MW01641205

BLUEJACKET

CLASSICS OF NAVAL LITERATURE

JACK SWEETMAN, SERIES EDITOR

This series makes available attractive new editions of classic works of naval history, biography, and fiction. Each work contains an authoritative introduction written for the classics edition and, when appropriate, notes. The following are among the titles published or planned for the series:

Richard McKenna, *The Sand Pebbles.* Edited by Robert Shenk
Admiral Charles E. Clark, *My Fifty Years in the Navy.* Edited by Jack Sweetman
Rear Admiral William S. Sims and Burton J. Hendrick, *The Victory at Sea.* Edited by David F. Trask
Leonard F. Guttridge and Jay D. Smith, *The Commodores.* Edited by James C. Bradford
Captain William Harwar Parker, *Recollections of a Naval Officer, 1841–1865.* Edited by Craig L. Symonds
Charles Nordhoff, *Man-of-War Life.* Edited by John B. Hattendorf
Joshua Slocum, *Sailing Alone Around the World.* Edited by Robert W. McNitt
Captain David Porter, *Journal of a Cruise Made to the Pacific Ocean by Captain David Porter, in the United States Frigate Essex, in the Years 1812, 1813 and 1814.* Edited by Robert D. Madison
Fred J. Buenzle with A. Grove Day, *Bluejacket: An Autobiography.* Edited by Neville T. Kirk
Marcus Goodrich, *Delilah.* Edited by Neville T. Kirk
Edward L. Beach, *Run Silent, Run Deep.* Edited by Edward P. Stafford
Filson Young, *With the Battle Cruisers.* Edited by James V. P. Goldrick

BLUEJACKET

AN AUTOBIOGRAPHY

by Fred J. Buenzle
Chief Yeoman, USN, Retired

WITH A. GROVE DAY

PREFACE BY CAPTAIN FELIX REISENBERG

Introduction and Notes by Neville T. Kirk

NAVAL INSTITUTE PRESS
Annapolis, Maryland

This book was originally published in
1939 by W. W. Norton & Company, Inc.

The original edition of *Bluejacket* contained no photographic illustrations. Those that appear here have been specially selected for this edition of Classics of Naval Literature from the Neville T. Kirk Collection.

Library of Congress Cataloging-in-Publication Data

Buenzle, Fred J.
Bluejacket.

(Classics of naval literature)
Reprint. Originally published: New York : Norton, c1939.
Includes index.
1. Buenzle, Fred J. 2. Seamen—United States—Biography. 3. United States. Navy—Biography. 4. United States. Navy—Sea life. I. Day, A. Grove (Arthur Grove), 1904– . II. Kirk, Neville T. III. Title. IV. Series.
V63.B83A3 1986 387.5′092′4 [B] 86-8528
ISBN 0-87021-190-0

Printed in the United States of America

CONTENTS

LIST OF ILLUSTRATIONS

INTRODUCTION

The republication of *Bluejacket* now makes available the most comprehensive and graphic memoir of the enlisted man's life during the decade of the 1890s, when the Navy completed its transformation from wood, sail, and auxiliary steam power to steel, electricity, and the essential features of the modern warship. Episodes varying from a quest for hidden treasure to the fight against the "Uniforms Not Admitted" discrimination that, in an era when civilian clothing was prohibited for enlisted personnel made social outcasts of men wearing their country's uniform, combine to produce both a tale of adventure and a significant documentation of American social history.

In these pages, too, the reader feels the lift of the deck as the sloop-of-war *Portsmouth* heels to a quartering wind, or the strain of numb and freezing fingers on the spokes of the double wheel holding the Civil War veteran *Lancaster* on course against wintry gales and seas. Or, in midwatch blackness, he can vicariously brave stinging rain and lay out on a yard to grapple with viciously slatting canvas at the boatswain's call, "Reef topsails!"

Indignation will be felt at the arbitrary exercise of nearly absolute power granted to naval tyrants—with tragic consequences to subordinates—contrasting with the humane and intelligent leadership of a William T. Sampson or a Francis A. Cook. In Buenzle's day, as in Melville's, there were occasional press protests against the discipline of harsh punishment on shipboard—that ancient heritage of seafaring—and, in the United States Navy, enforced with the "sweat box" brig, double irons, and even the gag and the bucking stick. Only with the coming of the new steel Navy will the reader sense a transition to an ethos of reward, promotion, and carefully controlled punishment.

On the relationship between officer and enlisted man during the last days of sail, generalization presents difficulties in the absence of sufficient "clinical data" and the lapse of nearly a century. Suggestive fragments, however, survive from cruise notes set down at intervals by an anonymous seaman on board Admiral Dewey's flagship *Olympia.*

"It was quarters and Captain Reed, accompanied by a stranger, took the deck. Colors over, he said 'Captain Gridley, I turn over to you, not only the finest ship that ever rode the seas, but the finest crew that ever manned one!

"There were tears in his eyes and in his voice, and, what surprised us most of all, a smile benignant lit up his face. It was the first we had ever seen. Was he glad to go, or had the falling of the mantle disclosed the man?

"If from my humble station I dare address familiarly one so exalted, I would say, 'Captain Gridley, I know your motto,' and when I had quoted 'Write me as one who loves his fellow-men,' he might not answer, but he would not deny me."

And shortly after the victory at Manila Bay:

"On the morning of the battle Captain Gridley was so ill that the little commodore offered to excuse him from duty; but, gallantly as is characteristic of the man, he replied, 'Thank you, Commodore Dewey, but she is my ship and I will fight her.' And he did, although figuratively speaking, he was a dead man before he went on the bridge, and days had strung themselves into but few weeks when he was ordered home on sick leave.

"The *Olympia*'s officers rowed Captain Gridley across to the naval collier *Zafiro* for passage from Manila to Japan and a transpacific liner.

"A week later a telegram told us that he never reached home, having died on the fifth of June on board the *Coptic.* The grief that filled our hearts abated not, even when the prescribed time for mourning had passed and flags were released from half-mast."

On another occasion:

"I was on signal watch on the after-bridge; an ordnance officer stood looking shoreward through his binoculars as the admiral's barge rowed straight for the ship. At the proper moment he commanded 'Bugler, call the guard.' Then all the red tape required to get an admiral aboard was unwound. This accomplished, Lieutenant Dorn came at me fairly foaming at the mouth, 'What are you doing on the bridge?' he roared.

"'I am on signal watch sir.'

"'Then why did you not report the admiral's launch coming?'

"'Because you saw it, sir.'

"'Because I saw it! What right have you to say I saw it?'

"'I saw you looking at it through your glasses, sir.'

"'You don't know that I was looking at the admiral's barge; you have no right even to think what I am looking at. Your duty was to have reported to me what you saw coming toward the ship. Failing to do so, you shall answer to the stick on Saturday morning. I put you down for carelessness, disobedience, neglect of duty, and insolence.'

"I swallowed my rage, as I have done many a time and oft since I have worn this uniform, and, in fancy, saw myself going down into the brig for thirty days. The brig means handcuffs or ankle irons, a diet of two hardtacks, and a tumbler of water three times a day, with full rations every fifth day. I have seen men come out of the brig looking like the end of a forty-days' fast in a monastery. I have seen men in for three days wearing double irons. They looked like pirates. Their crime was smoking out of hours. . . .

"On Friday night Lieutenant Dorn sent for me and gave me a kindly talk, winding up with the promise that he would either make a sailor out of me or kill me. I was on the shore list for the next morning, but for reasons of my own tarried on the ship. This same officer, noticing me, asked why I was there.

"'Broke, sir,' I answered.

"He told me to go to his room and where to find ten dollars, which I was to take, get ashore as quickly as possible and not to forget to return it on the next pay-day."[1]

Buenzle interweaves fo'c'sle yarns with personal narrative and he brings the "iron men in wooden ships" vividly to life. He conveys the strength with which the code of mutual loyalty bound these shipmates. Nor do their frailties escape the attention of a sharp but understanding eye. Many—often speaking in foreign tongues—were recruited in ports of every continent, and they constituted no small element in the backbone of the Navy. Some officers preferred them to native Americans; others expressed doubts as to their basic loyalty and commitment to the Stars and Stripes. The war with Spain found them serving the guns with a devotion second to none.

Bluejacket's pages are also peopled with Old Navy characters whose like will not be seen again. Its author, the apprentice seaman who very literally sat at their feet, reveals himself as no uncritical enthusiast for the technological progress that banished them from our warships. Yet, with the adaptability of youth, he himself seized the opportunities presented by this same revolution and put his initiative and application to such good effect that he was able to shed his seaman's jumper for the coat of chief yeoman. Thus he is able to bring *Bluejacket* to a climax and conclusion with a stirring chapter on the naval battle of Santiago, which he witnessed standing at the elbow of the commander-in-chief of the victorious American squadron.

The reader is apt to come away with some puzzlement at the author's preference for duty in the crowded, ill-ventilated wooden

1. L. Tisdale, *Three Years behind the Guns* (New York, 1908), pp. 165–66, 264–66, passim, 126–27. Edward J. Dorn, the *Olympia's* Gunnery Officer, was then 43 years of age and still a lieutenant, as were also his Naval Academy classmates (1874), a commentary on the Navy's static rank structure in the years prior to the Spanish-American War.

vessels of the "sail and salt horse" era over assignment to the new steel cruisers with the comparative luxury of hot fresh water, steam heat, and refrigeration, and he will put down to prejudice the accompanying denigration of "greasy mechanics" of the rapidly expanding "smoke pot" Navy who were displacing the "real sailors." In point of fact, Buenzle was joined in these views by some high-ranking seniors, for seamanship, as in the past, was held to be the hallmark of the naval officer. Gunnery and engineering stood low in the accepted scale of values. Already in the late 1880s, a group of progressives was arguing that more emphasis should be placed on these specialties in naval education and training, but the weight of service opinion was against them.

At the least, training in sail was considered indispensable to the production of "audacious, adventurous, and efficient seamen." The arduous and complicated evolutions required for maneuvering a ship under sail, it was believed, promoted a spirit of teamwork and pride of achievement not possible among specialized personnel scattered through a machinery-filled hull. This aspect is well brought out by Admiral Caspar Goodrich in his recollection of a cruise to Rio de Janeiro:

"Imagine the *Portsmouth* moving easily up the bay, the wind dead aft, filling her sails, from foresail to royals and winged out on either side, all her stu'n-sails! As we drew near, the upper works of the other men-of-war, American and foreign, were crowded with men amazed at the unprecedented spectacle of a ship coming boldly to her anchorage under her kites. They climbed into the rigging while officers rushed up to quarter-deck and poop, moved possibly by apprehension that our people were all dead or asleep and grievous accident imminent. They could not believe the maneuver premeditated.

"On went the *Portsmouth,* silent as the grave, not a word spoken, save by the leadsman in the chains, reporting in low tones the depth of water. One might have heard a pin drop on her deck. Every officer, man and boy was at his post, the necessary ropes in hand—all waiting for the preconcerted order. We glided like a ghost through the maze of craft, whose ships' companies watched us spellbound, as we headed for the berth above them all which our eagle eyed commander had selected. We were to moor ship by dropping one anchor, running ahead, paying out ninety fathoms of chain, dropping the second, then heaving in on the first chain, veering on the second, until each stood at forty-five fathoms, when the ship would be held firmly at one spot like a horse tethered in a stall by straps from either side. This mode of coming to anchor is called a flying moor. It requires the utmost skill and judgment on the part of the captain for mistakes are easily made and hard to rectify. Generally speaking, the upstream anchor is let go first and the ship is backed down to the site of the second anchor. None of this for our skipper. He was making a grandstand play, serenely confident of himself and of his crew. He had tried the evolution too often out at sea not to be sure of the results. We kept on quietly, past the bow of one frigate, just under the stern of another, until we reached the proper place.

"'Let go the starboard anchor.'

"In came the stu'n-sails fluttering to the decks or the tops to disappear at once. Up flew the foresail and topsails, down came the jib, in came the to'gallant sails and royals. The crew scurried aloft like monkeys, lay out on the yards, gathered up the canvas, hurried down on deck again to reach it, every mother's son of 'em, before the ship had forged ahead and planted the second anchor.

"The whole thing seemed miraculous to the outsider, who did not know as much as we did the little devices by which it was made possible, or the constant preliminary rehearsals which made the play so complete a success. That such it was could not be denied. Indeed, the French Admiral when he called on board the *Portsmouth* the next day, voiced the universal sentiment as, hat in hand, with a low bow to Captain Semmes, he said:

"'*Monsieur le Commandant, je vous fais mes compliments. Vous avez l'equipage parfait.*'"[2]

2. Caspar F. Goodrich, *Rope Yarns from the Old Navy* (New York, 1931), pp. 72–73.

In May 1889, when Fred Buenzle enlisted, the Navy's active strength consisted of twenty warships. Three of these were steel cruisers; of the others—designated "3rd-rate unarmored"—fifteen were built of wood and two of iron. The steel *Atlanta, Boston,* and *Chicago* mounted modern breech-loading rifles, though they were still fitted with full-rigged sail auxiliary to their steam main propulsion. They had been laid down in 1883, when the technological gap between the United States and foreign navies had literally forced Congress to take action. However, long delays in construction—including bankruptcy of the contractor—had made them outmoded when they went into commission.

The 3rd-rate cruisers not only comprised the large majority of ships in service, but their complements absorbed more than three-quarters of the Navy's 1,500 officers and 8,800 men. All had been built before, during, or shortly after the Civil War. All normally operated under sail at sea and limited their reliance on steam to port entry and departure. The Navy Department order requiring log entries of steam use to be in red ink has provided naval historians with a target for amused criticism. The order was not, however, merely a whimsical product of bureaucratic conservatism. Rather, it reflected hard realities: limited coal capacities and fuel consumption per horsepower roughly three times greater than would be normal in their successors at the turn of the twentieth century. Lean appropriations for navy coal also contributed to impose economy, but the prime reason lay in the necessities of protracted cruising in distant seas as commerce raiders—their designated mission in the rather remote eventuality of an outbreak of war. The national defense policy of the day mandated a navy consisting of cruisers and an offensive strategy of destroying enemy commerce. The post–Civil War generation of senior officers had been deeply impressed by the performance of the *Alabama*—her remarkable endurance and the extent of her depredations. Cruising under sail at sea and reverting to steam only for approach to contacts, her sally of twenty-two months ranged from the North Atlantic to the East Indies.

But the Navy's screw sloops and corvettes were chiefly vulnerable by reason of their obsolete armaments. Their eight-inch, cast-iron Dahlgren smooth-bore muzzle-loaders were fundamentally similar, except in size, to those on board *Old Ironsides* in 1812 or on the squadrons that repelled the Spanish Armada.

The two decades after the close of the Civil War saw the Navy pass through a period of stagnation that has been called the "nadir" of its historical development. A rapidly expanding, self-contained American economy, with strategic security assured by geographic isolation and the absence of military or ideological threat from abroad, produced a national complacency that fostered both deterioration of defenses by land and sea and mismanagement by a Navy Department in which incentive and directive energy were largely stifled. In the service, the talents of the ablest officers were spent on the production of reports and studies of technological and professional developments in Europe.

These circumstances prompted New York street traction magnate and Secretary of the Navy William C. Whitney to an exasperated outburst in his annual report for the year 1885:

"The country has expended since July 1, 1868—more than three years subsequent to the close of the late civil war—over seventy-five millions of money on the construction, repair, equipment, and ordnance of vessels, which sum, with a very slight exception, has been substantially thrown away; the exception being a few ships now in process of construction. I do not overlook the sloops constructed in 1874 and coasting three or four millions of dollars, and to avoid discussion they may be excepted also. The fact still remains that for about seventy of the seventy-five millions of dollars which have been expended by the Department for the creation of a navy we have practically nothing to show.

"It is questionable whether we have a single naval vessel finished and afloat at the present time that could be trusted to encounter the ships of any important power—a single vessel that has either the necessary armor for protection, speed for escape, or weapons for defense. This is no secret; the fact has been repeatedly commented upon in Congress by the leading members of both parties, confessed by our highest naval authorities, and deprecated by all. Such is not the kind of navy which this country, with its extensive coast line, its enormous territorial area, and incalculable commercial resources, requires, nor such as it is entitled to have. This country can afford to have, and it cannot afford to lack, a naval force at least so formidable that its dealings with foreign powers will not be influenced at any time, nor even be suspected of being influenced, by a consciousness of weakness on the sea. While still striving to build up its merchant marine and to multiply its relations with foreign markets, it cannot be expected much longer to tolerate such expenditures for a navy which could not for a moment defend even its diminutive commerce against any considerable power."

European authorities that year ranked the United States eleventh among the naval powers. Rated higher were China, whose navy included two new German-built battleships, and Chile with the fast *Esmeralda,* the British-built prototype of the "protected" cruiser. This heavily gunned type relied upon speed and an armored deck at the waterline for protection and was the design adopted for the first fifteen cruisers constructed for the new steel Navy of the United States.

The national defense policy during the post–Civil War period of naval decline allocated to the Navy the prime mission of destroying enemy maritime commerce and the secondary one of supporting the coast defenses with monitors. Shallow approaches by sea and the string of antiquated masonry forts built prior to the Civil War constituted the defense of seaport towns on the Atlantic and Gulf coasts, which were assumed to be the most likely areas of attack or invasion. From 1870 on, however, these coastal batteries of smooth-bore muzzle-loaders would have been wholly ineffective against late-type battleships of the day.

Against the threat of invasion, elements of the regular army would, in theory, back up the coastal fortifications and hold the invaders until the state militias could be mobilized and called in for support. Less noticed were the realities of an annual desertion rate in the army approaching, in some posts, 25 percent, and that the state troops almost without exception were ill trained and worse equipped.

Such was the scheme of national defense with which generations of nineteenth century Americans, nurtured as they were in the "Minute Man" tradition, were entirely comfortable, and its attraction to the taxpayer could not be gainsaid. And it was a policy that drew in large part on the logic of contemporary international geopolitics.

Fundamental, as was mentioned above, was the security conferred on the United States by physical isolation from Europe and Asia. The nation's population, augmented by European immigration, reached 56,000,000 in 1885, a twenty-year increase of 60 percent. In the Old World, only the Russian Empire was more populous. The material requirements of war after 1861 provided the impetus that completed the transformation of the American economy from predominantly agricultural to industrial. The parallel development of the railroad-river net linked the four corners of the continent and made the nation independent of any foreign source of strategic raw materials. By 1883, the Carnegie mills were setting world records for iron production, and in that year the United States passed Great Britain to lead in the output of Bessemer steel. This economic performance, after a civil war in which a million-and-a-half men had been put under arms, convincingly showed European chancelleries the impossibility of invading the United States. Only England theoretically was capable of attempting a local blockade, but as always, Canada's vulnerability to attack by land stood hostage for amicable Anglo-American relations.

After 1865 the rapid internal development and industrialization of the United States also contributed to drive the Stars and Stripes from the high seas, as shipowners, confronted with increasing pressure from state-aided foreign competitors, transferred their capital to more attractive investments in internal development. The resulting disappearance of the American deep-water merchant marine reduced the need for the protection of trade in the event of war, a point seized on by congressional anti-navalists in debate. But even congressional supporters were taking advantage of national security, so cheaply bought geopolitically, to perpetuate the Navy's obsolescence by diverting funds to the political patronage of the shore establishment.

Though England still retained her traditional title "workshop of the world," the industrial revolution on the continent, which began with the termination of the Napoleonic wars, proceeded at a rate second only to that in the United States, and by 1870 Germany had outstripped France and had taken undisputed lead as the continent's chief producer of manufactured goods. The revolution was to affect all aspects of traditional society, but in none was its influence more far-reaching than in the development of European navies.

The creation of ironclads for a high-seas fleet was inspired by the brilliant Dupuy de Lome, *Directeur du Matériel* of the French Navy, whose designs were adopted in 1858 and four ships laid down. Four more followed in 1859. *La Gloire,* the first of these to be completed, ran her trials in August 1860. The British quickly followed suit with the handsome, ship-rigged *Warrior* of 6,109 tons, constructed of iron throughout, which completed fitting out for sea in October 1861. She was protected, like *La Gloire,* with a belt of iron armor four inches thick and mounted forty Armstrong breech-loading rifled guns.

The "first fight of ironclads" in Hampton Roads on 9 March 1862 was, therefore, more an incident than an innovation in the progress of naval technology, for both the *Monitor* and *Virginia* (*Merrimack*) were specialized types, limited by design and construction to coastal and sheltered water operation. Less than ten years later, the 9,000-ton seagoing "turret battleship" *Devastation* was nearing completion in Great Britain, and the London *Times* could announce on 15 August 1875, "We now carry 85-ton guns on board ships in turrets protected by 14-inch plates." The following year saw the launch of the battleship *Inflexible* with 24-inch side armor and a main battery of four 81-ton 16-inch guns moved and loaded hydraulically.

During this period Krupp had already introduced steel-barreled artillery; the French had perfected the interrupted-screw breech mechanism; the British in the early '80s were first to manufacture and use nitrocellulose smokeless powder; and the American Augustus Harvey would invent the first universally adopted process for face-hardening steel armor plate. Robert Whitehead, an English manager of an Austrian engine-manufacturing plant in Fiume, perfected the automotive torpedo in 1876 after twelve years of development.

The public and congressional apathy that, meanwhile, had brought about the stagnation of the Navy was equally crippling to defensive capability ashore. The coast defenses of the United States in 1860 were as powerful and effective as those of other nations, but the introduction of armor and rifled ordnance in the navies of France and England, against which their smooth-bore guns were practically useless, rapidly made the fortifications obsolete. The first notes of alarm were sounded by the press on the Atlantic seaboard in 1880 on completion of the Italian *Duilio,* mounting 100-ton, 17-inch Armstrong rifles capable of hitting the centers of Boston, New York, and Philadelphia from beyond the range of the antiquated cannon and masonry that provided their only protection.

Secretary of the Navy William H. Hunt took action on his own initiative, and in July 1881 convened the "First Naval Advisory Board" of 16 officers headed by Rear Admiral John Rodgers. In November, the board reported on the progress of foreign navies and set out a program for a 100-ship Navy to consist of the existing 32 wooden cruisers plus 8 large "unarmored" steel cruisers, 10 smaller "unarmored" steel cruisers, 20 wooden gunboats, and 30 auxiliaries—5 steel rams and 25 torpedo boats—to be constructed. Though some dissent was expressed during the board's deliberations, the composition of its recommended building program underscores the persistence with which most American naval officers adhered to the doctrine of cruiser warfare against commerce in the era that produced the modern battleship in Europe.

Two years later, Congress, by the Act of 3 March 1883, authorized three cruisers (*Atlanta, Boston,* and *Chicago*) to be constructed of mild steel "of domestic manufacture." The last provision was critical, since the United States possessed limited facilities for producing the required open-hearth steel. The Siemens-Martin process had been perfected in England a few years before, and the Royal Navy had completed its first two steel ships, *Iris* and *Mercury,* in 1878 and 1879. International litigation had held up introduction of the process in the United States, and Bessemer steel, of which the United States was the leading producer, principally for railroad rails, could not meet standards required for shipbuilding or the manufacture of high-powered ordnance or high-pressure boilers. The John Roach firm, contractors for the "ABC" cruisers, was bankrupted by efforts to meet the Navy's exacting requirements for steel, and the government had to take over construction of these vessels and complete them. Also lacking were forging mills capable of handling heavy ordnance and marine engine components. The tubes for the 8-inch guns of the first steel cruisers were forged at the Whitworth works in Manchester, England. In 1887 the crankshafts for the triple-expansion reciprocating engines of the *Baltimore* were imported from the same firm.

The problem of securing adequate military ordnance was addressed by Congress in the Act of 3 March 1883, providing for a joint Army-Navy board known as the Gun Foundry Board. This body in its report recommended that the government manufacture its ordnance and that armor be procured from private manufacturers. The board also called public attention to the defenseless condition of the coasts and the need for a comprehensive plan for harbor protection. Congress, accordingly, on 3 March 1885, provided for another board, the joint Army-Navy "Endicott Board," to study the problem of coast defense. Basing its conclusions on the assumption of a small navy charged with the primary mission of destroying enemy commerce, since an American high seas merchant marine was virtually nonexistent, the Endicott Board in January 1886 presented a plan for the defense of every important harbor on the coasts and even on the lakes. This comprehensive scheme, modified as needed by technological advances in ordnance, constituted the basic plan for coast defense up to the entry of the United States in the First World War.

Secretary Whitney, an exponent of naval expansion and administrative reform, came to the State, War, and Navy Building in March 1885. He would have preferred grappling with the inefficiencies of his department's decentralized and ill-coordinated bureau system as his first order of business, but he found himself confronted with problems of materials procurement that would continue to engage his best energies during the remainder of his tenure. The gravity of the problems is indicated by resulting delays in the commencement of construction of cruisers already authorized—one year and ten months in the case of the *Charleston,* and for the *Newark,* a record two years and three months. With Whitney's support, in 1886 Congress required that armor and ordnance be of domestic manufacture, and in 1888 this included all materials going into the construction and equipment of naval vessels.

During the 1880s, American steelmakers readily adapted to the requirements for steel shipbuilding. The manufacture of armor for the second-class battleships *Texas* and *Maine,* authorized in 1886, presented a problem of greater complexity, and at this point Whitney was obliged to turn to Europe, where the competition between guns and armor in the previous twenty years had led to continuous and extensive experimentation. There the British firms of John Brown and Charles Cammell supplied the Royal Navy with compound armor—plates with a hard steel face and backed with tough wrought iron—while, in France, Henri Schneider at Le Creusot had developed armor plates of homogeneous steel throughout. Whitney decided in favor of the Schneider product. The Bethlehem Iron Company was then induced, by offer of a contract for the Navy's whole supply of armor, to negotiate a profit-sharing agreement with the French steelmaker. Under its terms Bethlehem received full manufacturing rights, the complete technology of the Schneider process, and the benefit of the firm's experience. On 9 June 1887, the Navy awarded Bethlehem a contract for 6,703 tons of steel armor, and to provide adequate lead time for the installation of manufacturing equipment, the date of delivery was set at December 1890.

To create a capacity in the United States for the production of heavy ordnance, the Gun Foundry Board had recommended, and Congress had approved, that contracts for the initial forging and boring of gun tubes be let to private manufacturers, but that the machining and assembly operations be reserved for government gun factories. Whitney pressed Congress for action on the Naval Gun Factory, which had been designated for the Washington Navy Yard, where the long-established anchor and chain foundry had in recent years been equipped for the forging and finishing of small-caliber naval rifles. Construction of the new shops was begun in 1887 and completed two years later.

In the meantime, the country's coast defenses had entered the initial phase of modernization. The Army's gun factory was planned for Watervliet Arsenal, and in 1888 Congress, taking up the Endicott Board's report, made the initial appropriation of a 90-million-dollar program of refortification, which, during the next two decades, would line the coasts near major seaports with concrete emplacements and pits mounting disappearing guns and mortars of large caliber. None of these guns and mortars were destined ever to fire a shot in anger.

On Whitney's departure from office in 1889, he could regard with satisfaction a Navy that was largely self-sufficient and quite independent of foreign designs, technology, and materials. True, he had failed in a major objective—to effect significant reform in the administrative operation of the Navy Department—but that problem area would continue to frustrate his successors until well into the twentieth century. In later years, he was wont to relate, with some acidity, the probably apocryphal case of the ship ordered to sea by the Bureau of Navigation a dozen days after the Bureau of Steam Engineering had directed her boilers to be removed for replacement.

At the outset of President Cleveland's first term, the new steel Navy comprised three unfinished protected cruisers and the dispatch boat *Dolphin,* which was undergoing sea trials. Four years later, in 1889, seven protected cruisers and two second-class battleships were under construction. Five more protected cruisers and the Navy's first armored cruiser, the *New York,* had been authorized and were programmed for construction beginning in 1890.

With the completion of this program the United States would possess a respectable force of fast, heavily gunned, unarmored vessels designed to outfight anything they could not outrun. Essentially it constituted a cruiser navy adapted to hit-and-run raiding and to the longtime American naval policy of offensive deployment against enemy commerce and defensive deployment for coastwise protection. Six monitors were under construction for harbor defense, and a dozen more, all veterans of the Civil War, lay rusting at anchor in backwaters. Of the wooden cruisers, each was quite without value, save for showing the flag.

Early in the 1880s, however, dissent from the prevailing policy was becoming audible within the service. Rear Admirals Edward Simpson and Robert Schufelt, respectively chairmen of the Gun Foundry and Second Naval Advisory Boards, had argued the incongruity of an American cruiser navy in a world of developing battleship fleets.

Whitney was followed in office by Benjamin F. Tracy, a Brooklyn lawyer and a brigadier general of volunteers during the Civil War, who, like Whitney, would earn stature as a distinguished Secretary of the Navy. Like Whitney, too, he turned his attention to ensuring the Navy's self-sufficiency. To promote competition in the domestic manufacture of armor, he took advantage of the development of nickel steel in 1888 and of the Bethlehem Iron Company's failure to deliver armor plate on schedule in 1890 to induce Carnegie, Phipps and Company to install an armor mill and to contract with the company for nickel-steel armor at much less cost to the government. Du Pont was encouraged to manufacture smokeless powder for naval guns, and E. W. Bliss Company of Brooklyn undertook production of an American version of the Whitehead type of automotive torpedo. To another firm were awarded contracts for the manufacture of armor-piercing shells. But Tracy's major achievement was the shepherding through Congress of the naval bill of 30 June 1890, which provided for the construction of the battleships *Massachusetts, Indiana,* and *Oregon.* In a gesture to tradition-minded members of Congress and inland newspaper editors, they were officially designated "coast defense sea-going battleships," but actually they carried the most powerful batteries yet put afloat, and their 18-inch-thick side armor of Harveyized nickel steel exceeded that of any foreign contemporary.

At this time the press was viewing with increasing alarm the threat to American strategic communications and to the Monroe Doctrine posed by the construction of an isthmian canal in Panama by French interests. Of greater concern was the steady buildup of the British, French, Italian, and German navies—stemming from the international tensions accompanying the surging imperialism that was partitioning Africa and penetrating the Chinese Empire, the Middle East, the Balkans, and even the islands of the South Seas. The 1880s also witnessed the revival of Russia as a naval power in Europe. This unprecedented naval expansion was paced by advances in naval technology that by the end of the decade had produced 14,000-ton, 18-knot battleships able to cross and recross the Atlantic with coal to spare.

The British Admiralty at this juncture announced its "two-power" policy—a navy to be stronger than those of any other two powers—and Parliament enacted implementing legislation in the landmark Naval Defence Act of 1889. This measure authorized the building of 12 battleships, 42 cruisers, and 18 torpedo gunboats (predecessors of the modern destroyer), all to be completed in four and a half years at a cost of approximately $100,000,000—the largest single appropriation in British naval history.

To Tracy and a growing segment of the press and public, these developments very clearly indicated that the time for change had arrived. For nearly thirty years administrations in Washington had followed a policy of watchful waiting, comfortably able to watch the progress of naval technology in Europe from afar and thriftily waiting until naval armament there had reached a size and power that could no longer with safety be ignored.

In his first annual report, issued in November 1889, Tracy set forth his own independently arrived at views, reflecting the influence of his association with retired Rear Admiral Stephen B. Luce and with Captain Alfred Thayer Mahan, just then relinquishing his presidency of the Naval War College, and called for a new and revolutionary policy of a navy of battleship fleets capable of barring entry into the waters of the American hemisphere by any hostile naval force. Reinforcing his appeal was the report of the Policy Board he had appointed four months previously, which recommended a naval strength to consist of 30 battleships of varying sizes and endurance, 41 cruisers, and 101 torpedo boats.

The effect of these reports did not immediately become apparent, since, in 1891, Congress authorized construction of but a single battleship, the 11,300-ton *Iowa,* which did not go into service until June 1897, four months before her first commanding officer, Captain William T. Sampson, requested the detail of Ships Writer Fred Buenzle as his yeoman. But the momentum initiated by Tracy was by no means checked. Vigorous support was furnished by a broad spectrum of manufacturers who had been brought into the logistic network created by the construction and supply needs of the growing new steel Navy. Even stronger was pressure from the financial, managerial, and labor interests associated with the iron and steel shipbuilding industry. By the 1890s its new yards at Bath, Boston, Baltimore, Newport News, and San Francisco had come to depend on naval construction to cushion the historically cyclical character of the industry.

The second Cleveland administration secured congressional approval for five battleships; the McKinley administration laid down ten; and the Theodore Roosevelt administrations added another twelve, including the 20,000-ton dreadnoughts *Delaware* and *North Dakota*. With this growing armada to back him, Roosevelt enunciated for the first time in the Navy's history a clear, concise, and consistent naval policy: "A Navy equal to the second strongest"—in this case, the burgeoning High Seas Fleet of Kaiser Wilhelm II and Admiral von Tirpitz. After the involvement of the European nations in the First World War, with its world-circling impact, the Wilson administration, seeking to preserve the neutrality of the United States, sponsored the Naval Act of 29 August 1916, which provided for battleships and battle cruisers more powerful than any yet built by any navy, scout cruisers, destroyers, and submarines in numbers sufficient to assure a navy "Second to None." After the entry of the United States into the war, the wartime Supplementary Bill (1918), which was rejected, would have given the Navy superiority over all other navies combined. But enough of the 1916 Act ships survived the postwar naval limitation and economy drives to maintain the Navy's "Second to None" strength until World War II, when it rose to unquestioned leadership among the world's navies, a position it has since retained.

Fred Buenzle, permanently deafened in 1898 from gun blast at San Juan and Santiago, lived to see the Navy he cherished emerge from its low estate in the era of wood-steam-sail to become victor in the greatest of all sea wars. For his faithful account of naval life "before the mast" during the most colorful period of that revolutionary transition, both navyman and "the gentle reader" must remain deeply in his debt.

NEVILLE T. KIRK

BLUEJACKET

To
Amelia Louise
Ever, in the voyage of life,
the best of shipmates

CONTENTS

PREFACE

Some years ago, drawing up before a neatly fenced homestead in Palo Alto, California, I walked under the torii into an enchanted garden, reminding me of China and Japan. High-arched bridges, a small lagoon with its lily pads, ferns, cherry trees, and goldfish swimming in the shadows, bespoke someone who had created this with loving care. Before me was a red-tiled cottage in shipshape order. Off to the right a one-story building of field stones gave off sounds. I knocked and then my louder summons brought a short, thick-set man to the door. Nothing could disguise the forthright look, the square seagoing figure of a sailor. So I met Mr. Buenzle, Chief Yeoman, U.S.N., retired. He is hard of hearing, his deafness honorably come by in the din of battle.

In a world more or less given over to plausible and often successful imitations, it is something of a shock to be confronted by a living presence of the genuine. "Home is the sailor, home from the sea"—the line flashed upon me as I crossed the threshold of Fred J. Buenzle's Snug Harbor. Here in his study, his museum, and in his workshop, or, more properly, his shipyard, I was confronted by a scale model of the old U.S. Ship of the Line, *Vermont.* He had been working on her when I knocked.

Built up, as shipwrights say, from the keel, with ribs, stem, sternpost, and beams, Mr. Buenzle had planked her hull and laid her decks, had coppered her, stepped her masts, crossed her yards, bent her sails, and every shroud, every stay, and all running gear was shipshape and navy fashion. There was the smell of oak, of tar, and of hemp about the place. I inspected this model closely while her builder and rigger stood by, a smile of satisfaction on his honest face. I rounded the model, followed her lines, peered at her fittings, her anchors, boats, battery, and gear. This took some time.

"I can't find a damn thing the matter with her," I said. I backed off, across the wide room, and searched her from keel to trucks. All was in proportion, all was true. The builder heeled the model until she held a list to starboard. I hailed Buenzle: "Hold her!" I cried. "She's real; she lives!"

"She should, Captain," he replied, "for I have built into her the youth of one lifetime, the glories of liberties after long detentions over deep water. She spells something now irrevocably gone!"

Ship models, like verses, are either perfect masterpieces, or they are lousy. And the pure stanzas of this world are no rarer than are the few correct miniature ships of the sea.

We talked there amid the relics of the Battle of Santiago, when Buenzle stood on the flying bridge of the U.S.S. *New York* with that superb sailor, Admiral Sampson. Because so little damage had been done to the American ships wisecracking historians, who have never heard the bark of a naval gun fired in earnest, seem to overlook the terrific havoc wrought upon the enemy ships. It was all so easy, after it had been done.

We tacked back and forth across the seas of time, talked of long voyages in sail, of the old *Portsmouth,* the famous *Lancaster,* the *Monongahela,* ships in which young Fred had learned the ropes. In China he studied the art of stenography and so became the first ship's writer capable of taking dictation and in time secretary to the admiral.

On his desk was a bulky manuscript. Like almost everyone else, he was writing the story of his life. But, unlike the greater number, he has finished, and here, at last, is the first adequate personal story of our navy penned since Herman Melville, a foremast hand on the frigate *United States,* wrote his *White Jacket.*

To me this book seems history in its truest sense. He shows us the living navy, at its ebb following the Civil War and on the upswing of its re-creation when ships of the White Squadron were launched to form the first units of the great fleet we have today. The reader of this book will gain an insight into the heart of the naval service, its enlisted men, their life and struggles, their joys, tragedies, and heroisms. A masterly presentation of many humble shipmates, it deserves high praise.

Mr. Buenzle entered the navy as an apprentice because of his love for the sea. His successful fight to bring home the honor of the naval service to his fellow citizens, in which effort he was encouraged by Theodore Roosevelt, is one of the forgotten stories of the navy. Only a few decades ago the uniform of an Amercian bluejacket was looked upon by many thoughtless citizens as a badge of dishonor. Army and navy men, in uniform, were barred from supposedly respectable restaurants and hotels. Their heroic heritage meant nothing to stupid hotelkeepers, headwaiters, and the soup servers of the shore. Seaman Fred Buenzle set a course for the Supreme Court to right this insult, and it did.

But I must take up no more time in writing of a book that breathes the very life of our fighting ships. Here are men of all ratings and all ranks, human documents as worthy as they are true. No writer, since Melville, has caught the spirit of the navy, its humor and nobility, as has Mr. Buenzle. The personnel of our great armada of today is based on the story, the absorbing, truthful story, set down in this book. Ships of sail, treasure found in wild Formosa, the Far East on the eve of Japan's awakening, and the flash of guns that made the United States a world power, drift like tear-starting smoke across these exciting pages written by a bluejacket of the U.S. Navy.

Bronxville, N.Y. FELIX RIESENBERG

BLUEJACKET

Chapter I

SOUNDINGS

He was a boy of sixteen, and he couldn't remember the time when he hadn't known that some day he would go to sea. Now that great day had come, and he was off to sign articles as an apprentice in his country's navy.

It was a splendid day. The sun never shone brighter than on that May afternoon in 1889, and the birds never sang sweeter. Every step took the lad away from his tavern home above the Wissahickon and nearer to the gates of the League Island Navy Yard, portals to every hope and dream of adventure that could be brewed from the pages of Melville and Marryat.

But the courage given by a full bumper of claret which his father had thrust upon him to celebrate the day was quickly fading, and already the boy was sick for home. The road he had to take led by a dreary way, down a hard-rutted country lane which in a few years was to become Philadelphia's proud thoroughfare of Broad Street, but which at this time was a most muddy and unromantic highway for a sea-questing boy. On he marched through a great city's ash heap, where the scavengers at their work were shadowed like phantoms against the ground-hugging smoke of scattered rubbish fires.[1]

Like smoke arose in the boy's brain the muffling questions: Where am I going? What am I doing here, walking alone? Why?

To become a sailor, of course. That was it. But at each step, smoky doubts spiraled in his mind, and the destiny he had always taken for granted now rose massive and chill.

Why had he, who had never seen the sea, always been certain that he was to become one of the men of the sea? Surely he had not inherited the seafaring hunger from his parents, for they were from the Swiss Alps, a place notoriously lacking in the mariner breed. His mother, in fact, with an impression of sailors gained only from watching the "so *schrecklich*" rough men who had brought her and her husband from the old country on an Atlantic packet, had desperately tried to dissuade him. He knew nothing official regarding navy life, for in those days the recruiting officer was unknown and there were no beckoning bright placards to advise the passer-by to "Join the Navy and See the World!"

1. The original navy yard in Philadelphia, known as the "Federal Street Yard," was located by the Schuylkill River on land that had been purchased from the city in 1801 by the federal government. The first ship to be built there, the 75-gun *Franklin,* completed in 1815, was followed by some of the best-known additions to the pre–Civil War Navy, including its largest, the 130-gun ship-of-the-line *Pennsylvania* in 1837, the side-wheeler *Mississippi* in 1839, later to be Commodore Perry's flagship in Japan, and the *Princeton,* the first American screw-propelled warship, in 1843.

Wartime need to expand the yard later caused the federal government, in 1868, to acquire 406 acres of marshland on the Delaware—on League Island—within the city limits. Landfill operations, principally municipal waste disposal, began in 1871 and ultimately enlarged the yard's area to 665 acres. By 1881, the Federal Street Yard had been dismantled and its plant equipment placed in storage on League Island—thereby contributing to the stark and desolate appearance of the new yard that so greatly depressed young Fred Buenzle at the time of his enlistment. During the same year, however—1889—construction of the dry dock and large repair basin commenced under the superintendence of Lieutenant Robert E. Peary, Civil Engineer Corps, who would later win fame in the Arctic.

What few facts he had picked up would seem to have been designed to make him flee from the life in horror. The mother of one of his playmates had been divorced from a sailor, and she had sometimes read to him parts of old letters from her former husband and other navy men. When he asked why she did not read all of them, her sister had whispered that he would learn such things soon enough. The navy wife said the life was too rough for any boy, and she should know. Again, an old Irishman who worked for his father and who had known naval service would, in his more coherent moments, tell the lad of the horrible food, the harshness of officers, and the unspeakable characters to be found in the deck department (he had served as a marine). The Irishman had not completed his first cruise, for he had been discharged—or, more likely, had deserted—at Rio de Janeiro, and his bitter hatred of the sea was so strongly expressed that the boy imagined he must have walked home.

And now he recalled the stories which only a fortnight before had filled all the newspapers, stories of brutalities committed against seamen in the merchant service. The ship *Solitaire* had arrived at Philadelphia to have her captain and mate charged with the murder of several members of the crew. One man was punched off the topsail yard by the mate. It was said that men were beaten to death for talking while at work, and atrocious food had provoked a mutiny. Was the navy like that? Once the boy was within the iron gate that now rose at the end of the road, and his name was signed on a certain page, there could be no drawing back.

But all these tales had only awakened a perversity in his spirit, a dogged willingness to suffer any hard treatment, to eat the rotten food, to do anything at all so long as it would bring him nearer to those beckoning isles he had pictured for himself while dreaming the days away along the Schuylkill's banks. Every port in the world, of course, was an island to him, and every island a tropical one, with royal breezes always. Now he would cast off his warps and lines from the lubberly drab life he had known; and if gales came—well, gales were meant to be fought.

The gates of the navy yard were before him now, the entrance guarded by marines who were joshing two young girls of a wise-looking sort the boy had never known. Refused permission to enter, the two retorted with the first curses he had ever heard from a woman's lips. Near by, also appearing shocked by such behavior, stood a bearded navy man whose easy trousers flapped in the breeze. His blue uniform was wrinkled and dirty, his every hair was an untidy spun yarn, and one eye was badly bruised. As the boy watched, this liberty man yanked up one flaring trouser leg, pulled a flask from his sock, and tauntingly extended the liquor toward a marine, calling him a sailor's hitching post and daring the duty-struck so-and-so to be a real man and take a drink.

Not to his surprise, the seaman saw his offer refused, and he was gurgling his fill when one of the girls asked him for a drink. Backing away in alarm, he tossed her the empty bottle with the advice: "There, young scupper-mouth, stow that under your spanker! Drink is awful bad stuff—for a woman!"

From the girl came a blast of blistering oaths that hit the boy between the eyes, and even the old man-o'warsman was put aback. He edged away as the girl, exhausted, clung to her companion and shook with sobs. Out of the corner of his mouth he growled: "Burn me! A man may sink mighty low and still act decent, but a ditched woman—never!"

With this bit of wisdom he turned about and swaggered up the lane toward the city. The boy watched him go, turning over the mouth-filling parlor oath. "Burn me!" That was the proper way to talk, no doubt about it. "Well, burn *me*," thought the boy, "I have in my pocket a certificate that I have passed the physical examination, and it will let me through this gate. I'll show it and be on out of this."

His papers took him through, and he passed into a long, roughly cobbled street extending between rows of quiet and deserted storehouses, where he walked amid cold piles of shot and shell left over from the Civil War. "Burn me!" That was a phrase to remember. He marched down a quay where boats rotted in foul-smelling sloughs beside the wharves jutting out into the Delaware.

At the end of a long pier loomed a ship. But what a crazy vessel she looked—part frigate, part cow barn. Never, thought the boy, since Noah set forth in his ark had such a ship been seen on the waters of the earth! Midships the craft had a sloperoofed superstructure above which rose bare poles and spars. She was the old *St. Louis,* an unseaworthy and noisome relic left over, like the piled shot on the quay, from the last war, and now good for nothing but use as a coast-station receiving depot. She was to be his first ship.

The recruit stared, and remembered a favorite story he had read again and again in the pages of the boys' paper *Golden Days,* a story called "Bill Rutherford's Cruise," which he had always accepted as gospel for life in his nation's navy. Every illustration in that story was sharp in his mind, men and guns and ships and all the tiny detail of a ship's deck. But never in any issue of *Golden Days* had he seen pictured a ship like this one. Nor had the tales of Captain Marryat prepared him for his first view of a sailor at work. An old man in dusty white uniform, spare as an anchor and with a face wrinkled like a black walnut, approached with crooked arms bent. He was pushing a wheelbarrow laden with warm ashes.

As the sailor came abreast of the watcher, he dropped his load, sat on the barrow, and at once jumped up cursing and rubbing his stern quarters. Then he filled his pipe slowly, staring at the boy quizzically.

"Visitor here?"

No, the boy said; he had been examined for enlistment as apprentice, third class, and had passed.

"Haven't signed articles yet, have you?"

No, the boy admitted again, but he was just on his way.

The old man spat on his hands, rubbed his hips, and a sharp crease showed between his brows. "Then I've got just one word for you, young fellow. Heave around smartly and to the rear, march! Get home hell for 'lection, for it's your last chance to quit. Go back to school and then try for the Acad'my. May need some pull, but at least as an officer you'll see the other end of a dog's life."

He seemed angered at the boy's reluctance to move. "Damn your bilge, don't I know? Been at this end of it for goin' on thirty-three years, and at the last of it see what I'm doing—moving the leavings of a gang of greasers. A navy of smoke-pots and filthy coal-heavers, that's what we've come to!"

The boy was loath to have him go on, for the old man wore a uniform that had always spelled romance. Yet he could not forbear asking: "You don't hate the navy, do you?"

"Hate it!" The old sailor turned purple and he bristled. "Why, it's the best damn navy in this world, and I'd give my last drop of blood for it as soon as would anybody, fore or aft! No, the trouble's outside. And it burns me to see a young fellow enlist in a service that isn't respected!"

He saw that the lad was puzzled, and tried a new tack.

"See here—don't you know that once you put on this uniform, nobody will let you on a dance-hall floor?"

"I wouldn't care for that, sir; I don't dance."

"You will later on, one way or another. And you'll maybe want to take a drink when you get to places like Norfolk or New York, won't you?"

"Yes. Why not?"

"Why not? Because the dirty lubbers and crooks on shore won't serve a man in uniform, not in any decent place they won't! And you won't be able to buy a good meal, or a clean bed, or go to a theater. Only the dive-keepers and the trollops will give the sailorman a hand, my boy, and don't say I didn't warn you! But go or stay, it's all the same to me." Lifting his dingy load he went off to the dump heaps.

The boy tried to believe that coal gas and the slow smoke from burning rubbish had caused the choking pain that rose in his throat. Why, the navy uniform was the most glorious garb that had ever been known! Why should anybody turn a man away from a public place as if the uniform of an ever victorious navy was something shameful to wear?

That question was to hold much of the boy's thoughts in his early years, and some of the later years of his life were to be devoted to fighting for a proper answer to the problem. But he could not guess any of that now as he braced his shoulders, pushed off the

Recruits for the New Navy. This particular group was photographed aboard the *Vermont* in the Brooklyn Navy Yard in 1893. The two burly men on the near end of the bench at left were probably enlisting as firemen.

wreathing hazy doubts for the last time that great day, and marched toward the gangway of the old receiving ship.

"Maybe I have made the biggest mistake of my life," he said to himself, "but if I have—well, burn me!"

And in that mood the boy I once was climbed the gangway of his first ship.

The tiresome job of signing articles was done. I had been successively taken in tow by a sentry, a corporal of marines, and finally the chief master-at-arms, and I had signed the papers that transformed me from a civilian into a man-o'-warsman. My name was put to a document promising to obey orders of all officers and petty officers until I had reached the age of twenty-one, and several of those petty officers had given me brief lectures on what would happen if I didn't. Under the guidance of my first naval acquaintance, Jack Wright, I had been shown how to cut my name on a stencil and mark the clothes which the paymaster had charged against my pay of nine dollars a month. Now, full-rigged in a suit of stiff whites—redolent with storeroom odors of camphor, turpentine, and chewing tobacco—heavy square-toed shoes, and a wide, grommeted cap, I ascended a short wooden ladder to the topgallant fo'c'sle deck and abashedly gazed upon my new shipmates.

The unaccustomed garments made me feel that everyone on board was staring at me and questioning my right to wear them. Most acutely I suffered from the woolly clutch of the skinny, long-legged blue flannel drawers that I had forced myself into, and every thread in them seemed to be working up its own particular itch on my tender skin; but here in the public eye I felt much too daunted to scratch. I need not have suffered, for the many men about me were too busy with their own concerns to bother about a new face among them.

The narrow spar deck of the old ship was cleared all the way back to the cabin doors, and the two gangways, clean as a *Hausfrau*'s kitchen floor, were crowded with men. The entire area of the ship covered only the space of an average city lot, but her three decks harbored more than three hundred men in apparent comfort. This is more suprising when one stops to think that more than half that living space was taken up by the accommodations of a dinghyload of officers.

None of the men I saw on the fo'c'sle head seemed to feel cramped, although many sat elbow to elbow, most of them making or mending clothing, darning socks, or doing intricate fancywork with yarn or cord. Several knots of men were obviously grouped by nationality or race, for it was by no means a crew of 100 per cent Americans.

Just below me a small band of swaggering Negroes, recently

returned from a foreign cruise, compared bargains in rolls of blue cloth and black silk neckerchiefs which they had swapped or bought from British man-o'-warsmen in China. Most were tall, broad-shouldered, and well-featured, except for one, a wizened and pock-marked mulatto who was something of a dandy and had just bent on a suit of much-embroidered blues that was greatly admired. One of the tallest of these men, who had been "Jack-o'-the-dust"—a sort of storekeeper's helper—on one of the Asiatic ships, was stripped to the waist and was washing down a dusky breast on which a faint portrait of Abraham Lincoln had been tattooed in colors. The gay temper and laughter of the group was infectious, although an old fellow who was polishing a plate on top of the capstan remarked to me with a sniff: "Them niggers thinks they is shellbacks and barnacles from clew to earin'."

Two Norwegians splicing rope on the deck talked to each other in their own strange tongue, but when a square-set Scandinavian petty officer began issuing orders in the same language, one of them retorted in exasperated English: "Gude Gode, you go to hal."

Amidships, near the galley, a Hawaiian, arms crossed, stared before him like the Diabutzu at Kamakura, his snow-white hair in odd contrast to his richly colored face. Next to him sat a petty officer with "hashmarks," or enlistment stripes, on one arm, and a "crow" or rating badge on the other. His skin was the color of rich mahogany, and his hair black as tar. With fingers hard as marlin-spikes he was braiding sennit for a knife lanyard. I was to come to know him as Basil Bono, a Greek who claimed he had been born on a pirate ship and weaned on sea water. He also claimed that he had no heart, but I was strangely attracted to him and later was glad to have been shipmates with him more than once. As he sat there working, he found time to put teasing questions to a man lying on a near-by bench, who was trying to read a German book with a lithographed rooster on the cover. The sight gave me a twinge of homesickness, because it reminded me of the many times I had seen my mother consult that selfsame book for poultry disease remedies.

Up the ladder came a boy of about twenty with an armful of spun yearn, and Jack Wright with him. Wright, a man of the old navy stamp, fully fitted to act as an instructor, began to show him how to spin nettles for his hammock clews. I was told to keep my eyes on the job, and soon was on friendly terms with the recruit, Durgin, who had enlisted as a coalheaver.

"Call me 'Happy,' and that's me!" he hailed me; and the name did fit. He was a handsome fellow with open blue eyes and a grin that showed perfect teeth. His face and hands were deeply tanned, for he had spent all his life so far on a farm near Wilkes-Barre, and their color accentuated the white and flawless skin above his elbows and below his neckline. Muscular, narrow-waisted, and well over six feet tall, he would, I thought, have made a fine seaman. It seemed a pity that he should have chosen to serve in the grime and heat of a fireroom, where he would be burned out in a few years. I don't know where I could have so early picked up the antagonism that exists between the "black gang" and the deck force even to this day and age.

Near the smoking lamp close by the scuttle butt, a ship's cook was stirring a mess of boiling tea in his coppers and telling a story, pausing to enact scenes that had occurred on a merchant ship he had served on. As he finished, a Negro listener said to a companion: "Well, Ah don't care, Ah still thinks a belayin' pin is better than a lawyer."

But the hawser of scuttle-butt stories was not yet paid out, and a tall Hollander named Jurgens took up the slack. He stood by the bitts with one foot on the great anchor cable, his broad collision-mat of a beard slatting back and forth as he spoke, like a mizzen royal getting the first of a breeze. With the stem of his dead pipe he emphasized the points as he spun his yarn.

This was old Doc Buchanan. You remember him, Dan, on our last ship, when he said he was going to vaccinate every mother's son on board, even himself? He thought he might lose out when he came to the captain with his scrapers and his poison. The skipper says: 'Smallpox be damned!' and he pointed to his four gold stripes. 'These things, sir, vaccinate me!' And then next day the old man couldn't get up in the morning because of a bellyache after a royal time ashore with the U.S. consul, and the doc told him it might be smallpox. Before the captain got over his topheaviness he had four vaccination sores, one for each gold stripe."

"Did the skipper's arms get very sore?" asked one of the listeners.

"Scandalize me mizzen, no! Not his arms! The old man never sat down for the next twenty-one days!

"Well, it was this same Doc Buchanan who examined me at Cob Dock in New York for another hitch when my enlistment expired a month ago. When he put that pipe of his on my chest to take soundings, he ordered 'Starn all!' and says to me: 'Put on your clothes. Coxswain, you got heart disease.' Next day I went up to Boston, and tear out my lanyards if they didn't ship me without blinking. 'What?' I asks them. 'My heart all right?,'Sure; sound as the tub of a tops'l.'

"Next thing, along comes Shorty Bray, and careen me for a lopsided Dutchman if the same thing hadn't happened to him. The old doc in New York says: 'Put on your clothes, Bray. You got heart disease.' So Shorty went up to Beantown, where they signed him right off the reel.

"Well, so many of our lads seemed to have the kind of heart trouble that dropped off them on the Boston train that the Navy Department started to make a check, because it's hard enough to get men to re-enlist. But Doc Buchanan got on his ear, and said that when he, a three-striper, claimed a man had heart disease, nobody down in Washington or anywheres else could make him change his mind.

"Pretty soon the commandant of the New York yard, old Admiral Wilson, keeled over one morning and yelled for a sawbones, and Buchanan drew alongside of him and stuck his earpieces up against the old hull. Cat me if he didn't say the same thing, only in different words. The 'pothecary told me. 'Admiral, says the doc, 'you are very ill, sir. You got grave and serious murmurs and other funny noises in your cardiac regions. The least excitement may kill you dead as a fish.' 'That's a damn lie!,hollered the admiral, and to prove it, he heaved a big inkstand at the old doctor and ordered him to get himself transferred to other duty.

"So then a young doc was sent to the guardo to take his place, and one of the first things he found was two warlike bull cockroaches in the bell of the stethyscope old Buchanan had been using on us. There ain't been many rejections for heart disease lately, you can lay to that!"

The old men standing around him made pregnant remarks about lubberly pillrollers, for nobody on board ship can be so unnecessary as the doctor—to a well man. The tale set off Gloomy Dan, a jaundiced fellow just returned from a European cruise, and he took the storytelling watch.

"Well, sir," he began, "our ship's corporal, a fellow named Grabowsky, fell in love with a little Frenchy girl in Villefranche and got the idea of smuggling her aboard as a cook in one of the officers' messes. She was pretty, all right, but a smooth and slim little thing with short hair who looked just fine in the boy's clothes he brought her aboard in. The scheme was that for the last part of the physical examination, the stripping part, one of our apprentices, Spider Walsh, would slip in and take her place.

"Now the doctor on the job was a fat, jolly young fellow who happened to be caterer of the wardroom mess, which needed the cook, and so he was pretty interested in the person that wanted to get the place. But he was in a hurry to get ashore for a last fling, and he just brushed into the sick bay where the girl was calling off the names of colored yarns—in French, or course—to one of the nurses. 'Never mind that!' says the doc, and Spider, who was tacking about the sick bay, winked at the corporal, thinking he was going to get off his play-acting.

" 'So this is the feller that want to spoil our grub!' goes on the doc. 'Pretty thin, ain't you? He feels the girl's arm, and she looks up and smiles at him, and then he touches her again. And right off quick he pushes her into his private office before the ship's corporal and Spider have a chance to do their stunt. 'Come in here—I think you'll do,' says the doc. 'Let's see you strip!'

"And so the poor girl went in and—and—"

The storyteller now saw close under his lee the newest apprentice with his ears flapping to windward, and dropped his voice. I never did hear the end of that story, but it must have been good, because at the end there was a burst of laughter unusual in the always repressed atmosphere of 'tween decks, and even the teller himself gave a melancholy smile. At once came the expected warning from aft: "Silence for'ard, there!"

The party piped down. The ship's writer at his desk near the cabin door once more bent his red head over enlistment records, while opposite him a recruit writer returned to copying the rough log.

In and out the door to the cabin hurried a little bent-backed, nimble Negro. He was the captain's cook, an important member of the crew. He wore a blue uniform resembling that of an officer, but without any brass or gold; and he was the first colored man I had ever seen wearing side whiskers and a goatee. The instant impression that I got of this old fellow, whose name was John R. Bell and who was to become one of my best friends in the old navy, was one that I always had whenever I saw him. He was extremely gentle and extremely polite; as he went to and fro he spoke to each man or smiled at him, and the humble little fellow breathed forth a sweet air of pervading good will.

"He has grown old in the service, has Bell," Wright told me. "He came in as body servant to a well-known officer in the Civil War, and I guess he'll stay till he dies."

The pipe of a boatswain's mate trilled along the decks, and mess tables began clatttering down for the coming meal. Two bells had just struck. There was a clinking of metal from the main hatch, and, guarded by a corporal of marines, a trio of prisoners, unshaven, haggard, and manacled hand and foot, hobbled up the ladder. The three men nodded dazedly to friends as they were herded across the deck toward the head.

I asked Durgin, who was putting away his gear, what terrible crime these men had committed.

"Nothing much. They didn't get back to the ship on time. They're chronic liberty-breakers."

It was plain that he did not share my horror at what seemed to be a most ignominious punishment for a small infraction. But then, I remembered, regulations were meant to be kept. I made a silent resolve.

Another offender, of a different kind, hove into sight. His stiff white uniform and the newness of his shoes marked him as a recruit like me, and there was a pained expression on his face. From a lanyard around his neck was suspended a shallow basin of wood, highly shellacked, and bound by shiny brass hoops. This was a spit-kit, or seagoing cuspidor, and the man was forced to make his rounds to receive the contributions of his quid-champing shipmates. The poor fellow would think twice before he again made the mistake of spitting on the deck of a navy vessel. Thus had the naval Pooh-Bahs of ancient times decreed that the punishment should neatly fit the crime; and the sight certainly never failed as a source of innocent merriment.

On the decks of the old naval sailing ships, cleanliness seldom took second place, even to godliness. The fo'c'sle was spick and span. The inside of the rails, the hammock nettings and beams, and even the ceiling overhead were all a spotless flat white. The decks were a creamy gray, offset by straight seams of black pitch. There was an air of smartness about the sentries at the cabin doors, the marine orderlies, and the cooks in their galleys. Even the air smelled clean—odors of oak and pine, tar and whitewash; and the antiseptic tang of tobacco almost wiped out the faint flavor of bilge.

Supper was served on oak tables which were swung from the beams overhead. The sloping roof above me gave a shut-in feeling that one would not expect on the deck of a ship. I longed to be able to eat in the shadow of lofty spars tapering to the clouds amid a maze of rigging. But I put such thoughts out of my head and fell to upon my ration of boiled rice and strong tea, hardtack and molasses, served on a tin dish and eaten with a heavy spoon seconded by the blunt-ended regulation seaman's jackknife. I could hardly swallow lest I might miss some scrap of the outlandish talk that eddied about me.

After the meal was over the leisurely air of the crowd did not vanish, for the men lounged about smoking, chatting, and playing games.

"Blimy, we couldn't do this in the Queen's navy," remarked a young Britisher who had sat next to me at table. "Maybe that's why, after serving twelve blinkin' years there as apprentice, I'm a recruity under the Hamerican flag."

His name was Fielding, and I plied him with questions. He said he preferred our service for many reasons. The pay was better, the food was better; but what he liked most was the period of rest after meals, and the privilege of smoking.

"Curse me, there's more life here in an hour than we had over there in a week. Why, after supper in the British navy we'd probably have to go to a singsong or else sit about telling each other's fortune with tea leaves. The only bleddy thing I don't like here is that there's so many bloomin' foreigners—"

A piped call for attention interrupted him, and, in the hush that followed, the voices of petty officers relayed the hoarse shout from aft:

"D'ye hear there! Lay aft one hand from each part of the ship to man dinghy for special duty!"

Fielding had to jump up, for the captain of his part of the ship ordered him to act as one of the boatmen. His years of service in the Queen's navy was reflected in the unquestioning readiness with which he joined the other four men who had been chosen to go overside. From these others came muttered complaints, and out of a port someone bawled at them the old adage: "Growl you may, but go you must!"

Seeing Happy Durgin among the picked dinghy crew, I was inspired to volunteer in the hope of a quiet row on the river. I was already on the gangway when Jack Wright pulled me back with the remark: "You'll get enough of boatwork, my lad, before you're twenty-one. Stay aboard and watch."

Some distance inshore I could see a scow holding a derrick with a boom rigged over one of the anchors of the *St. Louis.* The dinghy crew was ordered to shorten some of the warps that moored the scow to a pier. It did not seem to me to be an emergency, nor was there apparently any good reason for breaking into the rest period of the men, and some of the boat party had already shifted into clean clothes for the evening.

The dinghy had gone but a short distance when her forefoot stuck into a bottom of black, sticky ooze. It was low tide. The men were unused to boatwork, all except Fielding and the coxswain; they fumbled with their oars in an effort to reach hard bottom. From the after quarters of the ship came a string of loud and confusing bellows which seemed to upset the struggling men all the more. The captain himself had been watching the effect of his sudden order.

"Get out of that boat, you fair-weather sailors," he shouted, "and push her through. Bear a hand there, quick!"

The men were at first unable to understand that they were to climb overboard. They hesitated and were lost. The shouting rose in a crescendo, while Fielding jumped out and the others followed with reluctance. Sunk in mud, they put their shoulders to the boat and pushed it through the slime toward the scow. The coxswain then leaped to the warps and began to ease them in a seamanlike way, but the movements of his helpers, weighted down by mud, were slow.

All this time the angry tirade had continued, and now the captain wound up with what sounded to me like the toll of doom for those mates of mine there in the ooze.

"Officer of the deck! Master-at-arms! Where are all of you? Get those men on board at once. Put them in irons! Log 'em for refusing duty! By the holy, I'll show the genteel lubbers! They're afraid to touch dirt, but I'll make 'em eat it!"

Chapter II

THE MAST

Darkness had come on. Bats and swallows swooped over the ship's housing, and mosquitoes swarmed up from the sloughs. Lard-oil lamps had been lit on the bulkheads, and in their pale glow we watched in silence as the unlucky, muddy crew of the dinghy was brought up the side, tumbled down the ladder, and pushed into the stuffy brig on the berth deck to spend the night alone with their misery.

Undisturbed, the little colored steward Bell bustled about preparing a roast chicken for that noisy tyrant, the captain. I wondered how anyone could be unmoved by those despotic actions against my friends. The sight had touched me closely, for both Fielding and Durgin had been among the unfortunates, and I myself had been within a hair's breadth of joining them.

In the darkness another boat's crew was sent to the scow. The tide was coming in now, and the dinghy was easily skidded across the shoal by a line from the shore. The men had barely reached the scene of their work and laid out their tackle when an order from the captain returned them to the ship. Evidently the need for this special work was not so urgent as had at first appeared.

This incident of my first day in the navy was my earliest lesson in the need of prompt and unquestioning obedience to any order received from a superior in rank or rate. It made me also aware of the possibilities for tyranny at the hands of men clothed with absolute power, and of how easily a headache or any slight upon the dignity of the afterguard might be taken out upon the hapless lower ratings. In later years I was called upon more than once to carry out some obviously absurd command that a child would have recognized as foolish. Each time that a retort sprang to my lips a thought of those five men in the dinghy at League Island, and of the punishment that was meted out to them, came to mind. It saved me again and again. "Obey orders if you break owners," as the merchant seaman says.

The silver pipe of the boatswain's mate at the gangway sounded the call to hammocks. The "dream-sacks," as the hammocks were called, were served out from the port and starboard nettings, each man stepping forward as his number was called. Someone instructed me how to sling my dream-sack and how to climb aboard, but at the first attempt I fell out on the far side, much to the amusement of the men watching me. It was the little Negro Bell who picked me up, and showed me that lengthening the footrope would make the canvas swing more loosely and more safely. "Never mind those fellows," he said soothingly in his soft voice. "There isn't one of them who didn't fail, more or less, at everything he ever attempted."

As a final comfort he slipped me an appetizing dish of food. The newest apprentice on the ship lay back in his hammock and munched a drumstick from the selfsame roast chicken that was then regaling the captain in his palatial quarters aft.

Taps sounded at nine o'clock, but I lay awake for a long time, listening to the half-hour bells, the hails of sentries, the banging of gangway doors, the stumbling return of drunken liberty men, and the trumpeting of a hundred snores.

"This is the life!" I grinned to myself, turning over cautiously in the hammock. How different was this crowded, spreading dark place from the little upstairs bedroom my brother and I had always slept in at the old home when we were little!

I remembered how the lurid glare of distant furnaces at the Pencoyd Ironworks would flicker on the religious pictures and circus posters covering the walls, and how the reverberations of the blasts made us think of tomorrow's sermon on the pains of purgatory.

I thought of the Saturday nights when my mother sweated over the hot coal fire in the kitchen, preparing immense hams and steaming sauerkraut for the customers and filling a wooden tub of water on the floor for her small boys to take their baths in. After that soapy ceremony, in our nightshirts we would pass through the bar parlor, with its sanded floors, its ceiling hung with faded and fly-specked escaloped paper, and the weary fronds of asparagus fern hanging from the gas bracket. Here we would pause to shake hands and say good night one by one to the customers, almost all of them from the rolling mills across the river. Chiefly they were a rough class of Englishmen with scar-splotched faces and often cruelly injured hands. Accustomed to fierce labor and forceful language, they were always gentle and kind to us; and although they consumed huge amounts of beer, porter, and ale, they drank slowly as they ate and discussed heats, rollers, and payday, and I do not remember ever seeing one of them drunk. A few others were swarthy Lithuanians and Poles—deep-chested, mild men who spoke loudly in broken English and on holidays played heavy pranks on each other.

My father was a favorite of theirs, and they treated his "front room"—into which a woman never entered—as a sort of workmen's club. He was a tall man, my father, with bristling black hair and with something Napoleonic about the cut of his face. In every way, his were the opposite of my mother's traits of gentleness, tolerance, and self-sacrifice. His name was Nicholas, but everyone except his closest friends called him Nick, not so much because it was easier to say as because it never failed to anger him. He was eagle-eyed, gaunt, violent, and unforgiving; he was the czar around the home, and his boys learned to jump lively if they did not want a good old-fashioned German licking.

Nicholas had a good, quick, versatile brain, and always as if by right took charge of any neighborhood movement, whether it was a dance, some business for the sängerbund, a flurry of local politics, or an agitation against attempts to increase the liquor license fees. His favorite stunt, in great demand at functions where he served as host, was to make an extemporaneous address in French, Italian, and a mixture of Swiss and German called Plattdeutsch, with a good dash of Pennsylvania Dutch dialect imposed upon a fairly wide vocabulary of English.

Aided by the fame of my mother's cooking and her happy way of making many friends, my father had prospered in his little tavern, and soon was able to begin building, on a near-by height, a real inn which combined the ruggedness of his Switzerland with some of the comforts of the American seventies.

The new house had seemed a mansion to us. It bore a sign which said COMERCIAL HOTEL; I think the German painter had left out an *M* for the sake of economy. The place had three stories, with a weather vane on the roof mounted over a gold-leaf barrel, the contribution of a brewer. On the second floor was what I privately felt was the largest room in the world. It was used for banquets, and as a dance hall would accommodate no less than twenty couples. The bar and kitchen were on the first floor, and below that was a cellar cut out of rock.

I remembered that cellar especially, for nearly every night of my youth had been spent there, sitting on a hard stool and holding empty bottles to the brass faucet of a barrel of beer or porter. Each bottle, when filled, was passed over to my father, who held it between his leather-aproned knees, inserted a cork taken from a pail of hot water, and tapped it home with a short billet of wood. Tap, tap, tap—I could hear that sound now, and almost feel the sweet stickiness of spilled porter in my clothing. Through the meshed windows—prison-like in their appearance—often came the shouts of children of my own age having a last game before bedtime. But I dared not look up often, for if I happened to break the lip of a bottle I would be fined five cents, and five cents was the whole amount I got in return for helping to bottle an entire barrel. Usually it took a full evening to empty one barrel; but even at that rate I had saved sixty dollars at the age of eleven and had also paid for my own shoes and clothes. The extent of my father's bottling business can easily be calculated.

In that cellar, I also remembered, was an apparatus of heavy copper mounted on spindly legs which was used for making soda and other soft drinks. It had a terrifying habit of blowing off a spout of white marble dust after the week's supply of soda had been made. A large still lay in a near-by bricked room, and here my father manufactured gin and cordials from white spirits, juniper berries, and chemicals about which he was very secretive. My task was to work for hours pumping by hand, from one barrel to another, liquids whose fumes would sometimes overcome the men occasionally taken on to help. They would keel over or become gaily drunk, and even I was sometimes slightly dizzy from the effects.

Beneath this cellar was a subcellar blasted out of solid rock and arched with brick that dripped monotonously. It was nearly a hundred feet long, lined on both sides with barrels of whisky and white rum. The place housed generations of rats and spiders, and was marked with the trails of slugs. For such offenses as wasting straw when bedding down the horse, or breaking bottles in water too hot to touch with the bare hands, or losing some of the birdshot used in cleaning the glass, I would be sentenced to serve a longer or shorter period of detention in the dark, tomblike silence of this lower cellar. No sunshine ever reached the top of the steep stairs at the end, and even the rattle of the streetcars could not be heard there.

Yet I preferred the solitary confinement of this "brig" to a beating with whip or club, for here in the depths of silence I could mull over my plans for the future, and in spirit cast off into the deep waters that I knew awaited me. I made many a voyage of fancy in my fleets of majestic cloud-ships, running from haven to haven through narrow straits of silver and gold. It was strange that I, who had never seen the ocean, was so sure of its incomparable deep color. I seemed to know instinctively the angry moaning it made against weed-strewn rocks, and to sense the tickling clean odor of kelp. Just back of my eyes was always the vision of a frothing curl of white water on a comber that toppled and receded from a sunken reef.

In the summertime I built ships of planks and boards, and pretentious models framed with cigar-box wood planked with thin strips torn from old bushel baskets. The climax of aspiration was reached when I was able to rig a rope ladder from the roof of a barn to the upper crotch of an oak tree where I built a platform—my maintop. At times when my father was making deliveries with his horse and wagon and I did not have to go along, I would clamber up the sagging shrouds to the peace and power of this station on my ship. From here I could gaze across the rocky banks of the Schuylkill toward where, almost farther than mind could reach, I had heard lay the sea. Some day . . .

There was no man or boy in our little town who could or would correct all my dreamy notions of sea life. The school to which I walked twice a day was two miles off, in the mill town of Manayunk. Here I studied English and German, and learned a great deal of catechism, some mathematics, and a bit of grammar. My schoolmates, almost without exception, expected to work at the looms and spindles as soon as that important milestone, the first communion, had been passed. That I was going to sea was common knowledge, but none of them knew how one went about such a career, I least of all. But I did know that only robust boys were wanted for naval training, and under this spur I spent my spare time in solemn physical exercise, climbing and running. This hardening process was also advanced by working in a stone quarry in which my frugal father kept himself and his sons busy when there was nothing more important to do. Here I cultivated a fondness for the explosive powers of dynamite, at the expense of splitting headaches.

That experience and the discipline of my father's house had proved, as I realized, lying in my swaying canvas hammock, of some value as a training for the sea life I was now beginning to know. But I chuckled as I thought of the only real job I had ever had in the outside world. It was a most curious training for a navy man, I thought, but there was nonetheless a flavor of ships about that job. In fact, I had lost the post because of my love of ships.

I had been not quite twelve years old when I decided to become a printer's apprentice in Philadelphia. Many men, and one old long-locked wise Yankee in particular, have found in such a path the way to fortune; but for me it had proved a rather dull dog-watch. It had been my own idea, however, for my father seemed to care little what I became, expressing the opinion that I was soft like my mother and would probably end up as a "temperance man," the lowest degree in his scale of human values. So I had sentenced myself to stand on an elevated platform hour after hour, six days a week, setting eight- and ten-point type and breathing a mixture of dust, lead, and benzine. The matter I set was always German and English by-laws and rules for Herman societies—every Herman society, it seemed, that had ever been organized. The shop seemed to do no other kind of work, so that all went well and soon I could recite these constitutions and by-laws word for word; the name of the particular Herman society might vary, but the rules were always the same. The senior partner, who belonged to every one of the societies whose by-laws we printed, was a Don Juan who had a gay eye for any girl that came near. He spent long periods standing at a mirror near my case, admiring his brown beard, smiling at himself, baring his teeth, and looking upward beseechingly.

Another task was to keep filled the hungry furnace of a donkey engine in the third-floor loft, where power was needed to run the big press. The apprentice—myself—spent much time lugging coal upstairs to feed this monster. Also, every hour or so I was expected to travel to a saloon with a large can to bring back fourteen cents' worth of beer. In those days the world seemed filled with beer.

But Philadelphia, like all other seaports, has a Water Street, and more and more I found myself passing the wharves on my beer-laden way back to the shop. Here ships from every part of the world came to unload, and even arrogantly pointed their head booms into the windows of grogshops across the cobbled street. One day was filled with delight because I had been able to touch with my hand the end of a dolphin striker just above my head. Only think: that spear of metal below the head booms had torn the weed of the Gulf Stream, had dipped into the blue swells of the West Indies, and even threatened the backs of plunging dolphins in the Indian Ocean! Of course, for all I knew the ship may have been a coaster from Norfolk, and her oaken ribs may never have housed any cargo more romantic than scrap metal or lump coal; but I felt that way about her, anyhow. She was a ship!

Even the most foaming beer has a way of going flat and stale if it is left for many long moments in a can lying on a warm wharf; and since my trips by way of the water front became more protracted, I cannot say that my exit from the printing business was sudden or unexpected. No one grieved, for my pay had been only a dollar and a half a week.

Now I had parted from all that old life, and already it seemed more strange to me than the existence about me here in the sleeping *St. Louis*. I yawned and, weary at last, curled up in my swaying hammock. My last thought as I dropped off to sleep was of the old ash-carrying sailor who at the gangway of my first ship had told me I was entering the navy by the wrong door. Perhaps he was right; but after all, burn me, what a day!

"Up all hands! Up all hammocks! Shake a leg, now! Rise and *shi-i-ine!*"

It was five o'clock next morning, and bugles, whistles, and shouts were arousing the crew. Hammocks rasped against each other, and here and there a leg clad in blue flannel drawers put out, groping for the deck. A medley of calls, greetings, growls, and badinage filled the air as yawning men dressed with speed. Each seaman lashed up his hammock, making a sawing sound as he pulled the cord through its hitches. Then each hurried the canvas roll to the spar deck, to be stowed upright in the hammock nettings after a close scrutiny by the man acting as stower; for, as the old rhyme has it:

"Seven turns with the lashing so neatly must show
That all of one size through the hoop they must go."

Certain men of the crew, termed "idlers," were not required to get up at first call, but were privileged to sleep on for two hours longer. The idlers were the quartermasters of the night watch, the writers, the carpenter's mates, the sailmaker's mates, the Jack-o'-the-dust, the captain of the hold, and men on the sick list. But their snoring was invariably ended by the commotion around their hammocks, and particularly when a ship's corporal could not, or wickedly would not, remember where each of the idlers was berthed, and whacked dutifully on the bottom of the hammock with a club. Then from the aroused men came blasphemous howls of protest that died down only when the last of the early risers had vanished with his neatly lashed hammock over his shoulder. That would have been exactly six minutes from the time of the first whistle.

There was a clatter of tin about the galley as the mess cooks drew their rations of coffee, which they served to their messes in steaming cans. The brew, which was called "bootleg," was strong and unsweetened, and proved a stimulant for the labors to be performed before breakfast. I looked about for the friendly Bell, but he was already ashore, marketing for the captain's table.

Pumps were manned, the decks were flushed with water and then swabbed down. Every alternate morning, but particularly every Saturday, orders called for a vigorous scrubbing of all parts of the deck with sand and stones. The planks, ladders, hatch coamings, tables, benches, cooks' kettles, spit-kits, all were thoroughly scoured. In corners where the larger scrubbing blocks called "holystones" could not reach, smaller stones called "prayer books" were used. I was handed a piece of sailcloth and told to wet it in coarse sand and get busy on one of the ladders.

Mornings when the decks were not to be sanded, the order was given to do some scrubbing on our outfits. Dirty clothes were soaped, scrubbed with a ki-yi brush, rinsed, and then hung on gantlines forward. As a final morning touch, all the brasswork was carefully polished.

During this morning watch I had my first chance to observe my new shipmates at close range. Some of those who had returned from liberty during the night were of little use at the work, and clearer-minded men condoned their slipping away to escape the labors of cleaning. No one seemed to expect a man to return to sober from shore leave; to be three sheets in the wind or half-seas over was apparently the sort of thing that an old-timer was called upon to achieve.

There were a number of old-timers on board, men who had made two or three cruises and were now awaiting the completion of some of the first ships of the new navy—the *Newark, Yorktown, Vesuvius, Chicago, Baltimore*—which had been constructed upriver at Cramps' Shipyard.[1] A bunch of these older fellows were listening to the indignant story of a returned liberty man who on the previous night had been refused admission to a hotel dining room while accompanied by his sister. Someone made a sly remark, and the resentful man repeated: "Yes, my sister!" He continued: "And me sober as a judge!" It seemed that the manager of the hotel had expressed his regrets, but men wearing uniform were not to be admitted.

This to me was a sudden repetition of what the old ash-carrier had prophesied, and awoke further misgivings. I realized that in many such episodes the men were quiet and sober, and as respectable as any other guests at the same hotels or places of entertainment; for, as a rule, the rougher element among the enlisted men had their own particular haunts where they were welcomed, and no complaints were heard from those quarters. The objection admittedly was against the naval uniform and not against the behavior of any individual who might be wearing it; but as it was contrary to naval regulations for an enlisted man to wear civilian clothes at any time, it would be impossible to escape such rebuffs on shore merely by changing clothes. I could not understand why any of the officers should be indifferent to such persistent slights upon the American naval uniform, and said as much.

"Barnacles and seaweed!" cried "Baldy" Tom Dunn, an elderly coxswain. "*They* don't care, bless you! If a fellow has hell on shore,

1. The *Chicago* was built at Chester, Pa., by John Roach & Sons and was completed by the U.S. Government after the company failed.

they figure, he'll be all the more glad to get back on ship and will give less trouble all around. If he has nowhere to go ashore, he'll be more pleased to stay in the service. You get the idee? But," he wound up darkly, "if it had been me that got kicked out of the place, I'd have seen 'em in blazes and gone off to some other joint where me and my money would be welcome!"

My first *St. Louis* breakfast was of beans, hardtack, and coffee, and the crisp morning air and wet work on the deck had given me a good appetite for it. After the meal the men smoked, gossiped, and argued. A recruit from the merchant service unsuspectingly started something when he referred to the painter of a small boat as a piece of Manila hemp. The resulting argument spread from group to group, growing more and more heated, and blasphemous remarks drifted quickly into obscenity. I gathered that such a term had no place on a man-o'-war, and was fit only for the mouths of landlubbers or graduates of a state school ship (who, in the opinion of proper naval men, were all fathoms deep in ignorance). Later I learned how childish the argument was, because "Manila" by its name meant a rope made from raw material grown in the Philippines, and hemp was not grown in those islands. Men of the fo'c'sle sometimes came to blows over differences of no greater moment than that.

Jack Wright now began telling me what studies I was expected to complete under his tutelage, and arranged a daily routine. He said that as first member of a new draft it would become my duty to teach in turn the other boys as they arrived on the ship. My first order was to report to the chief master-at-arms, and at nine-fifteen that morning I came before this dignitary for preliminary inspection.

"Jimmylegs," as he was called, was fat, kindly, jolly, and lazy, but strict in line of duty. Untidy himself, he was a stickler for cleanliness in the apprentices under his command. He towered above me and took a bird's-eye view of my neck and ears. My fingernails, he cautioned me, must be trimmed to a nicety and kept immaculate. These instructions made eyes twinkle among the onlookers, who knew that before the morning was out someone would hand me a tarry rope to hold. Jimmylegs then gave me a lecture on the evils of tobacco, whose use in any form was considered a serious offense in boys. The men did not smoke cigars or cigarettes, but there were plenty of wood and clay pipes about me, and much chewing tobacco was consumed. Many of the foreign contingent took snuff. I was to be restrained from all these delights until I was twenty-one.

At three bells, or nine-thirty, call to quarters was piped by the boatswain and his mates, and the lines formed for inspection. There was a general straightening of collars and neckerchiefs, and a toeing of seams. The division officers made note of absentees, and then the men were marched off to their special work and drills.

The time had now come for the most ominous ceremony of the day—the trial and summary judgment of prisoners at "the mast," which is the name of that part of the deck where the commanding officer of a naval ship holds court. Actually the mainmast had long ago been taken out of the *St. Louis,* and its position on the spar deck was unmarked.

Under the custody of Jimmylegs in his capacity as chief of police, the members of the unlucky dinghy's crew were marched to "the mast." Since the evening before, they had been permitted to clean themselves and don fresh white uniforms. Manacles and leg irons were removed, and they stood at attention awaiting judgment.

The marine orderly went to report to the captain that "mast" was ready, and that pompous officer stalked out of the cabin, twisting the whiskers on each side of his face. He was small, gray-haired, and fidgety, and it was hard to believe that from this little man had issued the bellowed orders of the evening before.

He took his stand by the side of the executive officer, and the ship's writer held up the report book on a level with the eyes of his superior. The captain read aloud: "Refusing to obey orders and creating a disturbance."

"The only disturbance I heard came from the old man's cabin." A recruit standing near me said these words in a careful undertone.

The captain was glowering at the coxswain of the boat, Ferguson, a bearded Scotsman of some forty years.

"Well, coxswain, what have you to say for yourself?"

Ferguson stepped forward, saluted, and was about to deliver a carefully prepared declaration of the innocence of his intentions. But the sound of an argument between two petty officers forward now angered the captain; he turned to the executive officer and commanded: "Mr. Webb, have that confounded noise stopped. Put those men on the report."

Then he glanced irritably at Ferguson. "What was that you said?"

The flustered coxswain, who as yet had said nothing, became confused and stammered. He managed to gasp out: "Sir, my record will show that this is the first time I've ever been on the report, and—"

"Oh, shut up! Mr. Webb, there goes that damned noise again!"

A boatswain's mate and some orderlies were rushed to the fo'c'sle to quell the new disturbance. But by now Ferguson was almost ready to collapse. He was one of the few enlisted men on the ship who were married, and he had been expecting to take a week's leave to visit his wife and baby. When the commotion forward had been subdued, the captain, tapping his foot with impatience, turned again to the poor petty officer and stared at him from keel to truck as if seeking a possible fault in uniform.

"Again I ask you, what excuse have you for your insurbordination last night?"

Ferguson hesitated, and tried to remember what he had been going to say. The master-at-arms, standing behind him, officiously jabbed him in the ribs with his thumb and mumbled: "Hey, you! Stand at 'tenshun. Can't you hear the captain's talking to you?"

The captain missed this display of zeal, however. He was scanning Ferguson's enlistment record with a puzzled air. At last he gave judgment:

"Now that we've heard your poor attempt at an excuse, we'll

give you some extra duty. What I can't understand is how you have had a clear record so far. Now, have any of you others got anything to say? Speak up! I believe in being just to my men, and you can have all the time you need. Speak up, I say!"

Wisely they remained silent.

"All right. I'll give each of you a week's extra duty, and a month's quarantine. Wait! You men, there, what are you doing with nonregulation tape on your collar?"

He had caught sight of Happy Durgin, whose cheerful acceptance of punishment had displeased the captain. Happy turned back to his place, and saluted smartly enough.

"What's your name?"

"James Durgin, sir. I got this jumper from a homeward-bounder some time ago, and never wore it before. My other clothes got dirty in the dinghy last night, and this was all I had to wear. I am sorry, sir."

"Sorry!" The captain grabbed at his side whiskers in exasperation at such effrontery. "Then why didn't you shift into your working clothes before going out in the boat?"

"You didn't give us time, sir. I—"

Fierce red surged into the captain's face. He doubled both fists and hooked the thumbs into his sword belt. Behind thick lenses his eyes flashed angrily.

"Do you dare talk back to me? I'll have you down for being insubordinate—insolent, by God! You a recruit?"

"Yes, sir: enlisted nearly a month."

"Enlisted nearly a month—what?"

"Enlisted a month, *sir*." The way the boy said the word did not help matters.

The captain fiercely pawed at Durgin's enlistment record. Under the heading of "occupation" he saw the word "farmer," and read it aloud with apparent loathing.

"I'll teach you, farmer! In the service nearly a month, and still don't know how to address your officers! Put him down for another month's restriction, Mr. Webb—and another week of extra duty for being out of uniform."

He noted Durgin's indifference, and added: "Did you hear what I said? That's two months of no liberty for you."

"Yes, sir. I don't go ashore anyway, since I have no money to spend."

"Silence, you! Not another insolent word! Now we'll make it three months. Go forward!"

Chapter III

SHIPMATES

Happy's lips trembled, but as he went off down the deck with shoulders squared I felt that he had won a victory. A trivial thing like deprivation of liberty, it seemed, could not affect his masculine strength; and the enlisted boy's self-control in the face of injustice had contrasted bravely with the ill temper and pettiness of his persecutor—for that was what I had come to consider my captain to be.

The whole affair alarmed me. I knew nothing of shore justice, but I was puzzled that a navy man could be adjudged guilty unless he could prove his innocence, even of a charge which he could not understand. I remembered with a shiver that I myself had been eager to join the boat party, and only my inexperience had saved me from the fate of those men. How would I have acted at "the mast," when, as a mere observer at a safe distance, my knees had shaken visibly?

And what effect would handcuffs and leg irons have had on my navy career? Restriction of liberty did not impress me as a serious or painful punishment, because I myself, with an unblemished record, would be compelled to remain on board for months until I had accumulated sufficient money to repay the cost of my outfit. I mentioned this to my mentor, Jack Wright.

"Hah, but you don't get the idea yet," he said impatiently. "The trouble this morning is just a beginning for those men. The entry on their records will be against them for the rest of their enlistments, and will be brought up every time they ask for a privilege, or go up for promotion, or try for transfer to another ship. I'd rather serve a year in jail on shore and be done with it! When those men re-enlist, the marks on their record will follow them right along to their next cruise, and they'll always be under suspicion. It's a life sentence—that's what I call it."

That evening Happy Durgin and I went aboard a Civil War monitor which was anchored alongside the *St. Louis* in deep water. He seemed to be his old self again, and I felt that it would take more than a harsh captain to make that grin disappear for long.

In the early starlight we walked around the single battered turret of the old pillbox, listening to the waves lapping at the side plates and splashing over the deck, which was almost at the waterline. With our hands we measured the great dents made in the turret armor by the solid shot of the Confederates. An indescribable emotion welled in me, and I muttered a few words in an attempt to express my thought.

"I feel the same way as you do," said Happy, "when I think about all these old ships, empty and cast away, that once carried the honor of our country. My father was on one of these ironclads; he lost an arm and an eye on the Mississippi. Poor Dad; he won't like it when I tell him what the old man did to my record this morning!"

"Does he want you to be in the navy? My father doesn't care much one way or the other."

"Yes, he always did. You see, we're a navy family. My grandfather, and his father before him, were navy officers; one of them helped to pull the guns and anchors on sleds through the woods to Erie, and then fought the British with Perry. Many a time I held my great-grandfather's sword in my hands and thought that some day I would carry on the family name in the service. But now—"

He shrugged his shoulders. "Well, I guess I can always go back to the farm. Enlistment records don't count where you have just so much work to be done."

Could either of us have looked ahead a cruise or two and seen the desperate outcome of Happy's dreams of an honorable naval career, we would have realized, as we then could not, that the whole undeserved tragedy had begun with the scratch of a penpoint marking a boy's record that morning on the old *St. Louis*.

But we could not guess the future, and Happy stayed on in the navy. The Englishman, Fielding, who had started out so hopefully in the service of an adopted country, disappeared shortly after his sentencing at "the mast," and presumably continued his search for a place where he might find his hours of rest after meals less easily disturbed by dangerous orders. Ten days later he was declared a deserter and dropped from the navy rolls.

The loss of a man of his stamp was not small, for men discharged from the British navy, or even deserters, were considered handy additions to American ships' companies, where more than four-fifths of the men were likely to be foreigners not of Anglo-Saxon blood. The Britishers were trained to observe strict discipline, and were usually neat in dress and precise in manner. They fitted in well as topmen and coxswains. Although the American navy in the eighties had a complement of only eighty-five hundred, there was great difficulty in maintaining a full muster, and few native-born seamen were willing to join. The rumor persisted that the service was as cruel and hard as it had been described by Herman Melville in the antebellum period, and this was strengthened by tales of harsh treatment on some of the man-killing old "blood-ships" that were still in commission. Therefore, most of the shellbacks were of foreign birth, although all apprentices, of course, were American lads.

On the second day of my service a boy named Nesbitt enlisted. He was an orphan from Girard College. Hardy, who followed him the next day, was a nervous, delicate youngster who came aboard with many suitcases (all of them had to be returned to his home). Roy, a fourteen-year-old boy from Trenton, was the next apprentice to arrive; he was small even for his age, but well able to take care of himself. After another week Ketterer was enlisted, and then came curly-haired McCouch, the last and largest boy of the lot. About one boy a week was usually received on the *St. Louis,* which nonetheless was considered one of the best recruiting stations on the coast.

Our number now formed what was termed a draft, and we boys assumed the new dignity of having our own division at quarters and inspection, and ate at our own mess. But we had none of the other privileges of the men, and were not allowed on shore.

Liberty from sunset to sunrise was granted each day to a part of the crew, although not to any man undergoing punishment of any sort. Seamen who might not have had any tasks to perform all day were kept lounging about waiting for sundown, and then released for a few hours. There was almost no place for them to go except to the dives of Vine and Race Streets. they returned at all hours of the night, or even well into the following day, many of them in a helpless condition. Escorted as far as the gates by their drinking companions, they would be herded or carried from there to their berths by the marine guards. If they had exceeded their time they were thrown into the brig, and the expected sentence was three months' restriction to ship. They got that sentence invariably. Even to a recruit this seemed a senseless system, but not until nearly a score of years had passed did the custom of granting merely night leave give way to the more humane method of granting liberty for twenty-four or forty-eight hours, allowing self-respecting men to get away from the coast cities and to visit their homes.

Every morning except Sunday the apprentices were drilled by Marine Corporal Reddy, and afterwards Jack Wright took us out in the dinghy for boatwork. At other times we learned the points of the compass, the use of log and lead lines, the Morse code of signals, knotting and splicing, the care of bedding and clothing, and how to cut and sew our uniforms. In the evening some of the boys swam in the Delaware River from the deck of the old monitor.

Out of hours we learned a great deal of naval customs, traditions, and history from the lips of Baldy Tom Dunn, who never refused to entertain us in an instructive way. Among all my new friends of the *St. Louis,* I felt the greatest pleasure in this old man's company. In my mind he stood as a pattern for the sort of man-o'-warsman I hoped to become, a chap who performed all his duties with ease, and commanded respect fore and aft. Old Tom was a heart-strand sailor.

Tom was a small, grayish man of about fifty, with a pleasant and touching air about him. He was generally to be found at his sewing near the break of the fo'c'sle deck. There the warrant officers who had sailed with him in former years would come to sit on taut cables and smoke their pipes and yarn by the hour.

Dunn was lame in the left shoulder. When he was asked about this he evaded a direct answer by remarking that cruising on the stagnant waters to be found surrounding a "guardo"—or receiving ship—was likely to give a person rheumatism. Jack Robinson, boatswain's mate, said outright that Tom had got the business end of a knife in his shoulder while brawling once in South America, "And if he'd kept away from that rotgut whisky those greasers like to drink down there, he'd be able to lift his arm today." But Jack Robinson, I soon learned, was a mighty liar; and somehow I couldn't believe that Tom Dunn had ever been a hard drinker. He had open, sea-gray eyes that gazed at you unwaveringly. He rarely went ashore, and when he did go he always returned on time.

Another favorite character of mine was the white-haired old Hawaiian whom I had seen musing on the deck my first day aboard. Born in the Sandwich Islands, he was naturally nicknamed "Kanaka." Almost always he could be seen sitting and smoking on the breeching of one of the guns of the spar deck, for he had some mysterious connection with the gunner's gang. One day I dared to ask him his age.

"You mean yeahs. I born—mebbe sebenty yeahs."

Kanaka was always approachable, and when I got accustomed to his odd speech, and he for his part decided it was not my purpose to make fun of him, I was able to absorb from him much of the lore of the old ships on which he had served. For all his years, he knew nothing except the sea and ships and guns. I never saw him go ashore. He could not read, and marked the articles with a ragged cross. His greatest worry, impressed upon him by many a naval cruise, was the coming of the general muster of the first Sunday of each month; and after one of these ordeals was over he began preparing for the next one.

The Hawaiian's face was deeply pitted with the scars of smallpox, which he told me was leprosy; for all I know he may have believed this. The scars were so large that in them he could place nickel three-cent pieces and silver half-dimes, holding them there by some strange means. Sometimes he would stud his face with a dozen or more pieces, and strut up and down the decks with the pride of a female coolie wearing all her wealth as bodily adornment.

After many hours of talk with the old native I found out that just before entering the navy, many years before, he had served on a trading schooner which had been wrecked on the coast of the island of Formosa. Kanaka and the first mate, a Frenchman named Merci, were the only survivors. I listened in rapt delight as he told how the two had struggled through the breakers to the shore, but later returned to the ship to get a chest of gold which they were able to bring ashore and bury between two huge rocks along the beach.

Never had I expected to hear my fondest dreams of sea treasure embodied in such a tale of real adventure, told by one who had lived the story. It was a wonderful story, simply related by a harmless old fellow who was marking time at the end of a cheerless life. I was anxious to get every scrap of detail, but it was a tremendous job to worm out of him the least shred of fact. His halting English and his curious terms left me high and dry more than once. At first I only half believed him, and to find weak spots in the narrative I asked him day after day to repeat it.

He did not seem to tire of my questions, nor did he vary any of the essential points. The mate, he said, got a bad cut on the back of his head when he smashed against some wreckage. The treasure box was an ordinary carpenter's tool chest, tight as a boat. In it were ten canvas sacks, each containing one thousand dollars in gold. There was another sack of leather, half filled with pearls. Before they had buried the chest the mate had forced it open and carefully examined its contents. My questions were varied cunningly, but always drew the same replies. Ten thousand dollars! A colossal sum; at one time my father had been in a lawsuit involving three hundred dollars, and until now that had been the largest amount my mind could conceive. Ten thousand dollars in gold! And some pearls, too. Burn me!

I kept after the old Hawaiian. Why didn't he take along some of the treasure with him? He explained that they were afraid the natives might find money on them and suspect that they knew where there was more. The two castaways hoped to get a boat on the other side of the island, and returned in it for all the loot. Well, what had happened to his companion, the French mate? He had never heard of him again, and thought he might be dead. Why hadn't he ever told anybody about it, and gone partners to find the money? Kanaka said that he had thought of doing so several times, but had found that sharing with others would not leave him enough to recompense him for the loss of his accumulated naval benefits; three-quarters pay after thirty years in the American service was a big enough treasure for him nowadays. "You beliebee me." To buy a ship large enough to sail to the island would cost almost as much as the whole thing was worth, even if it could be found.

But could he find the place again? Oh, yes, even though he had made no map. "Whaffo mappee?" He pointed a crooked finger at his forehead. "Mappee here." A look of resignation came over him, and he slid one palm back and forth across the other. "I die, mappee die too." But Merci knew where the stuff was, if he were still alive. The two of them had wandered across the island and remained with the natives until at last a Japanese fishing boat had taken them to the mainland. At Foochow they had parted, the Frenchman to seek another billet as ship's officer, and Kanaka to enter the American navy. That was the end of the story.

But for my part I felt that the story should not end there; and I was right. Several years later, through the curious fictional aptness that sometimes touches real life, I was to know the excitement of hunting that treasure, buried on an island coast by a Hawaiian and a Frenchman before I was born. . . .

Kanaka, who had suffered on many ships for the color of his skin, was shy in the presence of officers and men, for he was very sensitive to ridicule. He underwent continual persecution from the tiny Greek petty officer called Basil Bono. This man missed no chance to drop pepper in Kanaka's pipe, salt in his coffee, or roaches in his soup. One day I heard Bono say in the hearing of the native: "Here it is Saturday, tomorrow general muster, and that nigger ain't got no clothes ready, by God!" Kanaka, whose terror of the monthly inspection was well known, immediately hurried to the berth deck and started to overhaul his outfit. I slipped down and whispered to him that it was only Wednesday, and nowhere near muster day; but he went right on with his preparations. The old fellow was too gentle in nature to try to retaliate upon the Greek, who besides had all the bullies of the ship with him.

Basil Bono was about five feet two in height, and full of nervous energy expressed in a steady stream of raw blue oaths. His face was homely enough to frighten a cat, with snaggled teeth projecting under a black mustache which was always kept greased and oiled. Moreover, he was fearsomely tattooed around his flickering black eyes and on his cheeks and lips. Every part of his body had been under the needle, and some of the designs were so startling that I wondered how he ever dared to appear in mixed company ashore. He boasted that, when stripped, he could show more identification marks than any other sanguinary so-and-so in the United States Navy—or any other beblanked navy.

If Bono took to a new man or boy, he would soon confide the awful history of his past. Gradually, under solemn oaths of silence, he would reveal that he had been a Mediterranean pirate when he was caught, dressed and forcibly shoed, and impressed into the Greek navy, from which he had deserted to ours. His dream was, he confessed, to go back to the freebooter's gory trade. As soon as he had a good payday he would kiss all hands good-by and get himself a fast bottom that would damned well outsail any other blank ship that got within a league of his guns. And so on and so on. He would grind his teeth and shake his black head so that the gold hoops in his ears beat fiercely against the tattooed blue stars on his neck.

Most of the new men believed Bono had been a pirate, in spite of the fact that older men said he was a fourflusher and that beneath his bloodcurdling manner and speech he masked a kindly heart. But I was properly impressed, even after I had sailed with him a year or two later in the West Indies. A good stretch of my enlistment had passed before I happened to see Bono sailing at last under his true colors. One night in New York as I was riding across the Brooklyn Bridge returning from liberty I heard a commotion at the rear of the car. A large, husky-voiced Irishwoman, with arms ponderously crossed over heavy breasts, was loudly scolding a little man in naval uniform. He was looking straight at me, but evidently without recognition. It was my former shipmate Bono.

"Basil," said the lady, "if you ever behave again in such a shocking manner when we are visiting my people, I'll—I'll—You know what I'll do to you?"

"Yes, yes, I know," he replied feebly.

"Is that the way to talk to your wife, Basil?"

"Yes—I mean no, my dear. You will flay me alive, and hang my skin on the navy yard gate. I know, my dear." And with that admission, in my opinion, the terror of the *St. Louis* and self-confessed bloody buccaneer struck his black flag and passed meekly to his proper haven.

On my first Sunday aboard the *St. Louis,* an air of hurried expectancy accompanied the usual washing down and swabbing of the decks. Breakfast was soon over, the woodwork and paint were given a final cleaning, and the brass fittings were polished at the double-quick. Stray ends were tucked in here and there. Ditty boxes disappeared. Quids of tobacco were surreptitiously jettisoned. Shoes were given a final polish. Men walked self-consciously and spoke in whispers, glancing aft frequently as officers began to appear from below in cocked hats, with sheathed dress swords at their sides.

The officer of the deck issued orders with studied care, and these were bawled forth by Jack Robinson without any change of tone. At last the call to quarters was sounded on the bugle, and each man and boy speedily toed the mark with his division. But there was still a delay. Each divisional officer must be satisfied that all was well, or he himself might merit a reprimand. Lanyards were straightened, handkerchiefs and pipes stowed out of sight, unruly buttons chastened. Then with a blare of quivering notes the captain and his staff were summoned to the review.

It seemed to me that a lot of hullabaloo and fuss about cocked hats and shiny swords and buttons had been stirred up merely to carry on the supercilious and hasty examination of a group of workingmen living on a decrepit hulk. Nevertheless, my frame quivered as the austere little man in his gold braid passed before me with his eyes darting here and there.

Immediately the men were released, they hastened to shake off the formal restraint and dropped into their old careless banter, with even more than its customary share of coarse language. Permission was received for getting ditty boxes from the berth deck, and they began rooting about among their prized trinkets, which never failed to give solace to their sailor owners. Amid such innocent diversions the minutes passed until the bugle sounded again, this time for divine service.

There was a clatter of mess benches, a shuffling of many feet, and a rustle of hymn books. As the church flag was hoisted over the national ensign aft, the captain came out of his cabin and took his place at the portable pulpit, giving a signal that the tones of the little collapsible organ should now be heard. The organist was a girl from shore, and the thought that she was one of the few girls or women that I had seen for some days gave me a touch of homesickness, for already I felt marooned far from shore life and the sights of home.

Happy Durgin sat next to me. He whispered proudly that he

knew the girl, had met her at a Christian Endeavor gathering in the city. She, in fact, was the one who had helped him to enlist, through a letter written to the executive officer, Mr. Webb. Regularly she sent Happy some good books to read, which he had occasionally passed on to me. Several times during the service the girl nodded plesantly to him. What girl, I mused, wouldn't be proud to know him? I couldn't understand why Happy had accepted so lightly the punishment which confined him to shipboard and kept him from visiting such a girl, when a few words of explanation in the proper quarters might have mitigated his sentence. But that, as I was to learn, was never Happy's way. His pride in himself was one of the things that were to undo him.

The captain, with his gray whiskers, looked the picture of benevolence as he began his sermon, and might have stirred me as a preacher if I hadn't remembered he was also my captain. He seemed to speak only to the officers, never once glancing at the massed, sober-faced seamen. I wondered if that was because he considered the officers more in need of spiritual advice, or because he had long ago decided to give up the guidance of "the people" forward as a hopeless task. As he talked on, the oddity of a high naval officer, used to commanding rough men, speaking Sunday platitudes struck me as being a sort of masquerade. The speaker showed asperity as the muffled ship's bell interrupted his discourse, and I almost expected him to break into a barked command to have somebody logged for creating the disturbance. But, noting that he seldom gave the men and boys a glance, I eased my stiff position and stared covertly at my shipmates. None of them appeared much interested in what was being said, but there was a notable absence of the hawking and clearing of throats so common among shore congregations. Sailors seemed immune to coughs—at least during divine worship.

I was vaguely uneasy, for this was my first attendance at any Protestant service. But there was nothing alarming, so far. My thoughts veered to our little church in Manayunk, where my father shared a choir-loft pew with two neighbors. These two had sat together at Mass every Sunday morning for ten years, and during that time had never spoken a word to each other. Suddenly I remembered the cause of the feud, which now seemed indescribably petty. There had been a difference over money, a trivial sum. But the neighbors continued to sit together in anger, for to change to a better pew would have cost one of them two dollars a year more.

The captain seemed to be making heavy weather of it. I wondered if I might ever become so bold as to refuse to attend naval church service, for I had been told that this was a man's privilege. Then my mind flitted to thoughts of my mother, who at this time, her pious obligations fulfilled earlier in the day, would be busily preparing heavy dinners for hungry churchgoers and their guests. The solemnness and the quiet gave my nostalgia full sway.

The captain was reading from a book. The girl sang sweetly, and we joined in with embarrassed chants. The officers did not sing, and seemed bored. Then the captain retired to his cabin, with a weary glance over his spectacles. I rose with the rest, wondering what there ever might be to make him tired. He seldom showed himself on deck, even at drills. He walked only as far as the end of the pier, where a carriage and two horses awaited his pleasure. How did he spend his time behind the tight shining doors of his cabin, ever guarded by a dutiful marine? He was captain and, if he wanted, could spend all his time in his hammock with no ship's corporal to whack him into wakefulness. Or did he, perhaps, sleep in a bunk or even a real bed?

Happy was escorting the young lady as far as the gangway, where his bounds of freedom ended. His face went for a moment suddenly cold, but he smiled again as he said good-by.

I had missed the face of Tom Dunn among those at the service, and hastened to look him up. I found him on the fo'c'sle head, and he greeted me in his whimsical way.

"The new sailor is now so full of spiritual cargo that he won't have room for his Sunday roast beef and soft bread!"

"You watch me. I'm as hungry as if I had done a morning's work in the boats. The service was quite a bit different from what I was used to ashore."

We talked about sermons and chaplains. "You'll find some good chaplains in the navy," Tom said. "The trouble with all of them, though, is that they live aft, too hell-an'-gone far aft. And when a captain who hazes his men all week gets up on his hind legs and preaches the gospel to the same crowd on Sunday, why, I take somebody else's shift of duty and keep away. I can't help knowing the old man will ship his quarterdeck face again the minute the show is over."

Baldy Tom knocked the dottle out of his pipe and wrinkled up his eyes. "And then this captain talks too much about hellfire to suit me."

"But don't you believe in hell?"

"No—at least not the kind of flaming brimstone place he talks on. I can't believe in a hell where your friends roast, and then at the same time believe in a generous and forgiving God."

The call for dinner sounded, and Tom rose and straightened his clothing. "No, my boy, I couldn't swallow that bilge, not even if the lord high admiral himself passed it out. Listen; I had a good friend in the navy years ago—an officer. He wasn't any saint; he could drink with any of us, and that was his one great weakness. But there never was a kinder heart or a better sailor afloat. We lost him down in South America. If I thought that man was suffering in the kind of hell the skipper shouts about, I'd break all the rules and regulations to get down there with him. How could you be livin' dead up there aloft, and look down over the clouds and see a chum of yours a-frizzlin' there in the hold—a fellow that you knew was no worse than most of us, and many times a blamed sight better? And whatever he had done, he did it maybe to make you happy. To me, heaven would be a hell if I had to watch even an enemy burn like that."

Tom said all this with an earnest intensity that jolted my mind more than anything that I had ever heard from my teachers or spiritual guides. To win to heaven, I had always been told, was the one great aim of life, and I had believed that it was only right that at the Judgment Day—a sort of "mast" to be held in the hereafter—all the sinners should be marched off in irons to a fiery brig. Now suddenly, a gale of rude, plain thinking had torn my orthodox sails of creed out of their boltropes. I was left with an upsetting suspicion that this grizzled old man-o'-warsman might be a sounder preacher than his captain.

Chapter IV

TRANSFERRED

The old men who were my shipmates during the earliest days of my navy life were of a breed whose like will never be seen again. They were unassuming fellows, hoary and hard-fisted, plodding graybeards with stubborn hair on their chests, seamen not entirely broken on the wheel of their simple vices. Their hands might be calloused, but not their hearts. Some of them had shocking manners and appalling morals, but they were lovable still. Each had led a colorful life; but all of them will soon be forgotten. Their untold stories are doomed to oblivion, faded and vanished like the clever work of their hands—marvelously intricate designs of silk and cord, stitch and sennit—which they loved to make as they sat in their accustomed places on the deck. Their kind will never again sail the seas under the American ensign.

One of the most picturesque of all these shellbacks on the *St. Louis* was the boatswain's mate, Jack Robinson (that was the name by which he appeared on the muster roll, and for all I know it may really have been his name). The exalted position he held in the eyes of the apprentices was expressed in the comment of one recruit: "Why, even the officers ask him questions!"

For a long time, Jack personified for me all that a true-blue man-o'-warsman should be. His snow-white hair, long and curly, covered a forehead strangely free from the seams and wrinkles of worried old age. When I knew him, he was well on to sixty years old, but he had the broadest shoulders and the loudest voice on the ship. He stood a good six feet above square-toed shoes that shone like binnacles. Light blue eyes, so common among seafaring men, were shaded by a bosky tangle of brow, and the directness of his gaze hovered on the verge of impudence. His thick-lipped mouth was partly hidden by a tobacco-streaked white mustache, and an expanse of white whiskers extended out from his rosy cheeks like stuns'ls, flowing down far below his collar. A silver whistle, emblematic of his rating, hung always from a lanyard of sennit formed of a chain of more than two hundred Turk's-heads, each one a complicated knot requiring vast skill and patience to weave.

His walk, as he paced back and forth by the gangway performing the important duty of calling out the time and announcing distinguished visitors approaching the ship, was a belligerent swagger. He was a potbellied sailor, bluff in the bow; and a tight lacing of black silk at the waistband failed to prevent his trousers from slipping as he strolled. For this reason, no matter what Jack might be doing, he kept both arms free if possible. With spyglass tucked under his arm, he marched to and fro on his station, and on reaching either end he would lift and swing his outboard leg around, at the same time hitching up his trousers fore and aft. He used his thumbs as hooks; no finger ever touched the cloth, for he kept them spread apart with his palms down. This habit held over from the days when a more slender Jack had to do dirty work involving tar and paint.

While on duty, Jack was a bear, and men and boys kept clear of his hawse. He answered their questions with a snarl, although this would give way to a smirk if an officer spoke to him. To my mind he sirred the higher ranks unnecessarily, and this was the first thing that made me wonder if he were a proper model for a young sailor after all. When not on duty, he could be seen under the break of the topgallant fo'c'sle, sitting on his ditty box and decorating hats and shirts with the fancy stitches, stars, and crow's-feet for which he was famed. Although his prices were high, his excellent work was much in demand. At other times he would be found wearing a patriarchal pair of steel-rimmed spectacles and reading a pocket Bible, and those who approached might expect to hear an elevating lecture on the good life, and especially the life of temperance. For Jack was unique on the ship in that he claimed to be a teetotaler of the whitest dye.

One day the clumsiness of a recruit who had landed his boat with a thump against the streaked side of the *St. Louis* drew from Jack a blast of vituperation that shocked me, although there was a complete absence of blasphemy or worse. He scorched the offender as a hornswoggled landlubber, a waterlogged human derelict, a turnpike sailor, a skipper-licking mucker, a "sooperfloous" awning stanchion, and the flotsam and jetsam of heaven's abomination. The stinging contempt in his manner brought a flush of anger to the first-cruiseman's face, although Jack had not used a single expletive that the world would expect from the lips of a profane sailor.

Then Jack turned to me and asked where I thought the forsaken outfit was heading when such rambustious lubbers were allowed to fill the navy. And where did I think the tin smokepots they were building and using in place of real ships would be after sixty and more years of service such as the *St. Louis* already had to her credit? Noting my interest, he closed his Bible reverently, put it in his pocket, and delivered a parting denunciation in the direction of the recruit, who had already fled from the scene.

I learned then from Jack that my first ship had been built at Washington in 1828 and cost $135,000. She was rated as a second-class sloop of war, with a length of 127 feet and a beam of 34 feet. She carried 20 officers and 170 men, and her armament consisted of eleven 8-inch smoothbores and sixteen 32-pounders. Her first cruise was to the Pacific, and in 1833 she sought out and attacked pirates in the West Indies. She was one of the forty-two Union ships in commission at the outbreak of the Civil War, and

Jack Robinson himself had been one of her crew when she accompanied the *Kearsarge* in search of the privateer steamer *Sumter.*

The old man was deeply proud of his ship and her record, and spoke with rare feeling of the men who had manned her. "Yes, we were a proper lot in those days! It was a rare Friday morning, God bless my soul, when we didn't have a dozen or more men to flog, triced up to that there grating over the gangway." He waited until I had identified the grating before he went on. "Yes, and we whipped 'em with ten to twenty lashes of the cat-o'-nine-tails on the bare back for just such things as that farmer did with his boat a minute ago. The rumsoaks and skulldoddering pirates got what they deserved—their two dozen, well laid on—in the good old days. Different from the mollycoddle outfit you've got yourself into, my boy."

He glared along the decks meditatively. "And we had rum served to us several times a day as a part of our ration. But none of that for old Jack Robinson! No, sirree! I got my money instead, and every time I was discharged I had a tidy sum."

Jack now launched upon his lecture against the Demon Rum, a sermon that would have done credit to a Bowery reformer. According to him, every officer and man in the navy would have benefited by the strict regime of total abstinence which had made Jack Robinson what he was. Jack had a way of pointing to various other members of the crew and loudly referring to them as horrid examples of what liquor could do to a man's moral fiber. They merely smiled in return, and I wondered what broad conspiracy could have kept this fine fellow in the uniform of a common sailor. Although Jack claimed to abhor "book larnin'," I was amazed at his facility in quoting Biblical proverbs and tags from Shakespeare to his purpose—which was usually a tirade against the evils of rum.

Some of old Jack's stories of life at sea thrilled me as no mere printed adventures could have done. He had many a tale of the Mediterranean, where he had once served on the *St. Louis* in an expedition against pirates and slave runners. But every narrative, whether of gales, losses of life at sea, battles of seamen with marines ashore, or the cruelty of some early officers, invariably ended with a certain lecture on temperance. Naturally this part began to bore me, but I never could pass the main hatch gratings without shrinking at the thought of the shrieks and the bloody backs of flogged men who had been so monstrously punished there.

Some doubt may have arisen regarding Jack's immunity from all the usual shore temptations, for one day I mentioned this to Tom Dunn.

"To listen to him," responded Tom in his quiet way, "he is everything he isn't. If he was twice as good as he claims to be, he'd be only about a tenth as good as he should be. The poor old plank-owner is a blank cartridge."

The term "plank-owner," which Tom might just as well have applied to himself, was a common designation for old fellows who, once they had secured an easy berth on a guardo, could thereafter be removed from their posts by nothing short of death. The air of proprietorship that they assumed when speaking of their vessel was credited to the fact that each of them was supposed to hold personal title to a particular plank on the spar deck. Considering the hard life that most of them had spent in the service to win to such security, this fictitious ownership was a small concession to give them.

About ten o'clock one night, shortly before my transfer from the *St. Louis,* all hands were roused from sleep by cries and shouts from the gangway leading to shore. The marine guard from the gate was having a stormy time of it trying to handle a bluejacket returning from liberty. This tartar had succeeded in disposing of two of his escort by throwing them over the rail into the lagoon; and the third would probably have followed had not the marines on the ship gone to the rescue. With the aid of some of the seamen of the anchor watch, the liberty man was at last subdued and clapped in irons, but not before the peaceful night air had turned a sizzling blue from the geyser of profanity that the disturber was erupting all the while.

Here was my first contact with the unadulterated invective of the sea. If that drunken offender left unsaid anything abusive or obscene that could be imagined regarding the captain, officers, or marines (especially the marines) of that ship, my ears must have missed it. Since then I have heard men curse in many languages, men who were acknowledged experts at the job; but none of them could compare with Jack Robinson when drunk. For it was Jack, my pattern man-o'-warsman, Jack the patriarchal Bible-reader and preacher of a hundred neat sermons against the demon by whom he had again been betrayed.

Later I heard men speak of Jack's thirty-five-year record of alternate sprees and repentances. The old man went ashore only once in three months because the law did not allow a commanding officer to confine a man longer without liberty. It ordinarily took Jack, they told me, about five hours to spend his three months' pay and fill himself to the gunnels with whatever there was handy in the way of strong drink (he was not at all choosy what it was). It usually took him about a week after his return and arraignment at "the mast" to clean himself inside and out, whereupon he would start on another period of contemplation of the weaknesses of shipmates who could not go ashore without making beasts of themselves. For Jack always considered each of his falls from grace to be his last one.

This quarterly dereliction of Jack Robinson, as it happened, almost brought my own downfall. As soon as I heard the rumpus on the dock I slipped from my hammock and hurried with the others out on the causeway. At the foot of the after landing place stood a man puffing at a black pipe and watching with interest the efforts of the marines to quell the white-haired old stormy petrel. My neighbor was garbed in a long raincoat over what seemed to be a nightshirt; a little black skullcap covered his head, and by the light of the moon I could see that his feet, spread wide apart, were bare and encased in carpet slippers.

The air was balmy, the tide was full, and there was an absence of the smell of rotted seaweed and sewage that at other times troubled our nostrils. The old ship groaned as she rubbed her bosom painfully against the sharp plates of the abandoned Civil War monitor. It was the sort of time and place that might make a boy want to talk to an older person, and I took my uncommunicative neighbor—whom I thought to be a yard watchman—into my confidence.

"That's old Jack Robinson they've got there. The old hypocrite! He's told me dozens of times that he never touched a drop of liquor, and just listen to him now!" In my excitment I nudged the other watcher with my elbow. "Say, won't our old man soak him in the morning when he hears about this!"

The man gave me a contemptuous look, and turned as if to leave. I didn't like to be ignored.

"What's the matter with you?" I asked. "Didn't you hear? You better blow the smoke out of your ears. I should think you'd get sick standing out here in that silly rig. And just you let the officer of the deck catch you smoking at this time of—"

The man suddenly pushed out his hand before my face as if to shove me overside, and spoke at last. At his bellow, every man on the causeway came to attention, and it occurred to me that I had heard that angry voice before.

"Officer of the deck! Mr. Hill! Get every damned man aboard ship at the double, and put that drunken sot in the brig! And as for you"—he turned full on me, his voice dropping to a loud whisper—"you get to hell into your hammock where you belong, and learn to mind you own business!"

Oh, my berth deck and sanguinary orlop! It was the captain! My skipper, whose august presence filled me with terror every time he came within three fathoms of me; and I had criticized, ridiculed him!

On the run, I headed for my hammock as he had commanded. But I shivered so that I couldn't sleep, a cold sweat broke out when a marine escorted two prisoners in chains past my hammock, and every time the bell rang I imagined that the time had come to face the terrors of a midnight court-martial.

Despite these fears, I never heard another word about my offense; and as I told my story to Steward Bell the next morning, it is possible that he may have had something to do with my immunity. Perhaps the captain was not unwilling to forget the affair, and I was more than willing that he should. My record stayed clean for a long time afterward—principally, I think, because I tried to remember his advice to mind my own business.

Two months of my enlistment had passed before I was permitted to visit ashore, although not before my father had appeared in person to pay a deposit of thirty dollars as security for my clothing outfit. A few weeks after I had signed up, a law went into effect allowing each apprentice forty-five dollars' worth of clothing. It seemed to me hard lines that I had missed by such a small margin what amounted to a bonus of five months' pay; but the law was not retroactive.

One day of my liberty was spent at home, and there I proudly displayed my blue uniform, which at that time was a novelty to the people of the neighborhood. Then I took leave of my parents, my brother, and a girl who was to be my companion on a later and longer cruise in life. I prepared my mind for a lengthy absence from that home, for soon I was to be transferred north.

The day arrived when our small draft of six apprentices was to set off for Newport, Rhode Island, then the only training station in the United States for navy boys. With our bags and hammocks scrubbed white (only to be quickly smirched in baggage cars and the storeroom of a steamer), we stood before the master-at-arms for a final inspection of our clothes. Jimmylegs pronounced us "real seagoin'," and a nod from the executive officer further rewarded our efforts to do credit to our *St. Louis* instruction. In our bags were rations of tinned hardtack and canned beef; but John R. Bell handed me a packet of sandwiches that he had made up from the captain's stores. We shared the sandwiches as soon as we got off the ship, for we were always hungry.

My leave-taking of Tom Dunn was brief. In response to my thanks for his advice and entertaining tales, he mentioned that a sailor's life was made up of partings. Some years later I was to take a more painful parting of Tom Dunn, and to hear from the lips of another a story more touching than any the old shellback had ever told me in my apprentice days.

Jack Robinson—once again his old magisterial self—had the gangway watch, and was stalking about with his locks ruffling in the breeze. As we were passing over the side into the launch that was to take us up the river to Camden, he drew me aside for a last lecture.

"Remember what I've told you, young fellow. Steer clear of rum! Many's the good officer, not to mention these blackguards and rowdies that I have to call shipmates, has gone down to perdition—Keelhaul me for a scandalized mizzen if that four-legged farmer hasn't left his ditty box right in the middle of the gangway! I'll nail his sanctified liver to the cathead! I ought to land a bow-chaser on his whiskers! Does he want this ship to look like an unraveled lime-juicer tramp steamer?" Poor old preserved-in-alcohol Jack!

As our launch left the side we saw Happy Durgin on the after roof of the housing, waving a signal flag at us. His cheerful face was aglow, for he too was to be transferred to a service ship the next day. It was to be a long time before we met again, and then the circumstances would not be cause for grins.

We cut into the stream, and at the head of the dock I saw a pock-marked and stoop-shouldered sailor trundling a wheel-barrow full of cinders over the uneven planks to dump the load into a scow. I asked Jack Wright, who was in charge of the launch, if the old man who had formerly taken that duty, and who had spoken to me on my first day in the navy, had been given something easier to do.

"You must mean Windy Jim," said Jack. "He was one of Farragut's men on the *Hartford* at Mobile Bay. Well, yes, he has an easier job now, I feel sure; and let's hope it has nothing to do with ashes. Poor Jim got afoul of some berth-deck shellac last Friday night and drank the wood alcohol off'n it. He went totally blind, then crazy. He died at the hospital last night."

Chapter V

MUTINEERS

Never before in my life had I seen such a large group of boys as the crowd that greeted us with jeers when our new ship loomed up, misty and gigantic, in the thick New England fog. Over the bulwarks showed scores of youthful heads all crying out the same time-worn jest:

"Ahoy, Philadelphia! You'll be sorry you ever left the farm to go to sea in the *New Hampshire!*"

Our little draft, with mouths full of mist and eyelashes beaded with the clinging moisture, were in no mood to retort in valiant spirit. We had been landed from a Sound steamer at the fish-smeared wharf of Newport at two that morning, and had been locked in a malodorous waiting room for three hours until the training-ship launch picked us up. It was the Fourth of July, 1889, but we were in no mood to celebrate. Philadelphia would have looked good to all of us then.

We were hustled through a large port cut in the belly of the *New Hampshire* and mustered on the gun deck, where a warrant officer examined our papers amid a riotous shouting from a swarm of boys, young and old, that hovered threateningly about the rookies. The tumult was terrifying, and when we were dismissed I found that my ditty box, full of cherished reminders of home and what little money I owned, had been stolen.

Aside from the anticipated fun of initiating a draft of greenhorns in proper style, the youthful crew was in high spirits because it was to take part in a parade at Newport. We new boys were not to have a place in that drill, however, and instead wrote letters, prowled about our new home, and made friends with apprentices in the sick bay. All of them did little to cheer our lot, prophesying dire doings when the Fo'c'sle Cadets gathered that night as an informal reception committee.

Sure enough, our squad had to make its appearance before these Cadets, composed chiefly of a tough lot of boys from the East Side of New York City. Philadelphia lads were always fair game, for some reason, and we were hazed with enthusiasm. It did no good to resist, for that made it all the worse for us. We had to answer questions in seamanship and gunnery on points we knew nothing about, and they pretended we were marked on our records for our failures. We had to go over the masthead barefoot—a painful proceeding—and were then compelled to do other stunts not mentioned in any *Bluejacket's Manual,* until our well-meant efforts caused such a commotion that the mate in charge of the deck could no longer ignore what was going on. This was my initiation into what was to prove a nine-month hitch at the Newport training station.

My new ship was, like the *St. Louis,* roofed over in a sort of Noah's ark fashion, and below the rail she was not at all graceful; but she retained her immense spars, sail was kept bent on some of the yards for drill purposes, and I envisioned some real work aloft at last. The masts and rigging did much to offset the toothless and senile appearance of a frigate with many gaping ports undefended by guns. I soon learned that the *New Hampshire* had formerly seen service as the ship-of-the-line *Alabama;* years later—in July, 1922—under her third name, the *Granite State,* as she was being towed to Eastport, Maine, to be broken up, she caught fire and sank off the coast of Massachusetts. At Newport she rested at the end of a long pier in a basin on the shallow side of Coasters Harbor Island in Narragansett Bay. Only at high tide could we feel that we were really afloat. She was an unsanitary old hulk even when compared to other guardos, and was manned by a bunch of lads who had not learned the need for tidiness in close quarters. Tons of slops and garbage were tossed overside and allowed to settle around the ship until she was almost always aground on an atoll of potato peelings and beef bones.

The island on our lee covered about a hundred acres, and had once been the county poor farm. On the hill was the War College, a building that was formerly the county hospital and was, of course, referred to by us as the "poorhouse." There was also a naval hospital, a gymnasium devoid of fittings, and some shacks that served as boathouse and carpenter shop.

Here on shore we practiced infantry drills, but seamanship and sail tactics were taught to classes on the roomy decks of the ship. Genial, gray-haired Gunner Chard here drilled us in elementary gunnery. Fencing and broadsword drill were given also, and the training station in its time turned out several fencing champions; but that part of the old navy curriculum gave way, shortly after my training period, to more modern forms of drill. Strangely enough, they did not teach the apprentice seamen how to swim, and throughout my life a terror of drowning has persisted.

Best of all I liked the seamanship classes and the boat drills. There was plenty of rowing to be done in cutters and whaleboats. It was hard work, especially when carried on for two-hour periods that sometimes left us far from the island, calling for a long pull back; but it did me good, broadening my shoulders and fitting me for the times when a man was expected to do boat duty for eight running hours at a stretch, in foreign ports and on the open sea. We likewise had much sail drill, in single boats and squadrons.

There were still many sail-minded officers in the service, and through their efforts our station had been given a pair of regulation sailing launches which were to be fitted out as diminutive square-riggers. After months of labor by carpenters, blacksmiths, and sailmakers, two handsome little brigs were turned over to us.

These beauties, full-rigged to t'ga'nts'ls, were a sight to see as they flew before a nor'west breeze over the waters of the bay. In these tiny vessels we learned to tack and wear, and even boxhaul, as well as to perform the ordinary evolutions of loosing and making sail, furling, and reefing. Of course the leads of some of the principal rigging, such as halyards and braces, were not according to Hoyle—or rather to that wise old sailorman, Admiral Luce, father of the naval apprentice system. The crews were cramped for space, and one man might have to tend the main brace and slack the jib sheet at the same time. But the training these little vessels gave us was sound—in fact, entirely too practical for our own good, as will be shown by this story of an unrecorded sea battle off Rhode Island.

On a Saturday afternoon when most of the officers were on shore or asleep, one of these small brigs was seen to hoist sail and, clearing the reef at the south end of the island in a seamanlike manner, head up the bay at a merry clip. It was manned, we soon learned, by three apprentices who had recently been punished for attempted desertion. They were apparently making another try for freedom; and they had chosen a good time to succeed, for to overtake them with cutters was out of the question, and the only steam launch on the station was over at Newport.

The commanding officer of the training station was Captain Francis J. Higginson, whom we called "Poppy." With his red face seeming about to explode, he ran half-clothed down the path from his quarters, shouting a command to get the remaining brig ready for the chase. I lost no time in tumbling aboard her, jumped into the little maintop, and cast off the harbor gaskets of the mainsail and topsail. Two other boys were at the same time similarly engaged at the fore. When I got to the deck I cast the spanker brails off the pins and hauled out the foot of that sail loosely.

Poppy meanwhile was jumping about the dock with excitement, urging us on and shouting for the boatswain to come and take command. But no warrant officer could be found, and in a frenzy the captain himself hopped aboard over the bow, reaching the stern sheets in three short leaps across the thwarts. He grabbed the tiller and put it hard aport as we were shoved out from the float;

the jib filled, and with jib and spanker we rounded the point. Here we found the boatswain, standing waist-deep in the water waiting to be taken aboard. He was hauled over the gunnels, and this unceremonious method of reporting for duty caused the crew, and even the captain, to break into laughter. In a few moments we had all sail set and drawing, with the port braces hauled in to give us a good reach to the western islands and afford us the weather gauge over the other boat, more than a mile ahead and west of us.

We had the advantage of a master sailor at the helm. The little vessel—no ranking officer of the American navy ever, I venture, had a tinier command—was quite as unfamiliar to him as it was to us volunteers, but he kept us trimming the braces and sheets until we were clipping at a fine speed. When we neared Conanicut Island it was "Rise tacks and sheets!" just as if we were handling a corvette under full sail. Around came the yards, and away we went on the port tack, heeling over until the water came in by the rowlock niches and caused us to scramble to the weather side.

Our commander, whom I had always considered as a sort of avenging deity appointed to see that we behaved ourselves, seemed quite like a human being as he sat in casual undress at the helm. He looked the real sailor he was, and my first fears that he might capsize a boatful of boys who couldn't swim now vanished. His face was as grim as though he were running down a shipload of Mediterranean pirates instead of a trio of runaway boys. As we approached the southern end of Prudence Island he called the boatswain aft and ordered him to see if there were any charges in the arms chest for the saluting gun in the bows.

The boatswain, whose clothing had quickly dried in the breeze, reported that he could find three blank cartridges.

"Load her up, then! Lay the gun on that boat, and we might bring them to with a shot. Wait—what are they about over there?"

The petty officer looked through his glasses, and almost dropped them. "Sir, I think they are loading their stern chaser and aiming her this way!"

"The hellions! Wonder how far they'll go with it? Swig up a

little on that maintops'l halyard; now trim the t'gallant. Those fellows must have at least one good sailor on board, but we're gaining on them." In an undertone he added: "Those lads know more about sailing than you might expect of deserters. But I suppose those chairwarmers in Washington will use this as an argument against further training in sail."

The mutineers had reached into the lee of Prudence Island and, with headway lost, were trying to make the mainland. Noting their efforts, the captain ordered: "Mr. Pierce, just let them have one shot. Aim high."

Bang! Our saluting gun cracked; smoke circled aloft, and the cartridge wad plopped halfway between the two vessels. At almost the same instant there was a puff of smoke from the fugitive ship. Something thudded above us, and a splinter flew from our mainmast just below the top, taking with it the fastening bolt of one of the futtock shrouds.

"Godamighty!" cried Poppy. "They've got hold of some ammunition, and they mean business. They must be crazy!"

Mr. Pierce, scowling, was hefting a piece of stone that had fallen from aloft. "They're using some of their pebble ballast, sir." It was my baptism of fire.

The captain sacrificed some of his weathering to bring our bows head on to the other vessel. "Lay low, all hands!" We crouched under the thwarts, wishing we might be midgets for the nonce. "Stand by to board quickly when we get alongside. Slack the starboard, haul in a little on the port braces!"

Just then we heard another shot, louder this time. We looked astern where spouts of water marked a shower of stones.

"God pity them—I'll hang them for this!" The captain stood up and glared at the enemy, now quite close. In lieu of a sword he brandished a boat stretcher. Then he ducked.

"Upsy-daisy, here comes another!"

This time the single rock projectile hit our foretops'l yard on the port quarter, and ricocheted with a screech over our heads through the mainsail. Down came part of the yard amid a mass of light canvas, pressing hard against the weather foreshrouds.

By this shrewd blow our craft had been knocked out of commission, but the captain's eyes gleamed and he threw his hat into the air. It went overboard unnoticed. "What do you think of that for a shot, Mr. Pierce?" demanded the skipper. "There's life in the navy still! Let me lay hands on the fellow that shot us and I'll make a man-o'-warsman of him, damn his eyes! Aha, they're in trouble now too!"

The keel of the other brig had grounded in the shallows of Dyer Island, and the boat was on her bilge, her rail pressed under by swollen sails which the boys were frantically trying to ease down by hand after cutting the halyards. Shortly they gave up and raced through mud and water to the shore, stumbling through the fringing marsh grass. Just before they disappeared over the central ridge of sand one of them waved and shouted something we could not hear. Captain Poppy replied with a wave of the boat stretcher, but it was far from being an angry gesture.

"We should have gotten those lads back," he muttered. "They have the makings of sailors!"

We cleared away the damaged spar and canvas and got out the oars, to pull back slowly until we were picked up by the steam launch. The three deserters—who by this time were all heroes in the eyes of their apprentice friends—swam a quarter of a mile to the mainland, where a railroad skirted the shore. They were apprehended in Providence shortly after, and returned to Newport for court-martial. The fact that their sentence to a federal prison was light was due, I feel sure, in great measure to the intercession of Captain Higginson and to his desire to keep the story of the mutiny out of the press.

But the incident spelled the doom of our little fleet of brigs. The two boats were neglected, and then abandoned and left to rot. Many years after, while rooting about in a pile of scrap lumber at the Newport station, I came upon a piece of spar, broken off near the center. It was topsail yard, with its jackstays, Flemish horse, footropes, and tub for parrel. It looked hardly larger than a part of some ship model. I dug around in the crevices of its jagged break and found pieces of flint rock, fragments from my first bombardment. "It's no good to us, so take it away!" said the carpenter's mate. I have it yet.

The boys who stole the brig were neither the first nor the last of the many apprentices who took French leave of the service during my training period. Although there were times when we had to work hard, there were other times when inaction drove many of us into a state of boredom which to a lively boy was even mor galling. Moreover, there was a distinct hazard to health.

In accordance with a custom that may have originated in the primordial time when vessels were first built with decks, hardly a day passed that the planks of the ship on which we lived were not washed down, soaped, and scrubbed. Even if the weather were extremely warm, the spar deck would be the only one to dry out during the day; the rest of the living quarters were almost perpetually damp. All the clothing of the crew was washed on deck, first with fresh water, and then with rinsing water drawn with pumps from the sewage-crusted slough in which the *New Hampshire* was moored.

It is not surprising, therefore, that shortly after my arrival at Newport an epidemic of typhoid fever broke out on the ship. A Philadelphia boy who had been confined to the brig for some trivial offense was the first one to die. A belated concern for the health of the crew then caused the authorities to have the vessel hauled off her garbage heap and out into the tideway, but clothes were washed as usual, and the decks were still soaked every day. Eventually about five hundred apprentices were freed from the "floating coffin," as she was called, and quartered in the gymnasium ashore, sleeping on wooden and concrete floors and eating in the basement of the "poorhouse." Although the disease was checked as soon as we left the infected ship, not until five of my companions had been carried over to the cemetery on a lane appropriately called Farewell Road, and we had been shifted again—this time to tents in the lee of the reservoir—did our health reports return to normal.

On shore our organization was called Camp Tracy, and there we followed a rigorous existence based on army routine, three boys to a tent. No extra clothing was issued, and we soon discovered our navy outfits to be grossly inadequate for this sort of life. When the cold New England months arrived we found ourselves cowering in leaky tents pitched in a bleak, unsheltered position. By wearing all our clothes, and standing up in the tents with our canvas hammocks over our heads when it rained, we could keep fairly warm and dry, but during guard mount we lacked even this poor protection. We had a guard on duty every day, rain or shine. Sometimes we walked our posts in heavy snow and hail, carrying rifles at the slope so that water would not freeze in the barrels. Had a desperate enemy force been within hailing distance, our camp life could not have been more rigid or more exhausting. It was discouraging to one who had dreamed of spending his first days in the navy cruising in sunny climes. When at last we were transferred from the island to a seagoing ship, I had a severe case of inflammatory rheumatism.

On shore we were divided into four companies of infantry and kept busy at daily drills. Occasionally sham battles were staged before an audience consisting of our little captain and his bewhiskered executive officer, sometimes accompanied by friends from town. Now and then one of these visitors would ask the officers to have us repeat an attack, or else take our fieldpieces back up a hill, dismount them, and roll the wheels and the pieces themselves down against an attacking force. This was fun to watch but not fun to do, and one day the artillerymen, by a rare mistake, started the wheels down the wrong side of the hill. When Poppy and his friends saw the heavy, iron-tired wheels bounding toward them, jolting high in the air over field stones, they departed with no great dignity for a place of safety. And from that place the captain ordered the same evolution to be performed over and over again for another hour.

The official view was that it was just as well to keep us busy at such drills, for all of us had qualified in seamanship and in what little gunnery instruction was thought to be enough for us; and it was too rough and cold for exercising in boats. The wigwag and

International codes of signaling formed the remainder of our education. It would have been a dull boy indeed who could not absorb all this in two or three weeks of instruction; but some of our number had been at the station a year waiting for a ship to take them on a training cruise.

There were no trade schools in the navy in those days. Six boys were selected each term to work as helpers to the carpenter, the blacksmith, and the sailmaker. There was great eagerness to get these posts and the competition was keen, but under the plan only eighteen boys a year were able to get special trade experience.

Here at Newport we worked with the last of the old-fashioned naval schoolmasters, forerunners of the chief petty officers of the later navy. There were John R. Daly (a bucko mate if ever there was one), Briggs, Wendell, Sam Fox, and several others. All were ex-apprentices, and all imbued with the faith in hard drill typical of the army sergeant. In seamanship instruction they shone brightly. In gunnery they slurred over such things as the weights and penetrating powers of projectiles used in heavy up-to-date guns, which they considered too intricate and quite unreliable. The most dependable defense for a ship, they were fond of remarking, was a smoothbore muzzle-loader, fired by a matchlock or a percussion cap—no cam springs, ratchets, or recoil checks to get out of gear on one of those old reliables! They were also expected to teach English, but at this they did not make much headway. The uniform of these schoolmasters was a sort of cheesecutter rig, with a celluloid collar, a black string tie, and a rating badge showing, as I remember, an open book above a chevron. A beard or mustache seemed one of the scholarly requisites. Each of the men was proud of the naval cutlass which he was required to wear while on duty. More often than not they appeared at drills without a shirt, but with a determination that was worth pounds of gold braid.

Absences from our ranks soon began to be noted as boys left the service for one reason or another. Some of them were discharged through death or ill health or transfer to hospitals. Some discharged themselves without ceremony; and it was not unusual, when counting noses on returning from a funeral, to discover that one or more lads had handed their rifles to comrades and slipped into a ditch along the road, not to be missed until after the return of the company to camp. Nesbitt, one of our Philadelphia draft, left the navy in this manner. Of the rest, Roy finished the first cruise but deserted on returning to New York. The frail Hardy was discharged by way of the hospital. McCouch deserted from the training ship *Jamestown* at Port Royal, South Carolina. Ketterer was handed a bad-conduct discharge. I survived as the sole member of the little Philadelphia detachment to stay in the navy. With one exception I was the smallest and lightest of them all, and if physical ability meant anything, every one of those boys except the misnamed Hardy would have made a promising young man-o'-warsman. Something was badly wrong when such wastage of hopeful and enterprising human material could be allowed.

The first graduate of the apprentice system in the American navy entered general service in 1877, and the system itself had continued thenceforward, with frequent intermissions, until the time I went to Newport.[1] In 1890 all our naval officers had taken

1. In 1837 Congress authorized the enlistment of boys from 14 to 17 years of age to serve until 21. Initially the scheme was highly successful, but it lapsed in the period just prior to the Civil War. Secretary of the Navy Welles, as a war measure, revived the system in 1863, and it was set up on a permanent basis in 1867 with the assignment of the frigate *Sabine* as training ship. Additional training ships were put in service during the following years, and Congress, by the Act of April 25, 1875, established an apprentice quota of 750.

The system received its greatest impetus in 1877, when Captain Stephen B. Luce was given command of the steam frigate *Minnesota*, attached to the Training Squadron. In addition, Luce was also made Inspector of Training. Known throughout the service as author of the standard American text on seamanship, he had also written and spoken extensively on the problems of manning the Navy and the training of its seamen. He now set about to introduce more efficient instruction in seamanship, navigation, and gunnery and, of equal importance as he considered it, to bring within the purview of the system the relatively neglected areas of apprentice morale and even personal morals. Medals and privileges were awarded in recognition of achievement, and he strove tirelessly to make the naval service appear attractive as a prospect for permanent careers leading to the rank of warrant officer.

their years of training under sail. These men were strict but as a rule fair-minded, and had spent nearly all their time at sea. Rear Admiral Stephen B. Luce, who had established the training service system, firmly believed with many of the older officers that nothing was so vital to a fine enlisted personnel as a backbone of young boys trained in cruising ships of their own. Some of these men declared that no boy could spend time aloft furling topsails on a breezy day or reefing sails in a gale without acquiring many qualities of a high order—courage, resourcefulness, strength, and manliness. They claimed, and rightly, that sailing ships test all a boy's faculties and develop his mental resources, ingrain useful habits of discipline and neatness, sharpen his nautical sense, and encourage self-reliance. Indeed, even today this is recognized by some European countries that require applicants for officers' posts on steamers to have had some sea experience under sail. But these wise commanders were at last overridden by those who believed that quantity of personnel rather than quality was wanted, and that the more men in the navy the better, regardless of their sea training.

Luce strongly advocated that the apprenticeship year of training and indoctrination before assignment to the general service should be spent on a cruise in a training ship. He opposed any move to quarter apprentices ashore for any phase of their instruction. In a day when bluejackets constituted the bulk of naval landing forces, and infantry drill and tactics occupied an important place in port routine, this viewpoint ran counter to official thinking. It therefore remained an unrealized ideal.

After Luce's departure in 1883, on promotion to rear admiral and subsequent designation as the first president of the Naval War College (of which he has been justly called the "founding father"), the size of the Training Squadron diminished. The value of training under sail, moreover, increasingly came into question as the new steel cruiser navy of the 'nineties became the battleship navy of the new century. Personnel shortages in the rapidly expanding fleet now forced the reduction of recruit training time, merged "Apprentice" and "Landsman" into "Seaman, Third Class," and concentrated all recruits in the naval training stations that had grown up on both coasts and on the Great Lakes. The last of the seagoing training ships was decommissioned in 1907.

During my earliest years in the service there were only two training ships, the *Jamestown* and the old *Portsmouth,* and each of these was supposed to take about a hundred and fifty boys on long cruises twice a year. But boys willing to give up the comforts of shore life for a job paying nine dollars a month and offering no great inducements to earn promotion were hard to find; and it sometimes happened that these ships took the same boys on a second cruise. In later years even these two ships were eliminated, and the shore course was reduced from six to four months, and then to three. Many a lad has gone to sea in general service before he has had a chance to learn the elements of his seafaring duties. In 1903 the adherents of the sail-training idea succeeded in having two bark-rigged vessels constructed for cruising use at a cost of more than half a million dollars; but these barks never had a chance to get the stiffness taken out of their frames before they were doomed as mere receiving ships.

In spite of the small numbers of boys that were required each year to fill up the ranks of the peacetime navy of the early nineties, enlistments frequently dropped far below replacement needs, and the proportion of deserters was high. The chief reasons for discontent among us were the hopelessness of advancement for an enlisted man, the arbitrariness of punishment for offenses great and small, and the changeable policies shown in successive recruiting systems, laws, promises, and fulfillments. For years many recruits were enticed into service, and men already in the ranks were induced to remain, by offers of civil service preferment after a certain term of honorable service. Later these wise provisions were ignored or forgotten in a mad scramble to provide large drafts of new men for the growing navy; new promises were made, and the old-timers had to subsist on broken pledges.

The most dangerous effect of the system was to discourage the entrance of Americans into the American navy, which was manned in large part by men of other nationalities. That doughty old hero, David D. Porter, said in his official report for 1888 as Admiral of the Navy that it was questionable if certain members of American naval crews would fire on the flag of any Scandinavian country in time of war, and came forth boldly with such statements as this: "When the *Trenton*, our best ship, lately went into commission, as fine a body of Germans, Huns, Norsemen, Gauls, Chinese, and other outside barbarians as one could wish to see, softened down by time and civilization, were on board. Out of the whole crew not more than 80 could speak the English language."

The government had always been more than generous in the training and betterment of naval officers; yet nothing was done, during my years in the navy, to study or understand the most important part of the naval machine—the enlisted man. He was a transient who remained just long enough to learn the rudiments of his job and who then, lawfully or unlawfully, dropped out to browse in more secure and more profitable pastures. In the late eighties it was not thought unusual to have a turnover of navy personnel of close to 60 percent in a single year! Although in 1888 more than a thousand apprentices were under training, in the entire service there were left from the previous decade fewer than sixty graduates of the apprentice system in the service.*

I feel confident that the money it cost to train and outfit those who found no hope of a career in the navy, or who were discharged before they could be of any real use, would have furnished the funds for salaries, buildings, equipment, and personal comforts adequate to build up a solid and devoted corps of men who, like the sailors of Great Britain, would have been content to serve their country usefully year after year. Was it sound business tactics to attract thousands of men from productive vocations ashore, train them at much expense to become experts in gunnery, electricity,

*In the *Report of the Secretary of the Navy* for 1888 the following figures are given: number of men and boys in the service, 8,354; men enlisted at various rendezvous, 2,348; men enlisted on board ships, 2,436; discharges during year, 3,680; desertions during year, 1,121; number of men enlisted formerly apprentices, 59; number of apprentices on board stationary and cruising ships, 522; number of apprentices on board cruising ships of general service, 542. The ratio of discharges and desertions to total number in service may be computed at 57.5 percent. (Author's note.)

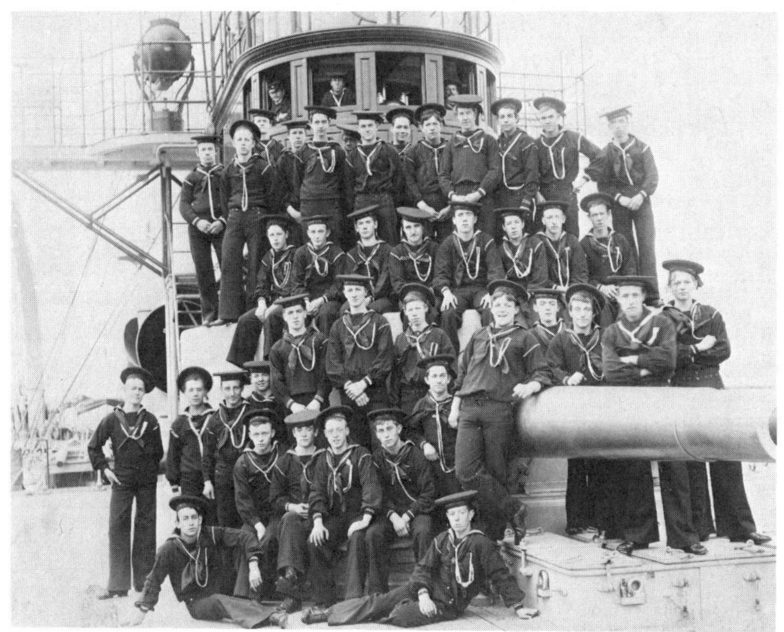

Apprentice seamen aboard the *Brooklyn* in 1897.

engineering, or seamanship, and then lose them because of ill treatment, insufficient reward for faithful service, lack of consideration for personal interests, or distrust of governmental promises? Moreover, these disappointed men were in their home communities always a permanent influence against the future enlistment of good men.

A close study of the possibilities of making the enlisted man's lot a comfortable one would have gone far toward building up a stable and alert fighting force; but it was not until many years had passed, and President Theodore Roosevelt had taken a peep below decks, that any real change for the better was brought about. In 1901 an amendment to the Naval Appropriation Bill provided for the promotion of enlisted men to warrant and commissioned rank, and in October of that year the first two of such promotions were made. Secretary of the Navy Daniels was the first official to recognize the need of a sound educational system for the lower ratings by providing schools that would aid them to advance; but it is a fact that these efforts were fought by officers who could see no wisdom in elevating the enlisted man to higher rank. Such thinking was responsible for the fact that for many years American battleships were manned by boys, and even in the war with Spain in 1898 were handled mainly by boys. Too often, when the boy became a man and a proficient sea fighter, he left the navy for more promising pursuits ashore.

Chapter VI

DOLDRUMS

In the autumn the training ship *Jamestown*, a full-rigged sailing vessel, arrived at the station from Europe with a crew of boys, and they and their Parisian purchases of silk neckerchiefs and cloth for uniforms were spilled into ships of the general service. Then the ship took on a hundred and fifty of the Newport boys who had been enlisted longest and sailed away to the West Indies, followed by the envious thoughts of all of us who were left behind.

Each morning my eyes were strained across the blue water of Narragansett Bay in hopes of a sight of the U.S.T.S. *Portsmouth*, a double-topsail corvette to which many of us had been detailed. Her arrival would free me from the irksome restraint of the rocky island whose every corner and crevice had long ago been explored. Living conditions ashore were still unhealthful and increasingly chilly, and we had been forced to strike our tents and sleep with our hammocks spread on the concrete floor of the unheated brick gymnasium.

My hopes of sailing blue seas amid sunny isles were raised in delight as one winter morning came the stirring hail of "Square-rigger in sight!" Then hove into my view the ship that in my

The U.S.T.S. *Portsmouth*.

opinion was the most graceful masterwork ever created by the hand of man. My dreams of beauty came true as I gazed at the *Portsmouth*. Although her hull was stubby and squat, with no sheer line, her slender spars and towering canvas made her a picture of white splendor as she drew through the narrows with all sail set except stuns'ls. She came about, dropped her light yards, took in the upper head sails, lifted her courses, and, as her headway gently eased, loosed one anchor, veered her chain, and then loosed the other.

The *Portsmouth* was in her time among the fastest sailing ships of the old navy and had a history of mighty deeds behind her. Second of that name, she was built at the navy yard at Portsmouth, New Hampshire, in 1843 as a 20-gun first-class sloop of war of 846 net tons' displacement, and cost $170,500. Under Commander J. B. Montgomery she sailed for the Pacific coast in the following year, arriving at San Francisco on June 3, 1846. During this cruise, war with Mexico had been declared, and on July 9 a detachment of seventy men from the *Portsmouth* landed in San Francisco and hoisted the American flag over what is still called Portsmouth Square, taking possession of the city in the name of the United States.

Later the ship captured several Mexican vessels in the Pacific, returning to Boston in 1848. During the following thirteen years she served in the African squadron, on the Pacific (especially in the East Indies and on the China coast, where she was under fire at the capture of the Canton forts), and again on the African station, capturing many slave traders. Some months after the outbreak of the Civil War she returned to New York and was assigned to the West Gulf squadron under Admiral Farragut, fighting many engagements there and on the lower Mississippi and taking a number of prizes. In 1866 she became the quarantine ship at New York for a year; then followed a first period as training ship. From '69 to '71 she was in the South Atlantic; from '72 to '75 the vessel was again in the Pacific, and in the following year served as training ship at San Francisco. In '78 she was on special duty at the Paris Exposition. Thenceforward until 1895, when the *Portsmouth* was transferred to the naval militia of the State of New Jersey, she was a training ship for U.S. navy apprentices on the Atlantic. She was to be returned to the navy in 1911, stricken from the naval list on April 17, 1915, and sold for junk.

The *Portsmouth* was not so kettle-bottomed as was, for example, the *St. Louis*, although both fell into the class said to have been built by the mile and cut off in fathoms. She had a length between perpendiculars of 150 feet, a maximum beam of 38 feet, and a mean draft of 16 feet 6 inches. In her best days, during the Mexican War, she averaged 128 miles a day during 496 days at sea, and was rated to log 11.6 knots close-hauled and 14 knots free. She was the only ship in our navy ever to carry double topsail yards, which had been adopted by the merchant service in the fifties; but her clews were hauled up into the quarters of the yard, a much snugger piece of seamanship than the usual merchant practice. Her spar deck was flush from the heads to the taffrail, frigate-fashion. The crew ate and slept on the berth deck, but we boys were to live on the gun deck, where were mounted eight 11-inch muzzle-loading smoothbores. Forward were a 60-pound Parrott rifle and two saluting guns, and there were a Gatling and a 3-inch field gun for landing in boats. This was the sole armament of an important ship of the United States Navy at a time when men now living served on her.

The arrival of the *Portsmouth* meant that two hundred and forty of us were free of the island and its dull round of cold and dismal training, mostly military. We had frozen or sweltered there, and all for nine dollars a month, less cost of clothing and hospital fees. In spite of that, I had grown fond of the place, for it was the only college I was ever to know, and it was one step upward in the service in which I was enrolled—for life, as I hoped.

We cheered the poor fellows left behind as we rowed ourselves in cuters through the ice across the mile of water separating us from our new ship. It was already night; the ports and cabin windows of our future home glowed with cheerful lamplight, promising shelter and warmth. As we rounded the counter toward the port gangway, there was the shrill call of a boatswain's whistle and the shuffle of many feet. On deck it was dark, except for the light of a portable lamp carried by a red-headed quartermaster. It was almost time for taps, and the animal warmth of many men living below decks rose from the canopy of the main hatch. We were mustered and checked, and when some of us dared to ask permission to go up into the maintop it was laughingly granted by the officer of the deck, to the amazement of a grumpy captain of the top who warned us not to capsize any gear and to leave things as we found them.

From the main jack I looked down nearly two hundred feet to the quiet dark deck and the rippling waves glinting in the light reflected from the cabin ports. We could feel the throb of the ship as drifting ice smashed against the stiffened cables. My heart overflowed, for this was now my ship, my sea home; I was registered in distant Washington as one of her crew, and in her I was to sail at last to the isles of my boyish fancy. This old square-rigger, like the dim island off there on the beam, was to most of my comrades merely another step in their progress toward a berth on one of the new iron ships then being built. But as for me, that night I would have been glad to cast my lot forever and aye with the lovely old wind-vessels whose stately masts aspired to the stars.

Cruising days were, however, still a long way in the future. On the following morning we were towed ignominiously through Long Island Sound to the Port of New York, there to spend many a weary week refitting and receiving stores, shivering and growling day and night as we tried to keep warm.

It was some time in November, 1889, that news reached us at New York of the loss of three United States warships in a hurricane at Apia, Samoa, on March 17.[1] The proud flagship *Trenton,* the

1. In dispatches from Apia dated 19 March 1889, Rear Admiral Lewis A. Kimberly, commanding the Pacific Station and the squadron at Samoa, and Captain Norman H. Farquhar of the *Trenton* reported that the three American ships were wrecked by the hurricane of March 15–16, with the loss of four

Vandalia, and the *Nipsic* were all piled on the beach with great loss of life. The log of our navy was blazoned with another entry of honor when the men of the wrecked *Trenton* manned the rigging to cheer H.M.S. *Calliope* as she beat her way out to sea and safety. When the British cruiser returned to the harbor after the storm, her captain made a speech to the American survivors in which he said:

"By God, it was splendid to see you lads standing at your posts on the deck of a vessel that was doomed without a chance to escape! Your cheers shall live forever in the memory of those who were privileged to hear them, and it was a proud day for us when we witnessed the heroism of our blood brothers of the sea."

The *Nipsic* was later floated and came home under her own sail. Some years later I was shipmates with one of the survivors of the tragedy—I think he was of the *Vandalia*—who with five others set out in a patched ship's boat to make the fourteen-hundred-mile trip to Australia, where they arrived safely and gave the news of the disaster to the world.

The destroyed American ships were fine vessels, and their loss

officers and 47 men. Three German warships were also in the harbor and all met disaster—one with the loss of all hands except four. The *Vandalia*'s Lieutenant John C. Wilson was sent to Auckland, New Zealand, to cable the dispatches to the Navy Department and then proceed to Sydney to charter a ship to bring the survivors back to the United States. Captain Henry C. Kane of the *Calliope* was given duplicate copies of the dispatches when he departed Apia on 27 March. These were duly forwarded when the *Calliope* arrived at Sydney on 4 April. Wilson, meanwhile, had reached Auckland by steamer and cabled his dispatches to London for transmission to Washington. On Saturday, March 31, the *New York Times* featured a summary of the disaster from London on its front page, and on Monday, April 2, a fuller account, based on the official reports, appeared. The newspaper did not publish on Sunday.

An undated letter from Admiral Kimberly to Captain Kane gives a clue to the means by which Wilson made his way from Samoa to New Zealand: "I thank you many times for your kind offer, but nothing can be done for us under the circumstances. We are trying to get a schooner off tomorrow to meet the steamer for Tutuila and Auckland, to send despatches for our Government and friends at home."

meant much to all of us. In those times our navy was one connected, if not contented, family of a little over eight thousand men and boys, many of whom were united by firm friendships made in the Civil War or on cruises. Nearly every one of the American seamen lost at Samoa was known to some member of the *Portsmouth* crew and was mourned as a friend. But it is not given to sailormen to mourn long, and soon from the older men we heard stories of gay escapades in which their dead friends were charitably, if not always truthfully, cast in the role of the heroes. The highest eulogy we heard of any man was: "That was a shipmate for you!" The ideal shipmate seemed to be one who was a good spendor ashore, who could take his liquor without too much quarreling, and who would fight for you without asking a reason. I preferred to think of the definition that old Tom Dunn had once given me on the *St. Louis*. Said he:

"A good shipmate is one who will stand back to back with you against a stronger force, especially British man-o'-warsmen; a man who will take your part against a company of your own marines; a fellow who can be depended on never to shirk his duty in storm or calm; a man who would lie for you! The best of a real shipmate is that he would do for you without witnesses what he would be proud to do before the whole world."

Ashore in New York we had many a chance to know who our best shipmates were. New York's Bowery, with the Barbary Coast of San Francisco in the West, was inseparably connected with the old navy man's idea of what shore pleasures could be, for at those two spots most of them habitually flung their paydays to the winds in the notorious dives that catered to sailormen. The city of New York, in the mind of a man on liberty, was narrowed to a zone encompassing Grand Street and the Bowery, and a few corners near the west end of Brooklyn Bridge. My recollection of what New York meant to a young sailor is comprised in the hustle and glare of the earliest white-and-tile restaurants, which were close to the dance halls whose names were known over the world wherever seamen gathered. (One of these places was called Suicide Hall because the street girls there pretended to take poison with their drinks.) It meant a roar of elevated trains and the hoarse hooting of ferryboats. It meant four saloons at every downtown intersection, and an oyster-counter at the middle of each block, where a boy could get large, succulent Baltimore oysters at a cent each with no extra charge for catsup. Most of all, it meant for me that nectar of the gods, the five-cent milk shake, which could be obtained anywhere, East Side, West Side, and down at Coney Island. Blue, thin milk, with a dash of vanilla flavoring and a handful of cracked ice, was poured into a large tin cone and screwed into an arrangement like an egg beater attached to a bicycle. The dealer jumped on a seat behind the counter and pedaled himself and my milk shake for a mile or so, until the mixture foamed over. "Drink it down, son, even if it kills you! What—another one?" "It's my last nickel, mister, but just shake one more!"

The play called *The Old Homestead* was in the heyday of its long run at a downtown theater. Here we enjoyed the acting quite uncritically, and kept warm and amused for two hours at little cost. The Eden Musée on Twenty-third Street, and Huber's, on Fourteenth Street, were also favorite spots to our men. At Huber's there was a fabulous glass staircase under which water, lighted by incandescent lamps, cascaded down. Exhibition freaks at a place on Grand Street were especially friendly to navy boys because one of the women believed she had a son in the service, although she had not heard from him in years. A tattooing artist on Pell Street had reformed and had dedicated himself to eradicating his own previous work. His intention was laudable because the work was terrible, but the pain of removal was just as great as was the initial tattooing, and the economics of the job were curious, because he charged twice as much to take off a picture as he had charged to punch it on. Along the Bowery were many museums "for men only" where a phrenologist, at absolutely no charge, offered to feel the bumps on your head. When a flattering epitome of your many fine traits had caused you to tingle with vanity, an assistant pointed to a placard which announced a charge of one dollar for character readings. I was once caught by this little dodge, but the "doctor" was forced to compromise for fifty cents. It was all I had, which meant that with not a penny more at hand my liberty was perforce over.

When apprentices who were out of money desired one more fling ashore, it was possible to raise a loan from the "six-for-five" fellows aboard ship, who charged a dollar interest for the use of five dollars for thirty days. Another common practice was to draw a new pea jacket from the paymaster on issuing day, signing a charge of ten dollars and eighty cents against our accounts. So general was this custom that all of us knew exactly what dealer on Baxter Street would give us five dollars for the new coat, or where at another place an hour of persuasive salesmanship might bring us a return of thirty cents more. To the frugal sailor a half eagle was sufficient for a snug twenty-four-hour liberty. One could get a box stall of a room in a Bowery hotel at twenty cents a day, with a penny newspaper thrown in. Meals were fifteen cents up. For those who needed rum to make the holiday complete, it could be had in the basements of barrel houses—five cents for a good-sized snifter. The last copper of the fund was reserved for pedestrian toll across Brooklyn Bridge.

Such amusements were the height of the enlisted man's ventures ashore. The reader of today might wonder at the threadbare and vulgar tone of our pleasures. Why did we not take in the sights in New York's splendid parks and public buildings? Why did we not visit those famous restaurants where fine dinners were served with wine at less than a dollar? Why not attend the free recitals and concerts, the lectures and other entertainments for which the city was famous? The answer is that we were not wanted, for we wore jackets of navy blue and flat caps marked with the name of an American naval vessel.

Nothing could be more calculated to arouse the feeling of ostracism in a man-o'-warsman than to be confronted with a notice: "No men in uniform admitted here!" Such a sign—and there were many of them—created a resentment against shore people that found a natural relief in abandoning attempts at respectability and frequenting those places where everything was open and warm, and where, at least so long as the money lasted, a man was received with hospitality even if he wore the uniform of one of his country's arms of defense. The churches did not welcome us; there was no Y.M.C.A. to furnish us with homelike comforts; and we were not even called to the Bethel Missions that sought out the seamen of the merchant service. It is true, of course, that many an old shellback released from long sea labors had earned a bad reputation for himself; but it seemed hard lines that young fellows should be barred from civilian fun for no better reason than that. And thus, as the strange excitements of the Bowery haunts vanished all too rapidly, we drifted back to the ship, feeling lost in a Sargasso Sea of disappointment and loneliness. For me, sailing-time could not arrive too soon.

Life at the New York Navy Yard was not by any means all bright lights and liberties. When the ship had been generally overhauled and heavy stores loaded, we were continually drilled, ashore and aboard, in order to keep us fit physically and to prepare us for our sea duties. This grinding work had one compensation—it kept us warm when nothing else could. It seemed to us that there were entirely too many of these endless drills, loosening and furling sail and hoisting up light masts and yards. We blamed the officers and considered it a piece of bad fortune to have been put under their command; but after some years had passed, it dawned on me that it had been the same on every ship, and that so long as there was one line officer aboard there had to be drills and more drills. We felt lucky when, on returning from a march in Brooklyn with rifle and full pack, we did not find some lady visitors on board who would tell their officer friends how curious they were to see how the work of reefing topsails was performed. Yet the drills kept us busy and hardened us and taught us our job, as we realized later in the lazy tropics.

At Christmastime some of the boys were permitted to go home on leave if transportation money was furnished them by their parents, and many of them did go, because in those days almost every apprentice was from some near-by coastal state. On my return from my first visit home after a year under training, I hardly recognized the ship. She had the same claw-footed look forward, but aloft it did not seem to be the same old *Portsmouth*. There were thrum mats in the rigging and chafing gear on shrouds and backstays, topping lifts, and guys; preventer backstays also had been fitted. All this spoiled her former jaunty appearance; her trimness was gone, but she looked ready to face the sea.

The boats were in their gripes, heavy gun breechings were doubled and frapped, and there were extra lashings on the guns. The port shutters had been calked, although the decks still leaked here and there (every boy swore that the biggest leak was right over his hammock). The ship was lumbered with casks of pork and beef and flour, bags of beans and waterproofed cases of coffee, barrels of sugar and hard bread, and plenty of molasses, in barrels and out. Eventually everything found its stowage place.

Getting to sea in the days of sail meant something more than hoisting the anchors and setting a bridge signal. The *Portsmouth* spent a full day making Sandy Hook, under tow at that. There we anchored inside the bight to await a favorable wind. All night we remained within sight of the inviting lights of Coney Island, stewing and grumbling as sailors will but remembering that what couldn't be cured had to be endured. If the men of the old navy in their later careers ashore sometimes showed a lack of initiative in the face of adversity, it should be remembered that they had been trained through years to a characteristic patience because of the necessity of awaiting a fair wind to insure any progress toward a fixed destination.

We were now placed in watches, and I was assigned to the port watch. My station on the ship, along with most of the other lighter boys of the crew, was among the afterguard, with special duties on mizzenmast and spanker.

The next morning, Sunday, arrived with its New York chill but lacking what we had prayed for—a fair wind. We wanted to be off. Men who had not yet quite rid themselves of bloodshot eyes and heavy heads growled and moved about discontentedly, preparing for the usual quarters in inspection. But the sight of the navigator coming up the wardroom hatch ladder with a chart under his arm brought the deck to life. Seamen anxiously questioned stewards and messmen, who were supposed to be repositories of all the secrets of officialdom, and got the bland answer: "Yes, bimeby mebbe makee wind."

The fat boatswain had come on deck and was talking to the men in charge of the watches on the fo'c'sle. Something in rumors, after all! The old-timers went below to their bags, and returned to the spar deck in nondescript but warmer garb; but I did not dare go below for fear of missing something. I was about to put to sea at last.

Now the captain and his executive officer, "Dickie" Rush, appeared on deck. The captain, a dark, undersized man with a low-spoken voice, was in many ways the opposite of the large and loud executive officer—who in the merchant service would have been called the first mate. Nothing happened. The two walked to the rail and noted the set of the current. The captain wet his finger and held it up; there was a general wetting of fingers about the deck, but no happy exclamations followed. The two officers asked questions of the quartermaster on duty, and then glanced over the low spit of land toward the ocean. The water remained unruffled in spite of all. Could no one whistle? Deep in my heart I was not discouraged. The captain represented to me the apogee of all authority, and I felt that if he really wanted a wind, a wind we should have. My hopes were raised further when two men went to the wheel and folded up its canvas covering.

It was after eight o'clock. Our foul-weather ensign hung limply from the dasher block at the end of the spanker gaff. It fluttered a trifle. Our glances went to the commission pennant at the main truck. At its broadest part it was lifting. "Here it comes!" someone said, as the surface of the water beyond showed a few tiny cat's-paws. The executive officer nodded to the navigator, and from many directions orders blared forth.

Some of the men disappeared into the chain lockers to tier up the cable as it came in. Many of us were herded to the gun deck to man the capstan and heave round. The chain seemed as willing to be off as we; it had lain in sand, and came in easily and clean. We hove in to a short stay—that is, with the cable pointing tautly down in line with the foretopmast stay. "Up and down, sir; short haul." " 'Vast heaving!" We hoisted each other to the spar deck, the ladders of the main hatch having been removed within the radius of the capstan bars. Overside the waters of the bay were rippling in a nor'west breeze that fanned our warm bodies pleasantly.

"Lay aloft, sail loosers!" Then, a moment later, "Lay out and loose!" Impatient fingers aloft worked at gaskets. On deck I was helping to clear the heavy canvas of the spanker and to get the sheets ready for running. I was rushed to haul one rope here and another there, seemingly without reason, but the work progressed.

"Stand by!" "Let fall!" "Sheet home the tawps'ls!" "Lay down from aloft! Hard down out of that now, and shake a leg. Man your topsail halyards!" The last order had hardly been lost in the rising gray mist when the deck again swarmed with men, leaving only a few of the topmen aloft like blackbirds among the canvas clouds.

Sails and gear began to tug and strain. "T'ga'nt and royal halyards! Overhaul lifts!" "Sheet home!" "Tail on here, you damned sojer!" "Let go that clewline; get off this bloody brace!" Words came like the crack of a rifle, and the neatness and precision of our harbor drills were cast aside in the excitement. The ancient, trim phrases of command gave way to: "Lend a hand here, you!" "Damn it, don't belay that over there!" and "Take your ugly hoofs out of that coil!" We hauled on the maintopsail halyard until it seemed the gear must split, and then rushed to the fore, far from our stations, to lend a hand. The ropes were stiff and wet, and the blocks and falls seemed stubborn and unwieldy. But those with experience thanked their stars that they were not handling single topsails with their much greater area of canvas and cordage.

The nine wrinkled sails of the *Portsmouth* beat back against the spars and shrouds as the sheets were painfully hauled close home. We were still at anchor, but raring to go—backwards. Once again to the halyards; now man the braces, port fore and main and starboard crojick braces, stand by the head halyards! Then back to the gun deck and the capstan bars, every man and boy that could be spared. It took only a few circles around to feel that we were stuck;

the ton anchor was well embedded, and the slight rise and fall of our bow was not enough to break ground. We heaved and heaved. The swifters at the ends of the bars stretched and sprung as young muscles were forced to make one more inch.

Suddenly something gave. Clumsily we fell forward; heads cracked against the keel of the sailing launch which was mortised through the spar deck. Had we broken the great chain? No; the anchor had decided to give up its hold on the bottom of the bay. The girls of New York had let us go. A loud call came from the fo'c'sle:

"Anchor's aweigh, sir!"

The *Portsmouth* was under sail. We were off to those tropic isles.

Chapter VII

UNDER SAIL

When we reached our stations on deck once more, we found that the executive officer had taken his place on the weather horse block and there, leaning his bulk over the pipe rail, was bellowing order after order. The ship was drifting astern, and the helm was put hard down.

"Let go fore and main clew garnets; sheet home the courses!" Two more great sails filled with the wind. Men ran away with the headsail halyards, and our bow fell off to the rattling accompaniment of sheet blocks and pendants. A few men left below at the capstan had run the anchor up to the hawsepipe, where it dangled and dripped as water from the clanking head pumps splashed on the broad flukes to wash away sand and seaweed. We were headed, I noticed, back toward New York—why was that? I was still unacquainted with the secrets of sailing a great ship against the wind.

The captain stood beside the brass canopy of a hatchway, alert to the movements of the helmsmen, glancing now at the pennant aloft and now at the buoys to right and left of us. A swarm of gray gulls rose from the beach and hovered over our stern, screeching so that we could scarcely hear the cries of the leadsmen in the chains. On up the roads we sailed, closehauled on the starboard tack, the captain's eye fixed on the leech of the main topgallantsail. Suddenly, with arm extended, he waved his hand to the right. The blare of the executive officer's voice through his trumpet frightened the gulls to silence. "Ready about! Helm's a-lee! . . . Rise tacks and sheets . . . Haul taut; mainsail ha-a-aul!"

The chanting call had barely blown down the wind when the yards were swung round and the ship seemed to pivot on her heel. The familiar orders heard in our peaceful harbor drills took on an urgent, new significance, and we cursed and stumbled in green anxiety, for now the safety of the great ship in a narrow channel hung on quick and sure action. It was not done with clever, practiced skill; but it was done. There was a tense moment when the ship stood still, as if to listen. Then her head wavered, drifted slowly to starboard. We hauled on the many braces, eased the spanker boom amidships and then over to the lee side, to the clatter and churr of jib and staysail sheets forward. When I could look up, I found we were safely on the port tack, heeled over and headed out to sea. Thousands of feet of rope were lying in a seemingly inextricable tangle about the decks; but the sails had filled robustly, the wind was on our quarter—the *Portsmouth*'s best sailing point—and a million bubbles swirled about the rudder and rippled in our wake.

Greenhorns as we were, we had put her about and taken her to sea. A few months later the same captain and crew worked the ship, piled with canvas, up the narrow reaches of the Elizabeth River and dropped both bowers, then put out a kedge so that we would not interfere with the traffic of the Norfolk Navy Yard. There was no turbulence or confusion, for by then our task had become second nature to us and we took pride in its swift accomplishment. We had come to know by the feel of a halyard when a yard was up or a sheet was home. We knew what rope to pull and how hard to pull it, and the precise pin of all pins where each was to be belayed. We had "learned the ropes," so that even on the darkest night we could work the ship by the manual of touch.

Now, as the *Portsmouth* dipped and curtsied to the Atlantic swells, we could feel the draw and lift of her upper sails and two courses before the freshening breeze. She was making six knots, which was not bad for her class. There was still plenty to be done. The decks were cleared of all shore gear, fenders, "pudding" mats, and the last of the sea stores. The two bower anchors were fished and brought inboard, and then secured to the billboards by frapping through their ring bolts. The cables, which had been unbent, were sent to the chain lockers. Conical "jackasses" of woven rope were drawn up through the empty hawsepipes to keep the seas out of the manger. It was beginning to rain, a cold and penetrating drizzle.

The deck had been given over to the starboard watch, and at seven bells we of the port watch went below for dinner. Few of my comrades had any appetite for the meal; most of them were queasy, and the calloused comments of the older men did little to reassure their stomachs. Nor was there any comfort or seclusion to be had, for after dinner we were all called to the rolling deck, where the rain continued and the sea was rising. Through the waves the hull heaved forward in a sickening series of plunges, scuppers under. We were battling an ocean.

We held southerly, and my first two hours were passed in jumping from the main braces to the crojick braces, swigging now and again at a halyard or sheet, pulling or slackening some of the spanker gear, tightening the vangs, letting go the topping lifts, or heaving the log (a special duty of the afterguard). Life seemed full of cares for a green hand, and I began to suspect that when a moment's respite came it was merely because the officer of the deck was forward superintending the trimming of gear there. For the first time I heard many sea commands that in future would stir me to automatic action, but which now were strange and frightening.

The world seemed to waver. I shivered, and my teeth rattled in my head. The sight of green water sliding by overside and the groaning of the ship's guts made me feel as if the vessel herself was sickened by the incessant pitching of the sea. A thin sour stream trickled from the sides of my mouth. I would have given much to be able to crawl into a warm and sheltered spot, to hide in a magazine or deep in the hold, or anywhere tht would take me away from the reach of rough duty calls amid a watery universe. At that moment Bob Hamilton, in charge of my part of the ship, ordered me to the wheel to take my first steering trick.

The flaxen-haired seaman at the weather side of the wheel, the post of honor, swore and spat when he saw me reach for the spokes opposite him. He needed a man, not a splinter of a boy, to help him handle the kicking old tub! His was the guiding hand, and I was barely able to follow his lead as he pulled or hung at the spokes, shifting my stand every minute or two, muscles shaking and head throbbing in the need to anticipate each contrary jerk of the rudder and flaw of the wind. The wheel seemed ready at any instant to pull my chest open.

During the first of the hundreds of weary hours I was destined to spend staring into the flighty black-and-white face of the compass card, I learned something of the malignant energy with which the wheel fights the man, and how numerous are the devilish forces that conspire to pull the "lubber's point" away from the helmsman's straining control. No one who has never steered a big sailing ship can understand what a sensitive and yet bullying task it may become. No matter how earnestly I strove to cling to the grating with my feet, the demoniac spokes would pull me up, up, until I came close to the scowling eyes of the big seaman on the other side. There was no duty on the whole ship that I would not then have preferred to this watch at the wheel. I yearned, rather, to forget all duty and lie with misery in the scuppers along with the boys already there.

Yet the demands of the work cleared my head and kept me on my feet until the sickness had passed; and when I went below I found that only one other boy in my mess was in any condition to enjoy the fare. The supper was of tea and bread, with a treat of jam that had retained no flavor except that of the soft-pine pail in which it had been kept. I had any part of twenty-two shares of this jam that I cared to eat, and, made greedy by the sea air, I forced down such a quantity that, for a long time afterward, jam was no sort of treat at all for me.

We drove steadily southward, and slowly our crew of tyros were broken in to the old routine of the sea, learning to perform all the tasks required for the safe handling of the ship, and of course doing the incessant cleaning demanded by the old navy ideal of washing and scrubbing everything in sight. As the misery of seasickness wore off, there was greater opportunity for the boys to become better acquainted with each other and with the older members of the *Portsmouth*'s company. Each day, it seemed, new faces appeared from the berth deck and the hold.

During the dogwatch of our first day out, a last breath of the Bowery was wafted to us when a stowaway was dragged forth by the chief master-at-arms and hauled to the quarterdeck. We recognized the culprit at once. It was "Tug" Waldron, lately a petty officer of the *Portsmouth* and one of the most confirmed liberty-breakers the old navy had ever known.

The stowing away of Tug Waldron had come about in curious fashion. Tug was a down-East barnacle, a good man on deck or aloft, but one who could never return from shore leave on time, or clean, or sober. He was an ugly man who prided himself on his ugly disposition and his reputation as a "Philadelphia lawyer" when arguing his case at "the mast," where his appearances were usually connected with bottles of liquor and usually ended in the brig with the rating badge removed from his arm. Whenever he was disrated he demanded to be excused from more menial duties on the ground that he was tubercular. He could give an instructive lecture on this topic, with graphic demonstrations of what his lungs looked like, although the men in the sick bay ascribed all these symptoms to too much cheap whisky.

One of his periods of detention expired a short time after we had tied up at the New York Navy Yard, and Tug was entitled to go ashore again. He declared, on leaving, that it would take the whole gang of yard leathernecks, in addition to the entire New York police force, to get him back on the rotten old hulk. This was not unusual talk, for there were always one or two men in every top who were aggressively sure that the ship couldn't operate without their invaluable services. We knew what he intended this time, naturally, and when he didn't return at the end of the day were almost sure of the course he was steering on shore. He would hang out at one of the Bowery dives until his money was spent and the affection of his current sweetheart had cooled, and then, when the ten-day period of grace had passed and he had been declared a deserter with a reward offered for his return, he would arrange with a friendly detective to deliver him to the ship. An arrangement was often made by which the sailor giving himself up would obtain a part of the twenty-dollar reward, and this seemed to many a confirmed deserter a smart stroke of business, even though the full amount was charged against him by the paymaster.

On the night that Tug had decided to surrender, he was reveling in McGurck's Saloon and awaiting the arrival of the detective who was to pay his debts from the reward money and escort him back to the ship. Tug was drunkenly boasting of how much he was worth in solid cash to the government when a disgruntled man in a derby hat entered and broke in on the proud oration.

"Say, listen up there, you half-baked faker! Don't try to make these people believe the navy would pay a nickel a bunch for a thing like you! Listen, you piker! I was over to the navy yard today and they offered me real money—big money—if I could do something to keep you out of the ship until after she sails!"

The detective had not lied. A day or so later, after recovering from the effects of the barroom free-for-all that had followed the announcement that Tug was a burden to the service he had so long disgraced, Waldron turned up on the deck of the *Portsmouth.* He had lost a few teeth, but he was clean, and there was still some swagger in his voice as he saluted and announced to the officer of the deck:

"Returned from liberty, sir."

"Yes?" growled Lieutenant Hodgson. "And who are you?"

"H.M. Waldron, sir."

"Never heard of you. What division?"

Tug fell back a few steps. "Why, yours, sir; I'm in the maintop!"

The officer shook his head. "Messenger, tell the executive officer there's a stranger on board who claims to be a member of this crew. I think he's an impostor. Ask him what shall be done with this man."

Tug was growing more and more uneasy. He looked about for sympathy, which was offered by one or two onlookers who had lent him money. The messenger came up from below.

"Sir, Mr. Rush says to turn him over to the marines at the gate with orders never to let him in again!"

Tug Waldron realized then that the story was true. He had lost the number of his mess. He was not needed on his ship; and losing a good ship is worse in some ways than losing a home, because the ship moves about and can't be found even though the captain might later get generous and want the lost man back again. That was why Tug stowed away in the hold a few days before the *Portsmouth* sailed, and why he was now appearing before an irate captain on the quarter-deck after the vessel had put to sea.

He was hungry, long-sobered, but still audacious Tug as he stood at "the mast" ready to take his medicine.

"Waldron," said the captain, "I'd like to know what traitor helped you to get back on this ship. We don't want you, and we've tried our best to get rid of you. Master-at-arms, cut that rating badge off this deserter's arm. Now I'll see what the bluebook will allow me to do to a man who doesn't belong to the service."

"Yes, sir; thank you, sir," grinned Waldron.

"Oh, that isn't all! I am holding you for a general court-martial, but in the meantime, if you overstep yourself, over the side you'll go, no matter what port we're in, and we'll keep rats like you off the ship if we have to use steel nets. Now, go forward!"

"Aye, aye, sir; thank you, sir." Tug saluted smartly and headed toward the galley and the first solid meal in a long time. Anyone could see how elated he was at the success of his ruse. As he passed some of us on the booms we heard him confiding hoarsely to a dubious seaman:

"It's great to be back again, Johnny, and to be welcomed by the old man in such a hearty way. He was trying to bluff me, but by God, I could tell he was tickled pink to have me back on his lousy old tub!"

On the third day out, the wind increased to a gale. The upper sails were doused and their yards were sent down to the deck to be lashed to the forward shrouds of the lower rigging. At sundown all sail was furled except the main lower topsail; a storm staysail and main trysail were bent, and under these three sails we hove to.

Thereafter for four days the ship rode sluggishly over angry seas, making no progress except a leeway that carried us well into the Gulf Stream off Cape Hatteras, and into a sea of universal ill humor. It rained all the time, a cold rain; each few minutes we shipped a sea over the weather side (through the brutal carelessness, it seemed, of the helmsman), and every man on deck was soaked through.

There was no evading deck duty, for on watch we were kept busy giving a pull here and slackening gear there, tugging at braces and preventer backstays that had not yet settled down to taut sea trim. Several times during our watches below we were roused out for night labor. All this while it was dangerous to be on deck, and to make progress one always had to cling to something—rail or lifeline or ends of gear; below decks, the body strained continually to keep in an upright position, legs seeming of themselves to wrap about cables or cling strainingly to coamings or gun carriages. Tumultuous great seas came out of the west in a grand procession under the keel, ponderously rolling up the lee side after slapping the gun muzzles with a frothing impudence. The innards of the ship whined a thousand timbery complaints at knees and beams; ladders gouged with their feet into the creaking planks of the deck; from the galley came the discordant clatter of pots and pans adrift.

For days the food was cold, eaten miserably off tarpaulins spread on the berth deck. All the ports of the gun deck were tightly sealed and calked to keep out the seas, and below the air was foul. At night the stuffiness and the smell of wet blankets, woolen clothing, unaired oilskins, and seasick boys became almost unbearable. The close-swung hammocks swayed and bumped together in a way that murdered sleep, and we apprentices were content to drowse off when and wherever we could about the ship.

Night and day the decks were swept with creaming surges from overside. Hatch hoods had been drawn over all the deck openings, and on the gratings under these tentlike canvas hoods the shivering members of the watch on deck crowded together, seeking shelter from the gale and wondering if this was a fair sample of navy life at sea. The privileged ones below protested loudly at the lack of air, and had the miserable wretches ordered out on deck. Below, on the berth deck, the faint glow of wan daylight that penetrated the thick glass ports continually faded to green, then darkened completely as the ship's side wallowed under. Beneath our feet on the gun deck the water that had seeped through the leaky gun ports swashed about from side to side.

On the pitching decks there was now little seamanship called for; after the second day of the gale, yards had been so braced and squeezed against the chafing gear on shrouds and backstays that the heart-strands of the ropes weeped and longjawed, and nothing more could be gained by swigging them for another inch of tautness. Sick and sleepy apprentices rolled in the waterways or tried to get out of sight under the boom cover amidships.

No matter what the weather or how hard the ship might be slapped and sluiced by heavy seas, the decks were invariably washed down and swabbed in the morning watch, and clothing was scrubbed on the forecastle. Quarters was always held at nine. We came to envy the equanimity of officers and older seamen in performing all the routine of a man-o'-war while we could hardly stand erect. Calmly amid all the tumult under the main hatch sat Wilson, the ship's tailor, carrying on his work as if he were in a warm and bright shop ashore. He never allowed the rolling of the vessel or the dimness of the light from the covered hatch overhead to interfere with his stitching or cutting, and his machine hummed gaily away. Beside him, when off watch, sat Billy

Thompson, a quartermaster, also stitching, embroidering long-pointed stars and silk diamonds on mustering clothes for men less handy with the needle. His red-bearded mate Stevens would also be there, overhauling the signal flags that were in his charge or reading his pocket edition of the works of Shakespeare. Men stamped back and forth around them, bellowing out orders or demands for light and standing room; the old mossbacks never bothered to look up from their labors.

I soon found that, strangely enough, the motion of the ship seemed easier if one climbed aloft; and high above the deck, if one remembered the old topman's rule—"one hand for the government and one for yourself"—it was safe and far from unpleasant. Because I didn't mind work in the rigging, I was often allowed to aid the mizzen topmen in reefing topsails or helping furl the great sail on the main yard; but my principal post on the southern passage was at the spanker. The spanker is the aftermost sail on a square-rigged ship, and runs fore and aft from sliders fastened to the mizzenmast. The sail is of little importance when the ship is running free, but owning to its position well aft it has a great influence on the steering of the ship—being, in fact, a sort of canvas rudder—and is of special value with the wind abeam or when the ship is clawing up to windward. The evolution of the spanker is, in little, a history of the development of modern sailing theory.

As late as the middle of the fifteenth century, the most common type of sail propulsion was the lateen ("Latin") rig, consisting of a single triangular sail to each mast. The longest leech of the sail was fastened to a yard which could be canted to catch the wind. There was no foot boom, and the sail was managed by halyards and sheets. The single-masted ships of the Romans had been replaced by vessels with three masts named, from forward to aft, the main, the mizzen, and the bonaventura; and although the two forward masts came to be rigged with square sails, on the rearmost the lateen rig was for centuries retained. It was depended upon as an aid to steering, and especially for maneuvering in battle when the square sails were brailed up; also, the lateen sail was always kept spread in port to prevent the ship from fouling her ground tackle. When running before the wind, the seaman unparreled the lateen spar from the mast and launched it over to leeward, with the heel of the spar bowsed to the deck on the starboard side. Near the end of the seventeenth century the part of the lateen sail forward of the mast was cut off, although the bare end of the yard remained for many decades, jutting out as a relic of its former shape. Gradually improvements were made to transform the lateen into the true modern fore-and-aft sail with gaff and boom. As the design of hulls improved the ease with which the ships could be steered, the length of the great spanker boom was shortened until it barely extended over the taffrail. Even so, the boom on the *Portsmouth* was heavy enough to call for all our strength.

As the heavy weather continued, all our clothing was sodden, and the skin on hands and feet became bleached and tender. Sea sores would not heal. If by chance any of us in the afterguard had remained fairly dry, he would sooner or later be called on to heave the log, and the wet line would inevitably soak him through.

Every hour on watch, in calm or storm, men of this part of the ship were mustered to measure our speed by an old-fashioned taffrail log, consisting of a wooden reel and an angular "chip" at the end of a knotted line. The knots were spaced forty-seven feet and four inches apart, and this distance with its divisions was marked out on the quarter-deck in brass-headed nails. The distance bears the same ratio to the nautical mile of 6,080 feet as twenty-eight seconds bear to the hour, and our speed could be computed by the simple rule of three. The run was timed by the quartermaster, who at a signal inverted a small sandglass and called for the mark when the glass had emptied after twenty-eight seconds. How accurate this method was I never knew, but it was the only way we had of computing our speed. Of course the effects of sea, tide, and wind had also to be taken into consideration. With the ship wallowing before a gale we would never have been able to bring the chip aboard again had it not been for an ingenious tripping device which by means of a toggle allowed the upright wedge of wood to flatten out on top of the waves.

Often we envied the boys in forward divisions who did not have to mess about with a log line each time the bell struck an even number; but in more clement weather, heaving the log was less unpleasant work, and even the wetting was more endurable, as the Gulf Stream water was many degrees warmer than the air. When we were in cheerful mood we made light of the work by singing the words written by an old sailorman to a well-known hymn tune:

"We read thee every hour,
Thou precious, faithful log;
Thy truthful line reveals
The distance as we jog.
We read thee, oh, we read thee,
Every hour we read thee;
The navigator needs thee,
O lo-o-ovely log!"

The storm blew itself out after four days. We were cheered by a smart wind from the east, and by the call: "Sheet home your tawps'ls!" Swiftly we were under light sails, and the ship, with a mind of her own once more, smashed ahead through the subsiding swells. The lofty, leaning spars glistened in the welcome sunlight. Clothes and bedding were laid out on the booms to dry, or hung up in the whipping breeze. Hatch hoods were thrown back and the precious sun slatted down into the steamy 'tween decks; gun ports on the weather side were flung open to the air. White-faced apprentices crawled forth and grinned shakily at each other, stretched in the sun, listened to the softer music of the waves, and at night gazed at stars whose brilliance held a promise of the soft tropics.

Life on board now became much more smooth and serene. We lounged about the decks after drill, or brought up strange sea-weeds and marine creatures in the temperature bucket. The older men of the crew were anxious to show us our duties and the finer points of seamanship, and most of the officers were patient and even kindly. However, rarely a day passed when the ship's court was not held to judge offenders from every division of the ship.

Most of their infractions might be considered trivial, such as being tardy in stowing hammocks or losing a piece of clothing or having a towel with one's name on it in the "lucky bag" kept in the charge of the chief master-at-arms. There was nothing lucky about having any of your possessions turn up in this lost-and-found department conducted by Jimmylegs, and many a bad record in the navy had its beginning in such a venial entry as "lost clothing." This and other misdemeanors were punished at the least by an order to toe a deck seam for an entire watch, with hammock on shoulder.

Treacherous little naval crimes like these were not easy to avoid. The civilian should try to imagine himself under the necessity of packing all his wearing apparel—Sunday clothes, dress clothes, working clothes, hats, shoes, and likewise cleaning gear and trinkets—into a canvas bag fourteen inches by thirty-six, including a tuck at the top for the draw-cord. Into that bag everything had to be packed so that there were no wrinkles. Access to one's possessions could be gained only at stated times, and nothing could be left about for a moment. My second ditty box disappeared shortly after we left New York, and when during the gale off Hatteras it rolled forth from its hiding place under a jackstay, it was found to have been broken open and rifled of everything of value.

When a man had washed clothing in the morning watch, his ears were pricked until in the afternoon the order was piped: "Stand by your scrubbing wash-clothes!" for it would be but a moment before the gantlines were thrown off their pins and the laden line drooped to the deck. You were fortunate if in the ensuing scramble you were directly underneath your own clothes, for otherwise someone would surely trample them in his haste to reach his own. If by chance you were at work in some distant part of the ship or did not hear the call, you might lose some of your outfit or discover that the master-at-arms had found them for you—and then another luckless boy would be down on the report. It was as easy as that. It seemed to me on this first cruise that the custody of my outfit, meager as it was, became my most corroding worry; and even today my most persistent nightmare is to dream of walking a chilly deck, naked and alone, seeking to find my clothes stowed in a bag whose number I have forgotten.

Our food was the regular navy sea ration which had been fixed by Congress twenty years before, and was not unlike the original ration list adopted for the enlisted man in 1801; it was not until thirteen years after our *Portsmouth* cruise that the general mess system was established. The weekly ration consisted of coffee, tea, beans, flour, pork, beef, canned mutton, and hard bread or "tack." We also had sugar, salt, and a few other condiments. After the first day out there were no fresh potatoes or meat. We apprentices soon became accustomed to this spare diet, except for the "salt horse" or beef in brine, which had a vile taste that no amount of boiling could kill. The common practice of the beginner was to eat with one hand and hold his nose with the other; but according to the older men on board there was nothing on land or sea that would encourage the growth of hair on the chest like a ration of salt horse. Even the wardroom officers ate it and seemed to like it; and after twenty-two men left their mess tables on salt-horse day there was little but bones and gristle left on the platter. It was served as a special treat at Saturday dinner, along with bean soup and a doughy, raisiny mass of sweetened "plum duff." The Jack-o'-the-dust was allowed, as storeroom assistant, to conduct a shop for his own profit, and if a fortunate apprentice had twenty-five cents he could get a glass of jelly or a can of sardines. A dish of marmalade bought from "Dusty," eaten with hardtack purloined from one of the chests on the berth deck, made many an otherwise dull midwatch pass cheerily enough.

The sweetest part of a work-filled day was the quiet and peace of the second dogwatch. Those who did not care to loiter amidships and join in the songs of the darky messmen went off with chums to gam in a corner, or hung over the rail and wove schemes for the future. In the minds of many of the apprentices these plans did not comprise a navy career; they had already learned enough to know that the inducements to remain after their enlistments expired were not tremendous.

Around the smoking lamp a knot of old tarry-breeks might be

boasting of their friendly association with the officers. One of them, with an almost insufferable air of self-importance, would say: "Aw, the skipper talks to me every time he sees me at the wheel. Just the usual chew-the-rag. He says to me, he says: 'Dammit, man how are you steerin' this ship anyway?' And I says to him: 'Sou'-sou'east, sir! And he comes right back at me, friendly as you please and twice as natural: 'Well, see that you keep her thataway and don't be yawin' all over the damn compass!'"

The proud fellow would be eyed admiringly by all his mates except a touchy old derelict who in thirty-five years in the service had never attained the dignity of a petty officer's rating. Jealously he might reply: "That ain't a thing to what he says to me. He says: 'Bowen, what become of old McCarthy of the mizzentop in the *Quinnebaug?*' I told him Mac was with me later on in the *Tuscarora.* Then he says: 'Fine ship, that *Quinnebaug,*' and I says, quick as a wink: 'Not near as good as she'd been with more officers like you, sir!' And the skipper he laughs and says to me: 'Later on, John, I want you to make application for transfer to go with me to the *Brooklyn.* I'll need you as my coxswain!'"

The glances that John Bowen got would be respectful but dubious. Everyone knew that the captain had spoken to him, but even if he had made any promises—and it was a signal honor to be asked by an officer to follow him to his next ship—it was a safe bet that next time Bowen came back from his liberty, as drunk and disorderly as usual, the captain would give him the limit of punishment and forget all about needing a coxswain on the *Brooklyn.*

Then: "Call the watch; relieve the wheel and lookouts!" One watch would go below for a sleep lasting four hours, provided it was not broken by special drill or some emergency. The other watch would be mustered around the lamp of the junior deck officer. Then would begin the silence, interrupted only by the half-hourly hails of the lookouts, and the surge of seas leaping along the ship's rugged sides.

The solemnest time of all was the early morning watch. Then somber clouds might shroud the stars, or tatter across a watery moon. A flurry of rain sends the afterguard to the shelter of the main hatch hoods. The decks are wet with scud. At the weather main-brace bumpkin stands a marine sentry leaning on the rail. Perhaps he is criminally asleep, and should anyone fall overboard he would fail in his duty of tripping the lanyard to release a life preserver and set off the attached flare. At the wheel amidships stand the two helmsmen, their faces reflecting the fitful gleam of the binnacle lamp, the only light visible on the empty sweep of deck. Even the officer on watch, for all one could tell, might be asleep, standing on the horse block, staring fixedly upward toward the weather leeches with the bell of his speaking trumpet pressed against his thigh. There would be no sound except the straining of hide wheel ropes, the melancholy chirrup of a sheet sheave aloft, the uneasy groans of the worn timbers of the ancient ship, the whinning of wind in the shrouds, and the bubbling of water sliding under the counter and of in an uneasy wake astern.

The bell tolls four strokes; two hours more before the watch can seek its hammocks and the warmth of the berth deck! Then is the time for two boys on lookout to draw close to each other and share their loneliness, peering over the taffrail to watch the phosphorescent streaks of dolphins flashing through the confused sea, until frightened into the depths by the twisting dash of a shark. The boys hunch closer, and in whispered tones talk together of sharks at sea and sharks ashore, and of human wolves, and of the loneliest time in boyhood that each of them could remember. . . .

"All's well!"

Chapter VIII

TROPICS

The *Portsmouth* was twenty days out from New York when the cry "Sail ho!" from the lookout on the foretopmast crosstrees brought every man and boy on deck. An hour later the stranger crossed our bows. It was a ship in distress, scudding along under a foresail lashed to a jury mast, and men on her poop were rigging another spar. No assistance was asked of us, and soon the ship disappeared toward the west, her broken bow catching the rays of the dying sun. For long after she vanished my mind dwelt on that British merchant ship, in trouble but proudly refusing aid from a man-o'-war. Perhaps she carried a cargo of fruit from Spain; I could envision the perishable stuff swamped with sea water. Or, perhaps, meat from the Argentine, or tea and silk from far China. I wondered if I really had seen a woman and a little girl on the poop of the low-lying vessel. Where were they going, and what were their hopes of reaching port?

Five days later we sighted land ahead, and at two o'clock sailed past the end of the breakwater and the small fort of Bridgetown, Barbados. Our two anchors rattled down near the moorings of a fleet of British warships. On the other side of us was the U.S.

flagship, a stately frigate with a flock of white boats about her at drill. The boys on a Royal Navy training ship cheered us as we passed them, and watched with appreciation as we deftly furled our sails and sent down our light yards. The first leg of the cruise was completed, and feeling like seasoned seamen we hurried through our tasks in anticipation of our first liberty on a tropical island.

As soon as our anchor splashed in the harbor of the lazy Caribbean port, the ship was surrounded by scores of bumboats, but only a few favored ones were permitted to reach the gangway by our Jimmylegs, whose position was rich in "cumshaws," or gratuities, at every port. The black native women who came aboard offered us flying fish fried in plantain leaf, oranges, bananas, cocoa, mangoes, and honey. Each woman assured us that she was not a "lime-juicer," meaning a British subject, but a "Yahnkee" born in New York—by which they meant the United States; but men and women alike spoke with a drawling cockney accent. Even the youngest of them were fine swimmers and expert divers. A flock of boys played about the vessel and dove for coins that we tossed overboard. Barking like a herd of trained seals, they uttered their enticing cry: "You heave—I dive!"

Early on the morning following our arrival we rigged out our boats and began the work of rattling down and setting up the rigging, which was sagging considerably as a result of the blow off Hatteras. Not until we had painted the ship alow and aloft, and had cleaned ourselves spick and span, did we hear the welcome call: "Lay aft the liberty party!"

We found a remarkable lack of points of interest for sightseers at Barbados, but no lack of guides. There was at least one native guide for each boy who touched foot on the seaweed draped wharf at Bridgetown. They offered their services for almost nothing, depending for reward mainly on commissions from storekeepers and harlots who might have trade steered their way. The guides we could not use began a fight among themselves until they were dispersed by native policemen who rushed down the stone quay shouting: "Gahngway for the Yahnkees!"

The water front was thronged with Negroes, male and female, every other one gnawing at a piece of cane and offering something to sell. Aside from short trips to the cane fields and mills and to the insane asylum, there seemed to be nothing much to do, and gradually, singly or in groups, boys drifted back to the town. In the little port there was a multitude of licensed rum shops and in addition many small grocery stores where more rum was sold than anything else. There was also a large district to which every guide tried to steer his charge because of the rake-off he would get from the girls who loudly advertised their vocation with cries of: "A shillin' for de use of me bawdy!"

Fate could not have devised a more devilish plot than the landing of two hundred boys, most of them away from home for the first time, on an island like Barbados. Not a word of caution was offered them as they stepped across the gangway into a dangerous realm, nor were they given any surveillance or instruction by officers. If ever there was a time when a worldly-wise chaplain was needed in the navy of those days, it was surely on a training ship. With a little money burning holes in their pockets, and left to their own devices for an entire afternoon in a sun-baked seaport, surrounded by touts and beachcombers and a few depraved older shipmates, it was no wonder that many of the apprentices soon drifted under the roofs of canteens and brothels to get out of the glaring sunlight. After a few drinks it was not easy for them to perceive the frightful mien of vice, and it was only too easy to mingle with natives whose livelihood depended on geniality and skill in temptation. It was indeed a miracle that many of the lads did not carry the mark of their first liberty with them through life; as it was, more than one soon realized the blasting effects of a few hours ashore, and thereafter the name "Barbados" would mean something more to them than a mere island.

Their sufferings could easily have been prevented, of course, if the authorities had not been possessed, consciously or unconsciously, with the idea that such indulgences were part of the sailor's life and that nothing else could be expected of the enlisted man. It was a survival of an old misconception that still persists, an attitude of official tolerance such as was revealed when in 1782 the great British man-o'-war *Royal George* overturned and drowned nearly three hundred women shipped for the use of her crew of seven hundred men.

Often in the port of Barbados we had spar drill at sundown. Many times the American flagship and the British training ship near-by would also engage in this evolution at the same moment, and there was considerable rivalry in attempting to outdo the others in the smartness with which it could be accomplished.

"Down topgallant and royal yards, and topgallant mast!" High on every mast of the *Portsmouth* four boys, two from each watch chosen for their lightness and agility, had been stationed, one pair on the crosstrees and the other on the jack above. They busied themselves in a dozen deft operations, stopping out the yard ropes, casting adrift the parrels attaching the two yards to the mast, and unhooking the braces and lifts and footropes, working with other boys in the tops below or out on the topsail yards, checking and overhauling the gear.

The lighter shrouds and backstays had been slackened, and with the topgallant mast swayed up an inch or so it was possible to loosen the wooden wedge or iron fid that held the mast in place. Then came a ticklish moment. The boys on the royal yards slid down the backstays to be out of the way. With a quick motion the fid was pulled free, and the entire weight of the top hamper swayed against the yard ropes and mast rope held by man on deck. Was everything clear? The boys on the lofty crosstrees spared a glance about the harbor below. On the other vessels, the upper masts were similarly swayed. What a critical audience would be ready to notice whatever might go wrong!

On deck the drum rolled, and at the third blast of the bugle the Stars and Stripes started down from the end of the gaff. "Stand by!" bawled the executive officer through his trumpet. The sun of the day was almost gone. Then: "Sway-e-e!"

The men on deck hauled briskly, and the topgallant and royal yards on each mast crossed scissorwise. Then, guided by tripping lines, great unwieldly masses of wood, iron, cordage, and canvas dropped downward with many a jerk and bounce. The stiff and steady mast that had been the security of a boy one hundred and sixty feet aloft was now shaking and sliding downward with the rest of the upper works of the ship. The taut rigging against which the boy had often braced himself hung pendant, swelling out and striving to escape his guiding hands. The topgallant mast rope tossed out hempen dust as it whirred through its sheave at the lower end of the mast and through the gin block at the topmast head. The Jacob's ladder leading to the jack shortened in little jerks, while loops of wire and snakes of cordage writhed downward. Everything, it seemed, was shaking deckwards, and even the crosstrees on which the topman was standing quivered and shook. At last the heavy capping funnel of iron, with its metal withe eyes and truck of lignum vitae, came within reach and was parted from the head of the topgallant mast, and settled creakingly into its nest at the topmast crosstrees. If everything went well, all the gear was quickly stowed and snugged into its proper bight, so that there would be no snarls when the spars were returned to their places in the morning.

All this time there was no room aloft for trepidation, or time for seeking the advice of an instructor. The swift completion of the complicated evolution, which soon came to be performed by us at a rapid pace, brought a confidence that thereafter marked the boys trained "in sail." All clear! With six yards and three masts deposited in unison in their lowered positions, the boys would slide through the dusk to the deck, perhaps to glow with pride at the captain's low call: "Well done, mizzentop!"

During the lazy anchor watches in the harbor, much discussion was caused by the solemn antics of a scalawag seaman called "Squeezer" Jacobsen. This fellow had a habit of grasping the skin on the back of a shipmate's hand, pinching it between a horny thumb and forefinger, and suddenly releasing it. Then he would gravely note how quickly or slowly the skin stretched back into place, looking the while at a large silver watch held in his other hand. The skin of apprentices sprang back like India rubber, that of the older men more slowly. Jacobsen claimed that this was an unfailing method of telling how hard a man's arteries were getting. To dismayed old mossbacks he would give such a diagnosis as this: "Your pipes is getting clogged and they needs flushing. It's time for you to see a plumber, or Chips will be framing up a nice box for you."

Some of the crew bitterly resented these unasked examinations, while others could be seen secretly pinching the skin on the backs of their hands. They would then look worried or pleased, depending on how quickly it went back into place. All over the ship, at all hours, men would be comparing notes on the flexibility of their hides. The fad extended even into the officers' quarters, and days passed before it ran its course.

Rascally Tug Waldron, of course, did not get leave to go ashore at Barbados, although had the ship been docked rather than moored he would surely have managed to make the nearest grogshop. As it was, enough liquor reached him to get him half-seas over, or mildly drunk.

The short ration had an amazing effect on his nature, for it merely removed the chip from his shoulder and made him startlingly polite. First off, he was found washing his clothes in a deck bucket belonging to another part of the ship. This was always a serious matter, comparable to horse stealing ashore; but Tug, when accused by the seaman who discovered the crime, instead of starting a fight calmly dumped the suds on the clean, dry deck and handed over the bucket with a bow and a yellow-fanged smile. That part of the deck belonged to the injured man's own division, but at his loud howl of fresh resentment Tug said innocently: "Why, sir, you wanted this bucket, didn't you?"

He bowed himself to the wash-deck gear locker, got a swab and squilgee, and mopped up the mess; but he was reported by the boatswain, who was more hurt by the complacence of the offender than by the offense itself. At "the mast," when the captain asked for his defense, Tug coughed delicately, put the back of his hand to his mouth, and said: "Excuse me, sir."

"Excuse you for causing a disturbance? I think you're under the influence of liquor right now! Do you remember what I told you when you were found on this ship after being warned you were not wanted?"

"Pardon me, sir. I asked you to excuse me because I had to cough, sir. The dirt and dust of these decks inadvertently tickled my esophagus, sir."

"So—my ship is dirty, is she? Well, now, my dear sir, we'll accept your apologies. Will you please accept from me and this ship, with my compliments, an award of thirty days' duty at cleaning the bilges? Now, Waldron, you scrap of rotten hemp, get forward!"

Tug bowed and saluted thrice. "Thank you, sir. You are very kind. I will report to the Negro custodian of the hold at once, sir."

He found the captain of the hold, a powerful black man, whistling and whitewashing the water tanks. "Ah, my dear friend Nevins! Pardon me a moment. I am requested by no less a person than our commanding officer to assist you in cleaning the bilges of this flash frigate!"

Nevins, who had had many quarrels with Waldron but who was irritated by the suspicions of the crew that he had helped the man to hide away at New York, was alarmed by this superfine politeness, and feared some new trick. "Pardon me, your warts! Damn if I'm wantin' you around me! Go on to hell out of here!"

"Hmm. I offered, sir, to clean your bilges for you, sir, but you spurn my friendly advances. Therefore, will you wait just a moment until I return?

Tug rushed to the spar deck, went to the rail, and appeared to be throwing something overboard—his Chesterfieldian manners, no doubt. Then he ran back to the hold, and faced the surprised Negro:

"Now, you black bootlicker, put up your dirty fists! You and the whole gang can burn in blazes before you get any more politeness out of me!"

Ten minutes later, an epic fight was over and Tug was shackled hand and foot in the stuffy brig. He opened his bag, dug deep and found a dime novel, and settled back with a sigh of content. "Thought they'd make me clean the bilges, did they? Hah!"

One of the apprentices, named Pennington, had the weather gauge of the rest of us because he had served a hitch in the merchant service, where he had learned how to sew on sails. He also had a lot of practical seamanship in his head, and became the logical candidate for the Bailey Medal competition, awarded each year to the apprentice getting the best ratings in professional skill and good conduct. Pennington was detailed as "striker," or assistant, to the sailmaker's mate, an old man with a Polish name whom his shipmates called "Cringle." I often visited Pennington on the fo'c'sle in the hope of getting some snatches of merchant-ship lore, and also to hear Cringle talk.

The old man was drawing toward his seventieth year, and was quite deaf. The advance of age on him was pitiable, for he had been accustomed to leave the navy at times and go back to the merchant service, so that he was still far from attaining the privileges of navy retirement. Yet he always seemed cheerful, and was a good yarner. He never could talk better than when he had a sailmaker's palm on his hand or was drawing his linen thread through wax. There was always a sweet odor of honeycomb about him. He was slight in build, but could fist and handle a sail on a yard with the best men in the ship. He sat always on the spar deck just forward of the fore hatch, where the backdraft of the big jib made a soft clean breeze. About him were spread the tools and materials of his trade: a large fid of wood for grommets, small fids for sail and hammock eyelets, hanks of glossy new Manila rope of all sizes, and sometimes remnants of heavy left-handed boltrope of tarry Russian hemp. A rank of needles—small and large, straight and curved—stuck out like porcupine quills from the old man's cap.

Cringle, with his loaded palm, shoved a glinting needle through four thicknesses of the heaviest canvas, the curved point following the lay of a thick strand of boltrope. He rubbed his gnarled hands down his cheeks to moisten the fingers, took a new hitch with the hook that secured his work to the bench, and answered a question that I had just put to him.

"Yah, dis is small sail, sure enough; but once I worked like all haal on sail half as small as dis. It save our ship, and our lifes too, I guess. Dis was on liddle brig from Calcutta to New York. All sails was rotten as punk. Mizzen topsail look ready to go any time, and captain—one of dese haaldrivers who run all night widout lights to save a fardin's worth of oil—say I must make old main t'ga'nts'l into new mizzen topsail. But everything on it was like paper, so I go over all old spares and take cloths and put dem into liddle topsail. I found good piece of boltrope from old jib and got new cloths for reef and bellybands. She was nice good topsail when I get done.

"De skipper he found out about it and says he take it from my wages. But when we been headed out north from Cape Town, one night de mate get caught by nor'wester and it take every stick out of her except de foremast. De yard hung dere widout lifts. We was waterlogged and de sea crawled all over us; de pumps was chocked. We try to put our rotten spares on dat foreyard; one by one dey blow down de wind like fedders. Den I get out my mizzen topsail, dat I make so good and careful. She held, poys. She held until we run back to Cape Town, and every mile de old man and de mate tell me I save de old hooker wid my liddle sail.

"We go to get paid off at Cape Town, and I see de captain comin' down de street. He shakes hands and talks about my topsail. I ask him to have a drink wid me, and he does it—two drinks. Den he shakes my hand and says good-by. I go to de office for my money, and dey tell me de captain he charge me more dan half my wages for de sail, because he says it is unauth'rized use of ship's material. Dat captain, he was sure a squeezer!"

"Burn me!" I said. "What a squeezer he was!"

And the silent Pennington took off his palm and said: "That goes for me, too!"

As we were about to get up anchor at Bridgetown and continue our Caribbean cruise, a cutter came alongside from the flagship to transfer two enlisted men who were being sent home with us. One was immediately taken to the brig under guard; he was to be confined until he could be removed to a federal prison. The other, to my delight, was Basil Bono, the Greek pirate, who was to be carried to New York as a time-expired man.

The inappropriateness of dumping this profane and lecherous little wretch into a training ship did not strike me as sinister at the time. The oil of the general service, in the official view, must be made to mix with the water of the apprentice system. The dark-skinned, earringed petty officer greeted me with a sulphurous shout of glee. When I asked him about former acquaintances on the *St. Louis,* he was full of scalding information.

"You remember that damn Jack Robinson? Sure you do. Well, he got transferred to another ship, the poor old plank-owner, and what does he do but go right off his keel! First thing, when the admiral comes aboard the new ship, Jack is told to pipe for side boys, and instead he pipes for mess gear. The ship's cooks all start a big fight in front of the big cheese himself. The captain, he's an old shipmate of Jack's and lets him off; but wait till I tell you how quick the skipper changes his mind. Next morning Jack gets out his cutlass and pushes the orderly away from the cabin door and rushes in hellity-hoot. He pulls the captain out of his bunk and sticks his cutlass up at his guts and hollers: 'What the hell you mean leavin' your punkee socks on my towel line, hey?' Jack's in the crazyhouse at Washington now, and he preaches and preaches about temp'rance and old Demon Rum. By God, I'd like to listen to it!"

I was about to ask Bono if he knew anything of Tom Dunn, when the boatswain and his mates filled the air with their shouts: "Up anchor! Make sail! . . . Lay aloft, sail loosers!"

The Greek jumped to his station on the foreyard, for whatever his morals might be he was an excellent seaman, and I hurried to the capstan. Negro bumboatwomen, hustled by a few marines, were crowding down the cleats overside, for the gangway ladders were already rigged in. Hundred of natives in their dugouts kept up the incessant cry of "You heave; I dive!" but all to no avail, for every seaman was at his post. It was a bright tropical day, the sea was a glinting blue, and the work of getting under weigh was exhilarating. When the topmen had shaken out the sails and returned to the deck they were sent to assist at the capstan, and the cables came in speedily. Then all hands were needed to break flukes out of the sucking sand of the bottom. "Heave ho; heave! Heave and pawl!" The bars bent and sprang with our weight on them.

"Anchor's aweigh, sir!" came from the fo'c'sle. Faster and faster the dripping cable passed beneath our feet, the loose links handled smartly by the gunner's gang. As the second cable began to come in, the men on deck hurried to sheets, halyards, and braces; the yards swung, the helm was righted, and to the screak of wheel ropes and the shouts of command we sailed out into the open sea.

I lost no time in seeking out Bono once more. When I mentioned Baldy Tom Dunn, the little man became serious.

"Why, old Tom, he's back there on the flagship! You didn't know? You bet your bleedin' eyes he's there, and having one blazin' hell of a time. Some young snot of an officer has got it in for him, and he'll stick him, sure. Tom's in the brig now, waiting for court-martial."

"Why, what for?" I could not imagine that staid, placid old fellow doing anything that would merit punishment of any kind.

"Nothin' at all. Nobody knows anything, except that this devil of a boy hates him and rides him every minute. Every day something; every drill something; new trouble for the old man. He can't move without gettin' jumped on. This young buck has got a big pull in Washington, and the captain can't help Tom a bit. Then Tom went on the sick list on account of his shoulder—you know he got a knife stuck in it down in South America. Maybe he can get a transfer—if he don't, it's too bad. Chrisamighty, if it was me, I'd put a bayonet in that bucko's belly."

A pilot was still aboard, and I hurried to the gun deck to write a note to Tom. When it was finished I handed it, with a shilling, to one of the Negroes in the small boat trailing alongside, hoping that Tom would get my message and perhaps a little comfort from my puzzled sympathy. Tom Dunn before a court-martial! If that fine old man could become a naval criminal, what hope was there for the rest of us?

Chapter IX

CRUISING

It was on February 12 that we left Barbados astern and payed off to the southward for Trinidad, also in the British West Indies and lying ten degrees north of the Equator. On the next day we entered the Dragon's Mouth leading into the Gulf of Paria, a narrow passage that was formerly an ideal lurking-spot for pirates. Before us to south and west rose the mile-high mountains of the Venezuelan mainland, while on the east spired the three tall peaks that caused Columbus to name the big island after the Holy Trinity. In the Gulf, about ten miles offshore, we anchored in shallow water and prepared for days of drill and target practice.

Our captain was heard to remark to some of his officers that he had been requested by bureau officers in Washington to drill the bottoms off his boys; and he was always a great one to follow orders. Almost every morning we raised our hook out of the mud and exercised the ship in tacking and wearing, in reefing topsails, and in taking down light yards and masts. At other times the daylight hours were passed in firing our broadside guns at a triangular piece of canvas spread above a beef barrel, the ship running all the while as nearly in a circle as a sailing ship could be made to run.

Before target practice, days had to be spent in careful and noisy preparations. Many were the precautions for preventing accidental fires—the ceremonial opening of the lead-lined magazine, the draping of fireproofed curtains, and the donning of special apparel by those who would enter the ammunition rooms; and all this for the transfer of a few bags of powder.

Then, when the ship was lolling ahead through the waves, the gun crews would be called to their stations, the heavy guns levered inboard by hand, the charge and saboted shot inserted in the muzzle, and the wad laboriously tamped. With the vent conscientiously filled with black powder, the guns would be run out with side tackles. Then came the anxious instant when the gun captain, feet apart, lanyard in one hand with the other held high in the air, gave on signal a sharp pull.

If all the work had been handily performed, the powder bag pierced, and the vent laid perfectly, there would follow a deafening roar and the gun would jump the length of its hemp breeching like an angry mule. On a great curving trajectory the shot would approach the target in a skipping series of splashes. Considering that the ship was moving ahead all the while, and rolling from side to side, it was surprising the number of times that the gunners could hit the mark. A spellbound "Ah!" would sound from the deck above, and from one of the tops would come a cry giving the range. That shot would have hit a ship! In those years the maritime safety of the American nation depended almost altogether upon the skill with which bewhiskered old gunners could hit a target with 11-inch smoothbores such as those that jutted from the sides of the *Portsmouth*.

None of the general drills, in fact, could by any stretch of the imagination be considered as a useful training for entrance into the new navy upon whose threshold we then stood. Daily we were called upon to perform evolutions that had reached the height of their usefulness a century before, when guns were fired with loggerheads and matches and ships were painted red inside so that the blood of battle would not show. The foolish cutlass drill was merely a form of calisthenics except that it was much more dangerous. The nonsensical snapping of revolver hammers only served to weaken the mechanisms. General quarters once a week was an abomination, especially at night. In fitful candlelight it was difficult to spread the rammers and sponges and the many other pieces of gear in their proper places on the deck. Boys and men stumbled over division tubs and walked on each others' feet and rammed their mates in the stomach, banging their fingers and filling the air with hissing curses. There was a pervading smell of gunpowder and the stench of lard-oil lamps.

"Clear ship for action!" was dreaded more than any other command, for it meant that even the boats had to go overboard. At the cry "Repel boarders!" we rushed on deck brandishing cutlasses and screaming like madmen—or rather, like Chinamen discouraging evil spirits by means of firecrackers and rattles. Shades of John Paul Jones! I wondered if everyone felt as silly as I did when performing such antiquated tactics.

At such times the hammocks on which we had spent so much elbow grease keeping them clean and white were torn from the nettings and piled on deck as breastworks, or else taken up into the tarry rigging and placed about the rims of the tops to serve as shields for sharpshooters. "Stand by to receive a raking fire from forward!" shouted Mr. Dicky Rush. That meant we had to throw ourselves flat on deck with rifles leveled over the hammock barricade. I began to consider those hammocks less as something to sleep in and hide our most precious letters in than as a heap of rags that would be our only protection against enemy rifle balls or shell splinters. In days gone by, some utilitarian officer had invented the idea of making a portable bulwark out of the beds of the enlisted men, because if the hammocks were destroyed the men themselves would have to pay for their replacement. Since the days when we drilled on the waters of the Gulf of Paria, bedding has come to be furnished by the government, so that now it is no longer considered suitable for use as splinter protection.

Another disheartening practice that seemed to come along far too often was fire drill. If there was a compartment or nook on the *Portsmouth* in which we were not called to fight an imaginary fire, it must have been inside one of the full water tanks. Our backs were nearly broken straining at the pumps. As soon as it appeared that one fire was under control, the fat executive would inform us explosively through his trumpet that another fire had just been discovered in the forehold or some other place equally difficult to reach. All these drills, of course, were planned by the captain; but it seemed to us that the executive officer charged with carrying them out had his own ideas about staging them at midnight or when the watch below was snoring along peacefully at fifteen knots.

Spare hours between drills were taken up with boatwork under oars or sail, and at this I was never bored. Of course the vessel was scrubbed from stem to stern daily, until she gleamed with cleanliness. If it is true that a hard-worked ship is a happy ship, then we were a happy crowd. We sought our dream-sacks the moment hammock call was piped, and I would barely have time to ponder on the healthful salty life I was living before sleep would spring and haul me down into unconsciousness.

Wednesday afternoon on board was "rope-yarn Sunday" for all hands. The time was given over to the care and mending of clothes. Every second Wednesday we had bag and hammock inspection. An hour was allowed for preparation, and then every piece of clothing was rolled into a neat bundle exactly seven inches long, held by a clothes-stop at each end and lined perfectly in a row. Some officers were perfunctory in their conduct of the inspections; other would take the slightest opportunity to make complaints and have the boys up for punishment. A pair of socks missing, a piece that was not neatly marked with a stencil, an unwhipped clothes-stop, a paper or book hidden in a hammock—any of these was sometimes enough to bring condemnation. One boy who had been operated on before leaving Newport was disciplined for having in his possession his vermiform appendix pickled in a bottle.

My first promotion came while the ship was sailing in the Gulf of Paria. The examinations of every boy under training were long and thorough, and the results depended on quick and accurate answers to questions put orally by division officers. Some of the questions were intended to deceive. How many ropes on a sailing ship? (There are only seven pieces of gear that are technically referred to as "ropes": boltrope, bellrope, wheelrope, manrope, footrope, mastrope, and yardrope.) How many pieces of gear did a fully rigged ship need? (None: if she needed any, she would not be fully rigged.) Other questions were honestly put, but laid a severe strain on a boy's memory. Did the foretopgallant brace reeve through a block over or under the maintopmast crosstrees? What was the longest rope in a ship? How did tacking or wearing a ship differ from box-hauling? In what order did the shrouds go over the mastheads? If the apprentice could not describe every detailed movement in the work of sending down and up the light yards and masts, and of bending sail, he had to remain in his old rating for another term. On the subject of ordnance it seemed important to know the exact number of Minié balls packed in different sizes of shrapnel, and I received a low mark on questions about grapeshot and shrapnel, chain shot and ball shot, none of which I had ever seen. We had also to enumerate the duties of each man at a broadside gun. The making repair of clothing was stressed, neat sewing and embroidering coming in importance second only to the marlinspike work of splicing, seizing, and using the serving mallet. Actually, little of the knowledge required was to be of use in future duty, as every boy expected that his next ship would be one with a steel hull, whose spars would be limited to storm trysail gaffs.

After this feverish period I was passed as an apprentice, second class, and allowed to add one stripe to my cuff and draw an extra dollar a month in pay. At that rate, I thought, in another year I would be able to keep up with my clothing expenditures, and even buy an extra bar or two of salt-water soap! Promotion also meant that I would be transferred to another division of the ship, to learn new duties under other instructors. I was thereafter assigned to the waist, or maintop.

My division officer now became Lieutenant Hodgson. He was the tallest man on the ship, with a luxuriant black beard and mustache always trimmed to perfection. We suspected that on shore he was a gallant man with the ladies, because on board he always dressed with meticulous care. The lieutenant had one obsession that soon became apparent to everyone—his keen eye for loose buttons. He could tell from a distance when a button on a man's clothing was merely thinking of shaking loose from its home, and would point it out with a passing nod. He seemed to care little about other points of inspection; his logic seemed to be that if the buttons were all right, everything else must be all right. We called him "Billy Buttons"—in private, of course, although one day when I was sent to his room with a message I discovered with horror, a moment too late, that I had breathlessly addressed him as "Mr. Buttons." He merely responded with "Great Caesar's ghost!" which was the limit of the good man's invective.

The executive officer, Mr. Rush, has already been mentioned more than once; and if his name has bobbed up more frequently than that of his superior, the captain, it is because of his high importance to the seamen and to the ship. He was the mouthpiece of command, and his responsibilities comprised everything about the vessel from the safety of all hands to the least item of the stores. He may have been christened James, but to us he was "Dicky" or, more respectfully, the first luff. At the mast you accosted him as Mr. Rush, with a salute. His rating was executive officer or first lieutenant, but you could not address him as Mr. Executive Officer or Mr. First Lieutenant; if you did, a dozen salutes could not redeem your reputation as a service man. To hear such a phrase aboard would be as strange as to hear a sailor say out in full the words "crossjack," "forecastle," "boatswain," or "studdingsail."

Fat Mr. Rush was a splendid sailorman, and never lost a rope-yarn of sail or a splinter of spar. His strictness came not only from his ideals of efficiency but from a fear that he might be led to grant too much leeway to any man under him, believing that to give a sailor an inch would tempt him to take an ell. His face was completely covered with red whiskers that joined without break the bristling hair of his head. He had a nervous habit of scratching his beard with perplexity, and any old seaman in his vicinity dared not get itchy whiskers for fear the First Luff would think he was being mocked. One day an apprentice stood near the horse block where Mr. Rush was shouting orders and scratching his side whiskers with both hands at once. The boy, thinking himself unobserved, mimicked these monkey-faces in an effort to entertain the helmsman; but the officer saw the antics out of the corner of his eye, and pretending to think that the lad actually was suffering from itch, sent him forward to have his body scrubbed with sand and canvas.

On Washington's Birthday the order was piped, "All hands skylark!" Officers and men of the permanent crew contributed money for prizes. The apprentices engaged in obstacle races and pie-eating contests and competed in swimming, high diving, and wrestling. As a climax, there was a race between a whaleboat and a gig, and another between boats manned respectively by marines and berth-deck cooks. The cooks were the favorites and won easily, to the great satisfaction of the deck department. The coxswain of the cooks' crew was a man who was covered with coarse hair on every part of his body except his head, which was completely bald. He ascribed this to wearing a watch cap through a long period of years. He claimed that, if he wanted to, he could get rid of every hair on his body by wearing extra-heavy woolen underclothes. This statement was loudly scouted by "Scupper-mouth" Hilgard, a Scandinavian with a fine head of blond hair, which he said resulted from wearing a watch cap for many years. . . . The interesting argument had not been settled at the end of the cruise.

After the morning drills on the twenty-eighth of February, we did not anchor in the Gulf as usual, but sailed across to Port of Spain, the British harbor at Trinidad. Here, after receiving pratique, we speedily stowed our sails and brought the *Portsmouth* to moorings amidst British men-o'-war and many merchant vessels.

The following morning, with the hoisting of our colors, the ceremonial saluting of ships and officers in the harbor began. The custom no doubt springs from feudal days when a host was expected to empty his guns to show the peacefulness of his intentions. It seemed to me a waste of good powder, but each officer was punctilious about the number of guns that were to be fired for a superior, and was equally ready to demand the number that were his due. Perhaps an insistence upon the forms of courtesy is of special importance among warriors of sea or land; if any slight upon dignity is suspected, the means to avenge it bloodily are always too dangerously ready to hand.

These noisy acts of civility performed, we were free to escape the cramped decks. Eagerly we lucky leave men answered the call, arrayed in our finest shore-going clothes, decorated with fancy-work encroaching so closely upon the nonregulation that we feared being stopped at the gangway with orders to change. Along its water front, Port of Spain seemed to be little different from Bridgetown, in Barbados. There were the same shining lazy bucks and saucy wenches, the same beachcombers smelling of gin, the same dark grogshops and godowns selling drinks, bread, rice, clothing, and household goods all jumbled up together. There were, it seemed, the same guides inviting the sailor to the same shabby vices.

But Port of Spain was city on the large island of Trinidad, and a lad could amuse himself for an afternoon by getting astride a donkey and seeing the town and the country roundabout. The governor's botanical gardens were famous the world over, but as I knew little about plants at that time, I could not appreciate their glories. There was also a fairly large zoo. Some of us went to the settlements for East Indian laborers, who were brought from India on contract for a period of years and thereafter were free. For every inhabitant of the town there seemed to be at least one buzzard, which birds were protected as useful scavengers.

From an elevated point we had a good view of the harbor, and like any Jack ashore I spent many minutes fondly enjoying the beauties of my own ship. I contrasted the lovely tracery of her rigging, etched against the sky, with the heavier spars of some of the British men-o'-war, and wondered how long it might be before such white-winged wooden birds of passage were chased from the sea by threshing steamers of steel. Few of my friends shared these sentiments. The new fleet that was being built was their chief topic of conversation morning, noon, and night; in a murky morning watch, when two lads drew together for company, they would whisper in awed tones of the iron ships where plenty of fresh water was to be had at any time. They spoke of a marvelous ice machine installed on the *Chicago* in the same hushed voice with which a boy of today might speak of a rocket-ship that could fly to the moon.

At Port of Spain a few of us took the trip to the famed Pitch Lake, or Devil's Lake, a sea of asphalt covering ninety acres, the surface hard enough to bear a railway track. We speculated upon the millions of dollars that it was worth to the British owners; for the tasks of mining seemed almost to perform themselves. The pitch broken out during the day was replaced during the night by oozings from below. The stuff was loaded on self-dumping cars which traveled by conveyor to the docks and there filled the holds of vessels carrying it to the United States for making roadways across the continent. The sulphur-and-brimstone fumes that rose from the breast of the lake could be smelled as far out as our anchorage in the harbor.

On this cruise I became better acquainted with a shipmate called "Sheeny" Byron, an older man with bleached white hair and a crimson face. During watches below he was a handsome performer at the handle of his lute-shaped hurdy-gurdy, but spent most of his time running a sewing machine, turning out beautiful "homeward-bounder" clothing for affluent and dressy companions. He was noted for his ability to "stand them on edge"—meaning the dollars—but like so many of the old-time navy men, after years of painful savings he would let it all slip through his hands like smoke. Sheeny had a remarkable memory for the dates of American history; and it was from him that I learned that, seventy-one years before, Commodore Oliver Hazard Perry of Lake Erie fame had died on a United States ship near our anchorage, of yellow fever contracted during an expedition up the Amazon River.[1] The man filled me with a desire to learn more about Perry, and especially the tragic treatment the hero of the War of 1812 got at the hands of his officer enemies. Perry found that battles are by no means over when they have been decisively fought, just as Admiral Sampson discovered after his conquests in the West Indies in 1898. Perry was buried ashore in Trinidad, but his body was later removed to his home at Newport, Rhode Island.

The fate of Perry was merely one of the reasons why Byron was so bitter about the conduct of some naval officers he had known or read about. One afternoon, as we were handling lines over the bow rail in hopes of hooking some catfish for supper, he said to me:

"Show me any of these cursed stories of naval life written by officers, and there you have me dismasted. They are so eternally afeared that a lowly flatfoot might get any praise for having a bit of courage or even human decency. There's a case of it in this book." He pulled a bound volume from his jumper and handed it over to me. "In there you'll find a story about the loss of the U.S.S. *Sagamore,* which is twisted around so that an officer gets the credit that was due solely to an enlisted man."

We all knew that Sheeny had been one of the crew of the ill-fated *Sagamore,* which had been lost in the Midway Island group (now a base for American air-clippers). Then he told me the tale of that disastrous pile-up in mid-Pacific.[2]

"We got into the breakers on Ocean Island early in November, 1870. The swells kicked the bottom out from under us, and

1. Commodore Oliver Hazard Perry died of yellow fever on arrival off Port of Spain, Trinidad, on 23 August 1819. He was returning from a diplomatic mission to Angostura, Venezuela, 300 miles up the Orinoco River, where he and several of his officers and crew had contracted the disease.

2. The USS *Saginaw,* Commander Montgomery Sicard, took on board a contractor's crew that had been engaged in deepening the harbor entrance at Midway Island and departed for San Francisco on 28 October 1870. On making a hundred-mile detour to Ocean Island to search for castaway seamen, the *Saginaw* was wrecked on the island's reef early in the morning of the 29th. To obtain assistance, Lieutenant John G. Talbot, the executive officer, volunteered to attempt a voyage to the Hawaiian Islands in the whaleboat. With a crew of

smashed every boat on the weather side; but in the rest of the boats, loaded with what fresh water and provisions we could take off before she came apart, we got ashore.

"That was one hell of an island to get cast away on! There wasn't an inch of shade, and we were almost broiled alive. We couldn't find a single animal that was living on the place. Our captain, Sicard, decided to send a boat to Honolulu, fifteen hundred miles away. We patched up our gig, put water and provisions aboard her, and the executive officer, Lieutenant Talbot, the coxswain, William Halford, and three others left in her on November 10 to try and make Oahu.

"Their provisions soon got wet and fermented. The whole crew of the little boat were sick. There was nothing to eat but some potatoes and a little sperm oil; they killed a booby bird one day, and another time caught some flying fish, which they ate raw. On the twenty-eighth day after leaving us they sighted the islands, and for two days more they tried to make a landing. So near and yet so far! Then a gale came up and threw them into the surf, and everyone died fighting except Halford. He made shore, was picked up and taken to Honolulu, and there he reported us and in due time we were saved.

"Now I call that a plain, unvarnished tale of pluck. Any man who can endure a hungry month's trip in an open boat and survive

---

four volunteers, Talbot left Ocean Island on November 18 and on December 19 reached Oahu, where he and his crew were drowned in the surf—except for William Halford, who survived and carried the news to Honolulu.

When the rescue steamer arrived at Ocean Island early in January 1871, the *Saginaw*'s crew had nearly completed a small schooner to carry them to a more hospitable refuge. Since Lieutenant Talbot had been furnished with the only sextant to be salvaged from the *Saginaw,* it became necessary to improvise a replacement. This task was accomplished by Assistant Engineer Herschel Main, an 1868 graduate of the Naval Academy. With great ingenuity he adapted the few available tools and salvaged pieces of metal to construct a precision instrument that met the requirements of celestial navigation. This sextant, with body formed from the dial plate of an engine-room gauge, is on exhibit at the U.S. Naval Academy Museum; the whaleboat remains a prized possession of the Saginaw County Historical Society in Saginaw, Michigan.

every hardship is a hero, no matter what his rating. How would we ninety-six men left on a sand pile in the middle of the Pacific have ended if it hadn't been for the guts and grit of that one man? But what does this pen-pushing prevaricator do but have every enlisted man drown in the surf and let the executive officer survive to save the day?"

Disgustedly, Sheeny spat overside. "Breakers don't respect a man because he wears a gold stripe on his sleeve. Why couldn't this fellow stick to the facts and give Halford the credit that he earned? When you get through with that book, heave it overboard!"

Halford was later promoted to warrant rank and was awarded the Congressional Medal of Honor.

In the cramped quarters aboard ship, every inch of space was taken up through ingenious skill in stowage. From a sail locker a heap of sails and awnings could be drawn like stuff pulled out of a magician's hat, and still there would be a full suit of canvas left within. The bread room, the paint locker, the spirit room, and the many compartments of the hold could contain amazing quantities of things.

No compartment on the whole ship, however, could be stuffed so full of anything as the dungeonlike brig was crammed with human misery. In that narrow and dark place of confinement there was scarcely room for one man to lie down, and yet sometimes two or three men were locked behind the marine-guarded door. There was a round port that could be opened in good weather; at other times, the little cell was like a medieval torture box. It must have seemed so to Tim Walsh, the prisoner who had been sent aboard from the flagship at Barbados. He was in poor health to begin with, and at night could be heard coughing so that his chains rattled. The *Portsmouth*'s doctor became so alarmed about the man's condition that at Trinidad he ordered him taken out of the brig and had his irons removed.

Walsh, an educated man, was far from being the monster that his treatment would indicate. His crime was neither murder nor arson nor treason; he had not struck a superior officer or robbed his shipmates. His record in the navy was good. He was facing a term of two years in a federal prison, with loss of "all pay that may become due him," because he had once deserted from the United States Army.

Later Walsh told me that he had done this because a girl had promised to marry him; but she lifted what money he had and shoved off with another fellow. Then Walsh thought that if he could serve one enlistment honorably in the navy, he might be given a chance of reinstatement in his old army rank. But after a year of service he was apprehended and condemned for his old desertion. His former sweetheart had betrayed him for the head money.

Several times I had tried to get into conversation with this prisoner in order to learn something more about Tom Dunn, for Basil Bono's attempts to enlighten me were merely a tantalizing thin strip of fact amid a huge sandwich slab of oaths. As I was going ashore one afternoon, Walsh asked me to bring him some tooth soap and a brush; and this I did gladly, adding a bottle of lime juice and a few alligator pears. He was grateful, and willing to tell me what he knew about Tom, in whose division he had served on the flagship.

Tom Dunn, he said, had been given his choice of remaining on the peaceful *St. Louis* at Philadelphia or going on the flagship cruise. He preferred the cruise because he could save more money, and also earn more by sewing clothing for others. "That old man had us all puzzled," said Walsh. "He was forever saving and stinting himself of the barest comforts. Did you know he sent all his money to some woman down south? No—she wasn't any relative; it came out later at 'the mast' that he had no next of kin. But of course it was his own money."

Walsh had to recover from a spell of coughing before he was able to resume.

"Tom was reported for insolence to a commissioned officer, an ensign named Thompson, the junior officer of our division. You never know how these things start; but it seems the ensign was in charge of the racing-boat fund, and Tom didn't want to contribute anything. Anyway, the officer got sarcastic and said something insulting about a woman ashore that was pulling the old man's leg. He wouldn't be be surprised, he said, if it was some nigger wench. Well, Tom lit into that cock-o'-the-walk and would have given him what he deserved if we hadn't pulled them apart. Of course old Tom should have reported to the captain what the young snotty had said; but it touched him on a sore spot. Now there was only one thing for it, and that was a general court.

"There our gunner, old Mr. Chard, came forth with a story that helped a lot in Tom's defense. The gunner had been sworn to secrecy by Tom, but thought he was justified in telling the truth because Dunn didn't seem to realize how serious was the trouble he was in. It seems, according to Chard, that about twenty years ago Tom, who was a roaring boy in his day, had got mixed up in a fight ashore in Caracas, while the ship lay at La Guaira. A native had got hurt fatally, and Tom, being drunk, couldn't prove that he hadn't been responsible. Tom's division officer was an old friend of his—they had shared many a cruise—and he hurried across the mountains to the capital and found that Tom was in danger of spending years in prison or even being shot by the civil authorities. The officer rushed around and pulled wires at the legation and got Tom released on payment of a heavy fine, which the officer laid out for him. Tom, of course, was mightily grateful, and knowing that a naval lieutenant's pay wouldn't stand such a strain, accepted the offer only on condition that he would pay it all back as soon as he could.

"A few days later, this officer was treacherously attacked on the wharf at La Guaira, and Tom pitched in to help and got an ugly knife wound in his shoulder. His friend died of injuries a few days later, but Tom arranged for Mr. Chard to act as his agent to pay back the loan to the dead man's estate. In spite of his wound, Tom scraped enough out of his pay and his sewing to square the account in a few months. Then Tom asked the gunner to arrange for continuing a regular allotment to the officer's widow and his baby son. It was fixed up through a bank, so that the woman wouldn't know the real source of the money.

"'And, captain,' the gunner wound up, putting his arm on Tom's shoulder, 'this man has been sending all his spare money to that family ever since. The boy must be old enough to support his mother now, and I have urged Dunn to stop these payments. But he says it's a debt of gratitude.'

"'I agree with you,' said the captain. 'How long have you been in the navy, Dunn? Twenty-seven years? Then you'll be able to retire in only three years more, and it's time you began to put something aside for yourself. Not my affair, of course, but I think you should follow Mr. Chard's advice. Now, as for this charge of insubordination, I'm going to dismiss it right here. I'll speak to Mr. Thomspon when he comes back on board. I'm going to have you transferred to another division, and you should be able to serve the rest of your time without further difficulties. You have too much to lose now.' We all hoped things would be better after that."

Walsh coughed again, while I pondered his words. "One Sunday morning on the *St.Louis,* Tom told me about an officer friend of his who was dead," I remarked. "He said that if he could choose, he'd rather go to hell along with that man than see him suffer alone."

"Yes; no doubt that was the fellow killed at La Guaira. I have met more than one old-timer in the navy who felt the same way about some officer who had befriended him—the kind of a man who would send a seaman below to sober up instead of logging him, or would praise him for a hard job well done. Maybe there are lots of officers like that in the service. But this young ensign Thompson—well, I don't know. He's proud as Lucifer and conceited about the influence he has with the senator that appointed him. The fact that he realizes he has treated Tom shabbily might make him hate the old man all the more. One morning, for some fancied slight, he made Tom salute him a dozen times. I needn't tell you what can happen on board a ship when two men are at odds and one is an enlisted man and the other a 'gentleman by act of Congress.' I'm terribly afraid, boy, that we haven't yet heard the last of the story of Tom Dunn and the young ensign."

Chapter X

SONGS AND HIGH SEAS

We weighed anchor at Port of Spain on March 26, headed out through the Dragon's Mouth, and once more were running through the Carribbean, bound for the French island of Martinique.

The sun vanished as we advanced; our swaying trucks scrawled on a sodden ceiling of cloud, and frequent squalls beat down the swells of a making sea. The barometer was still falling. I heard one man sing to himself.

> "When the wind's before the rain
> Hoist your topsails up again—
>   Do not fret!
> But when the rain's before the wind
> And your oilskins you can't find,
> Use a greenhorn's—he won't mind
>   Getting wet!"

The wind followed soon enough, and howled fiendishly in the rigging, as if magically conjuring up tumultuous seas to beat against the beam of the laboring old ship. Light yards had already been sent down, and now only the more seasoned men of the crew were allowed aloft to furl topsails. With blasphemous shouts they fisted the wind-deviled canvas that ballooned out against the stays and rattled like thunder. Hove to, we rode more easily in a shelterless ocean of moving hills and valleys, while under the *Portsmouth*'s coppered bottom the seas heaved and roared.

Rising above the thresh of the wind in the rigging came a terrifying loud crack. The boatswain hurried aloft and came down to report that the fore upper topsail yard was badly sprung. Seamen were called to the foretop. The foresail was close-reefed and set; both the foretopsails were furled and the upper one unbent entirely, an additional headsail being set to replace its spread.

The ship was rolling so heavily that it was not considered safe to send down the yard, which therefore must be repaired aloft. The carpenter's mates and the gunner's gang took charge and, disdainful of the tempest, hauled up a set of stuns'l booms and fished the weakened spar with boat chains, so that it would again be strong enough to bear canvas. The old men worked unhurriedly as though this were merely part of a day's work, but their skill in these tasks of saving the ship, without needing the word of an officer to urge them on, brought my grateful admiration.

The storm spent itself as quickly as it had come, and the sun sparkled on a blue sea, that fathoms-deep blue of West Indian waters, laced by swirls of white scud. The wind did not abate until we were driven past our haven at Martinique, however, and I was able merely to glimpse the town which a few years later was to be destroyed by eruption of the volcano that majestically towered above the island.

Nine days out from Trinidad we beat into the landlocked harbor of St.Thomas in the Danish West Indies. Mountains rich in emerald verdure, rising behind the lovely town of Charlotte Amalie, beckoned to lads who dreamed of liberties to be spent in the enticing shade. But first there was work to be done on board, removing the ravages of the blow, clearing up the hurrah's nest of temporary stays, lifts, and falls on deck and aloft, until the ship was trim again and unmarred by a streak of rust or a fluttering "Irish pennant."

As we dropped anchor, the gig of Her Majesty's Ship *Ready*, moored near us, cleared away and in a short time came alongside after making a wide sweep around our stern, skimming ahead like a water beetle to a quick English stroke—a quick pull, a long pause, and another quick pull. The commanding officer of the *Ready,* with cocked hat and epaulettes, came aboard to offer us any assistance that the sight of our fished topsail yard indicated we might need. The captain seemed to me a mere boy. His face was soft and close-shaven, and comparing him in my mind to the bearded, hard-faced, bull-voiced men who seemed hewed out to command naval vessels, I wagered to myself that he would never win to battle rank or advance greatly in the service of his country. He was handsome, and had a pleasant voice and easygoing air that contrasted with the constrained manner of the aide who accompanied him.

These two officers went below to confer with our captain, while I hastened down to the gun deck and found a starboard gun port where I could be close to the English gig held at the gangway. The trim old British salts, the first I had seen at close quarters, showed by their glances aloft a flattering interest in the way we had made our temporary repairs during the storm. I observed their natty uniforms, and wondered innocently at their similarity to our own. As I gazed, listening to their low-toned, clipped talk, our boatswain above on the spar deck began to pipe side boys. There was a hurried tramp of feet, and the Britons stiffened to attention. Two of our side boys had reached their stations on the lower platform just as I noticed that the boat cloth of the gig was drabbling in the water over its stern. The cloth carried a coat of arms, the most gorgeous blazon of needlework that my eyes had ever beheld; and I felt a quick desire to save it from the salt water.

I hissed a call, but the coxswain stood like a statue at salute, and the noise of an eleven-incher would not have moved him. But his young superior, the British captain, had now reached the grating, and he heard me, for we were not more than three feet apart. He looked in through the port, followed the direction of my pointing finger, and rewarded me with a smile and a "Thank you, lad!" as he stepped into his boat. Not until then did the coxswain unbend, but the beardless officer had already rescued the cloth.

Off went the gig with its smart racing-stroke, and I was called back to my duties. Not for forty-four years did I learn, in a letter from a *Portsmouth* shipmate, that the officer whose youth and gentleness I had deplored had, after all, made a name in his profession. He had become a full captain, and an admiral, and by then held the title of "George V, by the grace of God, of the United Kingdom of Great Britain and Ireland, and of all the British Dominions beyond the Seas, King, Defender of the Faith, Emperor of India." And his picture showed me that he had also acquired a fine sailorly beard. He looked, despite stars and ribbons, the kindly commander he was, and I wondered if he ever dreamed that a humble American bluejacket had once pitied him.

St. Thomas was a popular port of call for ships cruising north or south and was known for the large quantities of bay rum that it manufactured. The Danish group, which now lies under the American flag, was once the haunt of some of the most notorious pirates of history, among them the blackbearded and black-hearted Edward Teach, who in 1718 was boarded and killed by a king's officer. We stayed in the port nine days, enjoying its lazy shore existence, before we headed north with a long silken homeward-bound pennant at the main truck, rustling and bobbing with an inflated bladder at the end. Our first cruise was almost over.

Now at last we had fair winds, and all hands were turned out in an orgy of scrubbing and cleaning and tarring the rigging, so that on our homeward-bounder everything would be snug and gleaming. Gallons of "scoojie-moojie" were used on the brightwork of canopies and pins, and the decks were scrubbed until it seemed as if the planks would be sanded to destruction.

One morning Lieutenant Tyler, who had the deck, found on his order book directions for scrubbing and holystoning the decks once again. There were many other orders for the day and he wished to have this job over with as soon as possible, so unthinkingly he repeated to the boatswains's mate the words of the executive's written command:

"I want you to expedite the work today in your watch," he said. "Everything is to be scrubbed with alacrity."

The unusual order was repeated from deck to deck. "D'ye hear there! You will scrub everthing with alacrity!" The Swedes, the Dutch, the Africans passed on the words with various intonations. Down on the berth deck an educated ship's corporal mouthed the phrase with gusto. The limies looked wise, not giving themselves away. But Axel Swanson, up at the head, dared to admit that he was puzzled. As he started for the hold where sand and holystones were to be obtained, he pulled at his whiskers and mumbled to black Nevins in an aggrieved tone:

"Dey make me clean decks one time wid mud from de Godavari River in India, but dis is first time dey make me do it wid—what you call it?—alacricity. Well, hand me out some of de stuff, and I try!"

There were many men of Axel's kind on board the *Portsmouth*, and during the trade-wind days when the ship rolled steadily along at six knots, they often foregathered in the twilight to swap homeward-bounder stories. All these vikings seemed built for sailing the oceans of the world, but few of them dreamed of anything but escaping the fo'c'sle and getting rich ashore at trades they knew nothing whatever about. Seren Johansen, a foretopman with many hashmarks on his arm, was going to raise horses out in Ohio. He had already made payments on a percheron stallion, and soon the world would learn what fine horses could be raised and trained by an able seaman. Others eagerly read advertisements about growing mushrooms and breeding fancy chickens, rabbits, dogs, and fur animals. Many a sailor's payday was wrecked on Plymouth Rocks, stranded on Leghorn Reef,or sunk on Flemish Giant Shoal. One man had spent all his savings raising a fine crop of ginseng, the medicinal root so highly prized by the Chinese. But he was not able to sell any of it, and after returning to sea he complained that, with more than a ton of the stuff in his possession, it was just his luck never to have a single thing the matter with his health.

"Yaas," said Squantum, a waister, "I dink I try dat mushroom game. De New York *Herald* say de price is very goot now."

Squantum was a Dane who could barely sign his name; it was said that he could not tell the time if the hour hand of the clock was covered by the minute hand. He was sitting on a stuns'l boom and pressing the lighted coals of his pipe with a horny thumb. Someone protested: "Here, belay that! You'll be on the binnacle list with a sore thumb, and then we'll have to do your work."

"Not me!" said the Dane. "Me, I'm hard as de nails." He held out his hand for inspection; it looked as if made of sharkskin. "Do dis if you can!" He walked to the bulwark and rubbed his thumb over it with a rasping sound. Burn me if his hide didn't take off all the paint and leave the splintered wood showing!

"Squantum—what a name for a squarehead," said someone else. "Ain't that a town in Rhode Island?"

"Sure." The old Dane seemed pleased at the attention he had won. "I tell you. I come across from de old country on a bark wid China dings to New York, and run away. I go to see my uncle in Minnesota. He kick me back to sea, but first he tell me how to answer questions—I do not speak goot English den. First question, he say, is what is my name, and next one is where I been born. On de guardo, de man ask me de last question first. He write me down to be born at Christophersen—where is dat?—and my name he put as Squantum, de place my uncle want me to be born at. Ever since I been Squantum from Christophersen."

The fair weather lasted up to the capes, and there, as on the outward trip, we were hit by a howler and were forced to heave to. After tossing about for days we made Hampton Roads, Virginia. Back ashore in our own country, after the pleasing receptions we had been given in foreign ports, we saw once more the odious signs: "No Uniforms Allowed." At the great hotels at Hampton Roads, which were sponsored by the government, no enlisted man in uniform was allowed to enter, even though he had the money to pay for accommodation.

While we were at Norfolk, members of the crew of another navy ship were denied admission to a theater where a society musicale was being attended by many officers and their wives. When the indignant men made complaint to their executive officer the next morning, he pooh-poohed their protest and refused to pass it on to the commandant of the yard.

"Serves you damn well right for butting in where you were not wanted," he said. "If you yearn to get in the social swim, you'd better wait until you are discharged or get fired. You know you can't in those clothes."

Some of the men who had been slighted returned to the hall the next evening and started a public demonstration. They ended up in the brig of their ship or in the town jail, and were considered by the citizenry as blackguards who thus revealed how little their reputations had belied them. This incident and many another of the sort made a deep impression on the apprentices, and I could see that more than one was losing his dreams of glorious service in a corps that was denied in its own country the respect it deserved. So many years had passed since the nation had been engaged in a war that the real purpose of our ships and the handful of men who manned them had been forgotten. An enlisted man traveling inland hastened to get into civilian clothing, even though this was against regulations; otherwise he might be offered insults and abuse. The piling up of incidents of this sort made me determine that some day I would devote everything I had to removing that intolerance and that odium.

The obloquy was felt even by the case-hardened oldsters of the service, and their efforts to restore their own esteem were sometimes amusing when they were not pathetic. An incident of this sort occurred when, after dropping seventy-five boys into the general service at New York, we called at Newport to fill up their number with apprentices from the training station there. (The rest of us, to my delight, were to make a second cruise in the old *Portsmouth,* this time to European waters.) Most of the old fellows of the permanent crew took the opportunity to go up to Boston, the nearest place where they could enjoy a real spree.

The time approached when we were almost ready to get under weigh, and still a few stragglers had not returned; but we felt little alarm, for it was surprising how closely a semiconscious old salt could come to missing his ship without actually doing so. About six bells in the deep midwatch, a loud disturbance arose over in sedate Newport, and a boat was heard approaching through the night. The quartermaster sang out, as was required: "Boat ahoy!"

The answer came hoarsely: *"Portsmouth!"*

Now, had the boat contained merely enlisted men, the reply should have been "Hello!" A commissioned officer would have answered "Aye, aye, sir!" and other officers "No, no!" But there was only one person permitted to respond with the name of the ship, and that was the captain. The skipper had not been expected so soon, and there was an excited rush to receive him at the officers' gangway on the starboard side. The boat drew up to that gangway, and discharged Terence Riley, our blacksmith.

Terence insisted with drunken reasonableness that for thirty years he had been coming up the port gangway, and that now for once in his life he wanted to board his ship on the more stylish side. But the officer of the deck persuaded the boatman to transfer his freight to the other gangway, and then marked Riley down on a double charge. As the Irishman was taken to the brig he shook his fist in the direction of the quarterdeck and growled:

"Who'd sell a farm and go to sea? Begob, I'll use that sta'board gangway yet if it takes me last breath!"

As soon as we got clear of Newport, eastward bound, we ran into heavy weather with wind to spare. The backstays twanged like banjo strings, while below the woodwork incessantly creaked a straining song. I had always wanted to get a lofty view of the decks in a good gale, and found an excuse to go up on the mizzen royal yard. From this lofty perch the view was appalling. The deck looked like a narrow plank needling through acres of turbulent foam, a plank spotted here and there by tiny moving figures and others lying like logs in the waterways, indifferent to the swirling waters that poured over them through the scuppers. The great arc of swing soon made me feel that I might better get to a place closer to a convenient rail, and I lost no time in finishing my work and dropping back among my fellows.

Here I felt much more secure, and we old veterans of one cruise strutted about disdainful of the greenies who had yet to gain their sea legs. We now remembered the jokes and taunts that we ourselves had suffered not long since; and many a sick lad who wished he had never left Newport heard himself serenaded with the popular chorus:

"Oh, captain, stop the ship,
I want to get out and walk.
I feel so flippity, flappity, flop
That I'll never see New York.
The ocean's full of water,
I'm sick of the raging main—
Hi, hi, call me a cab
And take me home again!"

Four days later the storm had blown itself out, and we were cutting across the Gulf Stream among great brown patches of weed and schools of flying fish. The temperature of the water hauled up in a leather bucket every hour was much warmer than usual. One noonday the mainyard was hauled aback to stop our progress through the metallic blue waters, the ensign was dropped to half-mast, and at the mournful call of "All hands bury the dead!" we went to our stations on the deck.

It was my first sight of a burial at sea. The body had been neatly sewed in a canvas shroud, and lay draped with a flag on a plank resting on two halyard racks. In an awful hush broken only by the scraping of cordage aloft and the slapping of waves on the rolling side, the captain began in a low voice to read the solemn burial service. Under that flag, we knew, lay all that was left of Terence Riley; he had never recovered from the effects of too much cheap whisky taken on that last Newport spree.

At the words "We therefore commit this body to the deep," the inner end of the plank on which lay the body, weighted by three sixty-pounder cans of shrapnel, was lifted. Terence Riley obeyed the call to abandon ship, as all must sooner or later hear and obey; and forgetful of thirty years spent in being knocked about before the mast in American vessels, he embarked on a wider sea where officers and enlisted men must all start again on the same level.

The one honor he had sought through life was now thrust upon him after death; for by the irony of the sea, he left the ship over the starboard gangway.

The helm was shifted, the flag hoisted to the dasher block, and braces were trimmed. The boatswain piped down, and it was over.

Yet Terence was not forgotten, and amidships on the gun deck his name was spoken with fond recollection by the gunner's gang and their friends who foregathered there daily to swap yarns and talk of old shipmates and old ships. Sitting around on ditty boxes or on the oval division tubs used to hold water for swabs and sponges, the men would smoke and tell tales to their heart's content. A listener could hear again and again the names of the beautiful old wind-vessels of a vanished fleet—*Lackawanna, Yantic, Hartford, Adams, Brooklyn, Juniata, Susquehanna, Talapoosa, Swatara, Tuscarora*—and the names of vanished men who had sailed them.[1]

"Terence minds me some of Connie Woods," said Billy Stevens. "Same sad failin' for the drink. Connie was out with us on the *Asiatic* as equipment yeoman, and at Shanghai he came back from liberty badly under the weather. The deck officer let him sleep it off in the manger, and next day Connie stripped on the fo'c'sle and started swabbing himself down from truck to keel. Now, it happened that the skipper's wife was one of these nosies who like to take women visitors around and show them the ship, and a party of these females bobbed up just as Connie was goin' strong. One of the old girls screeched: 'It's a man!' Connie had his eyes full of soap and thought one of the kids of the crew was talkin' in a high voice to fool him. He took after that lady with a bucket of water, yelling: 'Hang me in a bottle like a cat! Yes, it's a man, and a real man, if

1. The *Susquehanna* and *Tallapoosa*, as side-wheelers, scarcely fit the description of beautiful wind-vessels, especially the latter ship, a "double-ender" gunboat built during the Civil War on the ferryboat principle to permit operation in narrow river channels without the need to turn in order to reverse course.

you ever saw one!' The captain's wife vowed she was mortified and would never set foot on that terrible ship again."

Alex Wills, one of the gun captains, chuckled and said: "Billy, do you recall the time we went after sand at Madagascar in the *Omaha?* Boys, we took a lot of trouble to find a guide who'd show us a place where we could go swimmin' without fear of bein' gobbled up by a crocodile. Finally we found a nigger who swore up and down that his place was all right. And it was fine, with deep green water and a clear sand bottom. After we had been swimmin' around for an hour or so and had paid the coon his dollar, I asked him: 'How it come no hab got crocodile in this place?' And he says, backin' into the bushes ready to run: 'Oh, it not safe here for um 'cause too many shark to eat um!' "

Alex had been in the navy since the Civil War. He was a quick-tempered man who was proud of his record of always being the first gunner to have his piece ready for firing; he even slept alongside his gun instead of in a comfortable hammock. One day during drill on the Atlantic cruise someone passed his powder boy a bag of plum duff instead of the expected charge, and the loader rammed it home without noting the substitution. As usual, Alex was the first gunner ready to fire, but no explosion followed the click of the hammer. That gun deck was not a safe place for officer or man for some time after the sodden mass of duff had been mucked out of the bore. Alex blamed the men of the Number Ten mess for the trick, and when that hungry crowd cut into their duff the next day they found in the center a sulphurous lump of gunpowder.

Whenever I could, I listened to the yarns of the old fellows and tried to pick up their seafaring oaths and peculiar expressions—among which, to my surprise, the two favorite phrases of the novelists, "shiver my timbers" and "splice the main brace," were notably absent. I was also fascinated by some of the nicknames to be heard. One man, a wizened cat of a topman but a great talker, was called "Euphroe" or "Uvro," which is the name of a piece of wood aboard ship that is drilled full of holes and used to spread the legs of a centipede on the backs of awnings. Uvro's arguments were as full of holes as that piece of wood; but he was always welcome in any group because he could lead them in a number of rollicking songs—"The Hat McGinnis Wore," and interminable ballads of Irish sweethearts who proved fickle. Uvro was, however, not Irish, but Scandinavian or perhaps Austrian or Swiss. His most popular and heartfelt piece began:

"Bad luck to the day I wandered away—
  Bad luck to the man on the guardo
Who wrote my name out to be tumbled about
  On board of the old *Colorado!*"

One mid-Atlantic drill I shall always remember. The ship was hove to in fair weather and we were ordered to rouse out the boats and get them overside. The huge sailing launch, with the cutter berthed inside it, rested in a space called the booms, cut through the spar deck between foremast and mainmast. A triatic stay of heavy hemp was rigged through great blocks from the caps of the two masts, and with purchases the heavy boat had to be lifted vertically until we we made "two blocks." Then yard tackles, fastened out near the brace bands, took up the strain while the vertical tackles were slacked away. With heavy jerks that shivered the whole ship, the heaving great boat was swung out over the rail and lowered into the sea.

To hoist this boat and replace it in the booms, the strength of every man and boy of the crew was required on tackles and jiggers. If it had come to the point of abandoning ship in a heavy sea, amid the tumult that could be expected on deck at such a time, the launch could never have been gotten overside, and the ninety men detailed to that boat would have had to seek some other means of floating to safety. I never passed under the great keel of the launch running along the ceiling of the gun deck without making a silent prayer that the necessity of abandoning ship would never arise while I was cruising aboard her. I was one of the ninety men who were detailed to that boat should catastrophe strike.

Twenty-one days out of Newport we entered the English Channel in the midst of a dismal British fog. That night stands out above all other naval nights as one of desperate labor and emptying exhaustion. Many a landsman believes that the sailor's strength and perseverance must be most highly tried in times of storm; but during a gale the things that can be done are few, for the ship is usually stripped of sail, and unless a spar goes there is nothing much that calls for the endeavor of all hands. The most trying times under sail are the days of variable airs when every muscle must be strained to make the most of the breezes without endangering the ship. Add the worries of shifting winds to the perils of a narrow channel and a lee shore lost in fog, and our struggles of the night may be faintly imagined.

Both watches were kept on deck all through the dark hours, reefing topsails and even courses, and then letting out the reefs again as soon as the topmen came down from the yards. We wore ship and we tacked. There was little haste that night to win the posts of honor at the weather earings; the challenge of windy danger was absent, and the work was mere drudgery. On deck we pulled and heaved hopelessly, like mules hauling coal in the depths of a mine. We were soon fagged from dropping anchors and pawling them in again, and at one time found ourselves with a fouled hawse near the unseen shore. The slow-moving half hours passed, marked only by soul-dulling labor and the fog-muffled sound of the ship's bell. Every word spoken on the ship—the repetition of orders by the men in the rigging, or a muttered curse on the deck—seemed amplified by the wreathing fog, and at times we caught our shouts repelled from the cold cliffs of old England. We scrambled heavily about the wet decks trying to keep warm, our teeth chattering, the biting drizzle reaching every part of us in spite of the "body-and-soul" lashings of our oilskins.

"Mainsail haul!" To the braces again at the double, our dimmed senses quickened by prods and oaths. We tangled ourselves in coils of lifts and the ropes of lighter gear. "Shift over your head sheets!" And on and back, drivers and driven. Frequently we had to heave the ship to, so that the deep-sea lead might be dropped for soundings. The line was passed outboard from aft forward, through a fair-leader in the mizzen rigging, over the sheave of which it had to be hoisted inboard again. The lead was heavy to handle, a billet of metal with a cup-shaped hollow bottom filled with tallow to catch the gravel or sand of the sea floor. When the line gave out after the order of "Stand by! Heave!" the doleful cry of "Watch, ohhhh, watch!" would ring along the sides from chains to chains, while our wet sails fluttered against the masts with a hollow thumping sound.

Listless with desperate weariness, we went below for the mockery of a breakfast. The meal was the worst I had ever tried to eat—bootleg coffee and a cold thin mess of molasses and hominy called "burgoo" when it was not called something much worse. Coming as a climax to that night of unceasing slavery and a fifteen-hour fast, that meal made me wish I were a few years younger so that I could weep unashamedly. There was no way to get extra food from the stores, for my payday had long ago been spent for necessities. I wondered if there was any trade in the world except that of the sailor where men were sweated for such long hours without food of any sort. And then, to top that, when something at last was put before them, to have it be a cold heap of stuff almost impossible to swallow!

At dawn we were sighted from shore, and a tugboat came out to help. She hauled the *Portsmouth* inside the breakwater at Plymouth Harbor, where we rode to an open hawse with sixty fathoms of chain to each cable. Now we were in a new land, and with youthful resilience the pangs of the night soon were thrown off. . . . Alongside us was anchored our sister training ship, the *Jamestown*.

Chapter XI

WESTERN OCEAN

The first boys ashore in England returned with honest praise for the welcome that had been given them, especially at the Sailors' Rest established by Miss Agnes Weston. We had heard a great deal about this lady who devoted her life to the shore comfort of Britain's seamen. We all made it a point to call at the Rest and see for ourselves the clean, soft beds and princely meals that were offered us at low cost. The clubrooms were snug, and when accommodations were crowded, cozy bedrooms in near-by private houses were placed at our disposal; no boy had an excuse to seek shelter in questionable places. We enjoyed several good liberties at Plymouth, and ate our fill of crisp sweet buns with plenty of unsalted butter. Some of the boys learned that a plug of navy tobacco would buy more from the dock loafers than its cost would buy in town, and they became smugglers in a small way.

We were puzzled but pleased to find that in England our uniform was more honored than it was in our own land. It entitled us, for instance, to travel anywhere we liked on the railways at half fare. The British people were proud of their own navy, and merely accorded us the same respect they gave to their own defenders of the sea. It seemed that we could find men in their navy who came from every village and town in the island. Often the son followed the father in choosing the navy as a vocation. Among the people the service was highly popular, and a sign "No Uniforms Allowed" would have caused a riot.

In the harbor about us were several British training ships—short, lofty brigs crowded with red-faced English boys, who were typically of beefier build than our tall, lithe fellows. On these ships, and others like them, the young seamen of Great Britain were given a thorough sail training before being passed into their general service. The training corps had been established in 1854. Boys remained in training until they reached the age of twenty-one, agreeing thereafter to remain in service for another nine years. They won retirement privileges after twenty-five years; the pay was small in comparison with ours, and increases came at the rate of about a penny a day, but there were other compensations.

Every weekday morning the little brigs sailed out to sea in formation. They drilled smartly, and there seemed to be much less confusion on their decks during maneuvers than on our own. The British boys raced aloft barefoot, and we were told that they were not permitted to wear shoes until they went ashore at the week's end. Our government didn't try to make us as hardened as that! Flogging in the British navy had been suspended a few years before we visited Plymouth, but we heard stories of birching for minor offenses on the little ships. This punishment consisted of caning with rattan on a tender part of the body over which a garment was tightly drawn. Flogging in our own navy was officially abolished as long ago as 1847,[1] but in our time it was not unusual to be chased about the decks with a rope's end in the hands of a captain of a top

1. On 28 September 1850, President John Tyler signed the bill that abolished flogging in the Navy. The long fight to terminate the practice was led by Senators John P. Hale of New Hampshire and Robert F. Stockton (formerly Commodore) of New Jersey, together with Captain Uriah P. Levy. Herman Melville's *White Jacket* appeared almost simultaneously in 1850; its influence on the legislation was therefore less than has generally been supposed.

or a boatswain's mate. The chaser always had to be prepared to turn the matter into a joke if an officer appeared.

In some ways the English boys were better treated than we were, on board ship as well as on shore. Their officers fraternized regularly with the boys, and no British dignity seemed to be endangered. On our side, it was felt that too often a graduate of Annapolis believed that gentility of speech and kindliness of manner were somehow incompatible with the duties of a naval officer. Such an attitude might be considered a sort of petty treason, because it nullified the efforts of the American government to secure and retain good men in its sea defense service.

I learned at Plymouth what many a man in the American navy today does not understand—that our uniform, like many other sea observances and customs, was taken over bodily from the British navy. It is told that George II so much admired a riding habit trimmed with blue and white, worn by the Duchess of Bedford, that one day he ordered all the men of his fleet to don a similar costume. A wide collar was added to protect the blouse from the grease on the pigtails that navy men of the day thought proper to wear. The three stripes were placed on the collar to commemorate the sea victories of Lord Nelson at the Nile, at Copenhagen, and at Trafalgar. When Nelson died, the black silk kerchief was ordered worn as a sign of mourning. We of the United States service still wear those marks, and the neckerchief is tied in the exact knot prescribed in the King's Regulations. . . . The American navy has plenty of victories and sea heroes to commemorate. Mightn't it be about time to find ways to honor them in their own service?

The Yankee naval man has always been uneasy when wearing clothes that seemed to submerge his individuality. Although in the earliest days of our navy's history there were a few attempts at uniformity, these were expressed merely in efforts by commanding officers to swank up their gig crews in family livery or clothing of their own design (one crew of enlisted men was for a while required to wear high beaver hats!). During the Revolution our men wore knee skirts of canvas over breeches of the same material—rather a fisherman's rig—but not until the close of the eighteenth century was any serious attention given to the adoption of a standard uniform; previous to that time it was considered an encroachment upon personal freedom to demand any odious conformity. The garb selected was in imitation of that of England's seamen—short jacket, trousers of wide cut, and a varnished flat hat. In fact, so much alike were the uniforms of the two national services that during the War of 1812 one of the crew of the American ship *Chesapeake,* rushing to the spar deck at the cry of "Repel boarders!" joined a party of the British, thinking them to be his own shipmates. It was to guard against a repetition of such awkward mistakes that our men, later in the same war, opened their jackets at the throat and embroidered their collars with a design of stars and stripes.

Although the two uniforms have always been closely related, the Englishmen differed from us ashore fifty years ago in that they were always attired in strictly regulation clothing and always wore each piece in the manner prescribed by law. Among a thousand of them ashore, the outfit of one always looked exactly like the others. But in any group of American bluejackets, either at home or in foreign ports, there would be as many variations in the wearing of clothes as there were men to wear them. This may be ascribed to our independence of character, but the general effect was bad. It would have been much worse had not lack of money and the strict enforcement of regulations kept us within bounds. But many a ship has been made unhappy by too much insistence on such rules. When Commodore Schley had command of the White Squadron in the nineties he almost had a mutiny on his hands when he attempted to compel his men to wear a flat blue cap with grommet of rope. Men who had served many years deserted rather than wear the "dinky" narrow hat with Dutch pennants in the rear. Schley's flagship, the *Baltimore,* while at Hampton Roads was labeled "White Slave" in large letters of coal dust because of uniform troubles.[2] (In the year 1934 the same type of cap was again issued to the enlisted men of the navy, without great opposition.)

2. This episode appears to have been fictitious. Captain Winfield S. Schley assumed command of the *Baltimore,* then under construction at Cramp's, on 1 June 1889 and commissioned the ship on 30 January 1890. The *Baltimore*

The ardent desire of American sailors of the old days for fancier uniforms, real "seagoin' " clothes, reached an extreme of display when they got free of the ship for a while and went on furlough. The men appeared in the streets and on trains in blue mustering caps fifteen inches across, spread tightly over an illegal grommet of steel, the tops emblazoned with ten-pointed bright stars, with smaller stars worked between the points. The name of the man's ship was shown in silver or gold letters on a silk ribbon whose ends fluttered over one ear as a reminder of the tarry pigtail once worn by his predecessors. The cap was tilted on two hairs at the back of the head or cockbilled over the starboard eye or ear, or, in fact,

joined the North Atlantic Squadron (Squadron of Evolution, White Squadron) at Key West and became flagship of Rear Admiral Bancroft Gherardi. The squadron then proceeded to New York, arriving on June 12. The months of July and August were spent off the coast of Maine, with visits to Portland, Bath, and Bar Harbor. On August 11, the *Baltimore* was ordered to convey the remains of John Ericsson to Sweden and departed from New York on the 23rd.

From Stockholm the Baltimore visited the Mediterranean and crossed the South Atlantic to the Straits of Magellan and thence to Valparaiso to protect American interests during a revolution. Here, on 16 October 1891, occurred the "*Baltimore* incident"—a mob attack on the ship's liberty party in which two of her men were killed and sixteen injured—which brought about a crisis in the relations between the United States and Chile. The ship left Valparaiso on December 11, arrived at San Francisco on 5 January 1892, and on February 24, Captain Schley turned over the command to his successor. He records: "As their old commander was about to pass over the side, the master-at arms stepped forward and said 'Captain, the boys wished me to present in their name this little souvenir of their service with you and of their affection for you. You know, sir, when you were captain we couldn't make you a present, but now that you are a plain gentleman we want you to have something to remind you of us and to remember us by.' Enclosed in a beautiful case was an exquisite gold-headed cane, made and finished by San Francisco artisans."

Schley was relieved in the *Baltimore,* however, by none other than the Captain Bligh of the receiving ship *St. Louis* at the time of Buenzle's enlistment three years previously. A "narrow hat with Dutch pennants" episode on the *Baltimore* might possibly have occurred, therefore, during the new regime, or perhaps later, since Schley's successor died within the year. Schley was promoted to the rank of commodore on 6 February 1898.

worn at any angle except squarely on the head as ordered by uniform regulations. The cap itself was usually made of the finest blue cloth, as were the mustering shirt and the trousers. Collars were heavily embroidered with stars, diamonds, and points, with herringbones of fine silk on the bosom and over pockets. About the man's neck, dangling over the English neckerchief clasped by a polished sea bean inlaid with silver, swelled a lanyard which, measured in painstaking hours of time, would have taken three months' pay to compensate. Beautifully designed of innumerable little Turk's-heads, diamond knots, and sennitwork, as white as many washings and bleachings under a tropic sun could make it, such a lanyard was more proudly worn than would have been a chain of silver or gold.

The monkey-jacket tightness of the clothing, so binding to a man who wanted to have his arms free aloft, was relaxed as much as the furlough man dared, so that his garments flared like a well-drawing staysail. His real courage was shown in the width of the trouser legs, flowing out fully as wide as the spreading hat he wore. The bell bottoms, so convenient to roll over the thighs for wet deckwork or for landing in surf, completely hid the foreign, sharp-pointed shoes, always shined to mirrorlike perfection. Wearing a silver apprentice mark, a rating badge, and even metal tape on his collar, and sporting a waxed mustache, Jack ashore was a rakish craft, resembling in outline the smart and trig vessels that he well knew how to sail around the world. He carried all with a grace calculated to arrest the eye of any lass he might chance to meet. Please do not smile, for the American man-o'-warsman of that day had few pleasures that were worthy of the name, and none was so satisfying to him as wearing a trim outfit of clothing and adornment which was all his own handiwork. Every item that he wore had been made on board his ship, even to rings fashioned from five-dollar gold pieces shaped on the point of a marlinspike.

The training ship *Jamestown,* which we found at Plymouth on our arrival, remained there during our stay. The two boyish crews swapped experiences like old-timers in the cozy rooms of the Sailors' Rest. Several times we competed with them at boat races and spar drills, and in performing the work of running up light yards the British brigs also gave us our money's worth. But the greatest bout of *Portsmouth* vs. *Jamestown* was not revealed to our commanding officers until a short time before we sailed for home.

We had pests on board ship as well as pets. First, there was the man who continually growled at everything while relating the great virtues of his last ship and her officers. There was the smallest apprentice who tried to pick fights with every larger boy. At times there were weevils in our hard bread, and ants and cockroaches in our sugar. Worst of all were the roaches, which, judging from their size, may have joined the *Portsmouth* during her San Francisco cruise in the forties. They were so large that they would stand without hitching while we scratched a date on their backs. We ran them in races across the decks.

At Plymouth our executive officer made an effort to reduce the numbers of roaches on board, for they were making serious inroads on our provisions, and some of them had been found even in the wardroom bean soup. Our captain offered special liberty to those of the crew who caught the largest numbers, and money prizes as well. One boy rigged a deep can with a finely balanced cover, using molasses for bait. He was the high winner for several days, until many other boys began reporting in the mornings with cupfuls of cockroaches, heaped so high that it looked as if the captain would have to get a promotion if he wanted to continue his money prizes. Our officers boasted of our thrift and enterprise. One day our captain and the commanding officer of the *Jamestown* were chatting on the quarter-deck, and I heard our skipper say:

"Believe me, old man, we'll soon get rid of roaches on this ship. We offer prizes to the boys for catching them. You must have a lot of the pesky things—why not follow our plan?"

"Not I," said the captain of the *Jamestown*. "We have found a much better way. We encourage visiting parties between ships."

"How does that help you?"

"Well, your boys visit our ship every evening, and they have just about cleaned the *Jimmy* of the last nasty roach we had!"

The prize offers were canceled at once.

We bade farewell to Plymouth on August 17, passing the famous Eddystone Lighthouse close on our starboard beam. Bound south, running before a fair wind, all my sailor instincts sharpened when for the first time I heard the order: "Set stuns'ls, all the watch!"

The studdingsails were beautiful sheets of virgin white, for they had never been broken out of the sailroom until this Middle Atlantic passage. Our older men considered it a nuisance to rig them on their booms and to fiddle about getting them to draw, but my admiration of these lovely extra wings never tired. I longed to see our ship from a distance, preferably from forward, as she curtsied and dipped with a steady breeze from aft, just strong enough to fill her sails and not stiff enough to prevent a gentle rustling now and then when the ship rolled. One of our officers told me that Nelson's *Victory* went into action with her stuns'ls set. What seamanship!

With the help of our extra canvas we made a steady ten knots. When the peaks of the Azores loomed in the distance, a head wind compelled us to douse our wings and we lay off and on for several days, until on the ninth day out we passed the Desertas Islands. A favorable slant helped us to bring the ship to safe anchorage in deep, clear water at Funchal, Madeira. As we entered the harbor the Pennsylvania State Schoolship *Saratoga* passed us, homeward bound. The *Saratoga* and the *Portsmouth* were unique among American training ships in having double-topsail yards.

At Funchal we were so close to the town that we could hear the shouts of the natives on the beach, and even the rattle of shingle in the surf. The natives of Madeira were famous fruit-growers and fishermen, and the island had since the voyage of Columbus been a port of call for Spanish ships to and from the New World. Yankee whalers often sought men for their crews here, and many a Portuguese fisherman came ashore at New Bedford to stay, so that now their descendants almost rule the old Massachusetts town.

Our boys enjoyed several visits on shore. Wine was good and very cheap, and the best fruit could be had for almost nothing. Even money was cheap, and when we changed our half dollars into *reis* and other Portuguese coins we had our pockets full. Some of the boys managed to spend theirs on a trip up and down the mountain in land sleds whose runners had been greased by gliding over sausagelike bags of tallow. The road was paved with smooth, round pebbles and was extremely steep. At the top, the oxen that had hauled the sled up were unyoked, and the sled came down the hill by gravity alone, steered by the driver in the rear using the toe of his boot. The approach of the vehicle was heralded far in advance by shouts and a great rumble, and half the town would turn out to watch its noisy arrival.

We were again at sea on September 1, and before we lost sight of the town astern we found a stowaway in the captain's gig. He was called Anton, a Portuguese who wished to escape a three-year term of military service without pay. Anton was at once given a complete outfit of clothes by the generous crew, and was duly enlisted as a landsman, taking his place naturally among the large number of foreigners we had already shipped. He began drawing his pay (about five dollars a month more than we apprentices got) and without loss of time learned a few American sea commands and a large vocabulary of American oaths. According to tradition, stowaways from the Azores or the Madeiras always become bumboatmen, and no doubt Anton has been harvesting the money of bluejackets for many years in the waters of his native islands.

During the voyage home, we second-cruise men were given examinations in seamanship, ordnance, and signaling. Some were promoted to the rank of seaman apprentice, second class, and pay was increased to nineteen dollars a month. I came near missing my promotion because I forgot to mention that a charge of powder must be inserted into the muzzle of a broadside gun with the seam away from the vent. My examining officer cautioned me seriously to be more careful, for a battle might be lost because of little things like that. I wondered why the powder wasn't provided in seamless bags, but did not mention this to the officer; I needed the promotion more than he needed the advice.

Cutting out sails, measuring lengths for standing rigging, splicing wire, and the making of dolphins and fenders were some of the more exacting practical points on which we had to pass muster. Our cruise experience counted most in preparing us to answer questions regarding the striking of topgallant masts, turning in deadeyes, passing a gammoning, and reeving burtons and other purchases; for in all of these we had been given plenty of instruction. What required careful memorizing was the list of duties of each man of a broadsider's crew, starting with "Number One—he steps directly off the gun carriage, lock lanyard in right hand, heft of his body on his right leg, right eye running over the piece, and thus awaits the co-instant of the target," and running along through Number Twenty and the powder monkey. And all this while I could not tell a co-instant from the doctrine of sublapsarianism.

The care of clothing was still stressed by the examiners; and that was ever a real and pressing problem. When navy men were seen ashore, clean and neat, with their tapes white as snow and their clothing hand-creased and immaculate, few civilians could guess under what handicaps this cleanliness had been achieved. On the *Portsmouth* we were allowed no fresh water for our clothes. Anyone without experience cannot realize how hard it is to work up suds in salt water, even with the use of the strong alkaline soap issued on board ship. The souls of good men have been harrowed by wrangles over fresh water in the sailing ships, and tops and watches bitterly arrayed against each other. Every morning after general cleaning, each division sent two men below to the captain of the hold, who measured out for them six gallons of fresh water in two buckets. This amount had to be passed along to serve the personal needs of twenty men and boys; it went first to the captain of the top, then to his chief striker, and then to each topman in a rigid line of precedence. When all had washed in it, the usefulness of the water was not ended; what was left was issued equally to all the men of the division for washing their clothes the next morning. The remainder was stowed in the chains and used over and over again until it was no longer fluid and had a thick gray consistency like liquid lye. It continued to be referred to as "fresh" water. If the condenser happened to get out of order, or the captain wished to punish us, the regular allowance of water was curtailed.[3] This happened also when a trip between ports took longer than was expected.

Drinking water was obtained from the scuttle butt near the main hatch on the gun deck, which was guarded at all times by a marine sentry. If he were friendly he might turn his back while you were drinking and give you time to take some of the waste water in a cup—perhaps enough to wash a prized lanyard or a piece of tape. It was good policy to be friends with any marine likely to get scuttle-butt duty.

There were no real friendships made on the ship, however, between bluejacket and marine. Collectively, the marines were always considered by the seamen to be the most obnoxious corps ever devised. Personally, I found the marines to be a friendly bunch, and often ashore I associated with them because they were usually sober and much more familiar with the ports visited than were the fun-loving sailors; but with good reason the leathernecks were suspicious of our advances.

Indeed, I often felt sorry for the marine contingent on the ship. They were poorly paid, even in comparison with our own low salaries. Their clothing seemed highly uncomfortable, although their stiff regalia of pipe-clayed belts and furred hats was at times put by; their cheap brass buttons had to be made always to shine like gold. They lacked a decent hangout in the ship. Their living quarters were far down on the berth deck, below the waterline; here they ate, slept, and loafed in a triangular space walled in by canvas bags, prison doors, cooks' chests, and the sick bay, amid a noxious odor of paint, iodoform, grease, pipe clay, and bilge. Anywhere else they were unwelcome, and rarely was one seen playing cards or chatting with seamen. The marines were always

3. None of the Navy's sailing sloops, including the *Portsmouth,* were equipped to condense sea water. Their fresh water was carried in iron tanks, and they carried neither the fuel nor the apparatus for evaporation. Hence the rigid rationing of fresh water on the training ships.

roused out at the call of all hands, and at drill were stationed at ropes and guns.

Inception of the corps of American soldiers of the sea antedated the organization of the navy, for it was established even before the Declaration of Independence. The marines have served with the ships in every war, but have always been made to feel out of place. The principal duty of the private marine was the most disagreeable one in the whole naval service. It consisted of watching his fellow men, spying on them, restraining them, and carrying out punishments ordained by officers. There we were, marines and bluejackets, nearly four hundred of us on one keel, serving one flag, and coming from the same states, towns, and even the same schools. Yet against each other we held a mutual contempt that grew into hatred as a cruise lengthened into months and years—for every man deprived of liberty or otherwise punished held some poor order-following marine as somehow responsible for his trouble.

We found marines at the gangway to search us when we first came aboard the ship; they were there on duty when we left the ship. We could appeal to no officer at cabin door or wardroom without submitting to the challenge of a "sailor's hitching post." When grog was issued in the navy, a marine watched the movements of the man who measured it out. At the scuttle butt, a menacing marine bayonet was a constant reminder not to waste or steal a drop. If a bluejacket was clapped in the brig, it was a marine who was stationed outside the perforated iron door to carry out the bread-and-water sentence. When the dread cry of "Abandon ship!" rang out in dead earnest and the sailor ran to his station, there was a sea soldier at every fall to see that no one entered the boat without authority. His bayonet was against the master-at-arms' force, the sailor police, as much as it was against the other seamen. It was a marvel that more often such antagonism did not break out into open internecine warfare, for it was encouraged and fostered by the naval officers, who believed that such animosity was an effective aid to discipline.

Our passage home was rather uneventful, as a gale now and then could not be considered unusual by veteran apprentices. Sometimes a steamer was sighted, but this caused little interest, men at work barely turning their heads and the people below not caring enough to come on deck. But when a sailing ship was sighted, then it was like a call of "All hands!" Men would crown the tops to make better guesses at the rig, and there would be excited discussions regarding the stranger's nationality and destination long before the hull rose above the horizon. Sail was in the blood of our men.

Naturally, we met dirty weather off Hatteras, which always seemed to be the *Portsmouth's* bad corner. There she met water-spouts, sudden squalls, head winds, and drenches of cold rain to harass ship and navigator. The studdingsails, which had come near to wearing out the last of the enthusiasts who remained in favor of them, had been neatly stowed many days back. The ship bowled along through seas veined with running white, seas that crashed over her quarters and made a beach of the deck. We seemed forever to be reefing or furling, sweating up topsail halyards and then letting them go again on the run, while the kevels smoked and the slatting canvas thundered a salvo. "More beef, more beef, you clodhoppers!" We scrambled aloft in inky darkness over weather shrouds whose incline seemed unfamiliar, and out on slanting footropes from which the stiff and slapping canvas threatened more than once to dislodge us. Above the roar of the wind rose the wild cries of invisible men.

Returned from the risky work aloft, we would be sent to stations at halyards, braces, and brails, with spouts of water pouring down our necks and shoes spurting salt water from their tops. "Tail on now!" A stiff rope is thrust into your fist and you pull and pull with the rest until the rope thins in your wrinkled and sea-softened hands. The tie block of the yard must be chock-a-block against the mast sheave. Now clap a jigger on it, and make her scream! "Bear a hand, now!" Blocks resound woodenly as they creep about the deck, and kinks flatten out as new ropes are swigged up. Now a rope weeps from its very heart, but the mastman jumps on the fife rail and hauls in and out for yet another inch, and again for just a strand's breadth. "Clap on to those sheets!" They are wet with kinks and snarls. "Pull your guts out, you farmer—ah, bust her!" More jiggers to haul on, and all creation full of wet knots.

A loud oath comes from the maintop, where a man's hand has been painfully pinched in a lift block. He presses the bleeding hand between his knees, and with the other crosses himself while loudly calling on his Maker to save him. From the horse block comes a sharp hail.

"Maintop there!"

"Aye, aye, sir!" answers the Swede captain of the top.

"Belay that swearing up there, d'ye hear? I'm paid to do that!"

On the second of October we dropped our hook in the North River, at New York, and furled sail on the good ship *Portsmouth* for the last time.

Our training period was over; but still I had not had my fill of the romantic life under sail and feared that I would now be drafted to some steaming man-o'-war with smoking funnels. There, I knew, I would never be privileged to fight a really terrifying storm with rollers coming over the bows and sending the gear off its pins to make a slatting hurrah's nest for a smart seaman to clear up amid the shriek of a hell-busting nor'wester. I knew also that our ship's company would now be scattered, and that I would see few of my friends again. I was sorry, for they were a gang of lively boys, and I had found during the cruise that there were few things that could down them.

While all hands were aloft furling sail at New York and putting on harbor gaskets, one of the lads slipped through the footropes on the starboard lower maintopsail yard, and fell. He landed across the main yard below, and although he must have had cause to be terrified, did not let out a cry. Krafft, the carpenter's mate, whose duty it was to help furl the mainsail at such times, with a big calloused hand grabbed the boy as he was slipping past, and coolly set him right side up on the footropes.

"Tamned kids," said Krafft, shaking his head. "Dey are alvays leaving dere shdations midoudt permission."

Chapter XII

PRIDE OF THE NAVY

A few days later I left the *Portsmouth,* never again to answer a muster on the quarter-deck of the gallant old vessel. I found myself on board the *Minnesota,* the New York receiving ship, whence a number of my companions were sent to the Pacific coast to man the new cruiser, *San Francisco.* I was to see few of those boys again.

I was ordered on November 20, 1890, to join the U.S.S. *Philadelphia,* the flagship of the Atlantic fleet. As was customary with any new ship, she was for a time called the "pride of the navy." To me the steel ship appeared tremendous. Her length was 335 feet, and she could easily be carried between the forward and after turrets of a battleship of today. Her best speed did not exceed twenty knots. What pleased me most about her was that she carried topsail and topgallant yards, and accordingly I chose to ignore the improved guns, the galleys, and the steel gangways.

One of the first wonders of my new ship was the lavish ration of fresh water—and hot water at that—which could be had at the spacious galleys. It seemed a great relief, and I felt that there could now be nothing more to worry about; but I was to learn that

The *Philadelphia*.

cleanliness is not so much the result of conveniences at hand as it is of character and habits. Somehow the men of the new navy did not seem as clean in person and clothing as those of the sailing ships, where any kind of fresh water was a luxury.

An innovation on the *Philadelphia* was an installation of steel lockers to take the place of regulation bags for storing the clothing of the crew. The lockers were arranged in tiers and had linings of white canvas, kept clean by scrubbing. The locker idea proved unsatisfactory, however, and bags were again used soon after this first cruise. The newspapers made special mention of the ship's electric-lighting plant. The battery of twelve 6-inch rifles with which this new ship was armed was most impressive when compared with the smoothbores I had fired during earlier cruises. It took me some days to get accustomed to these and other novelties on board.

Although she was a brand-new ship I was surprised, on joining her, to find the crew busy scraping the paint off her bottom in dry dock. My fate while on the *Philadelphia* seemed continually to be putting paint on her sides and scraping it off again.

Our first mission in the flagship was to receive the Brazilian cruisers *Aquidaban* and *Guanabara*, which were making a ceremonial visit to the United States. When this duty had been performed, we left the North River on January 19 for Haiti, in the West Indies. Our country was making an attempt to negotiate a treaty with the president of the black republic to cede us St. Nicholas Mole for use as a naval coal depot, and Rear Admiral Gherardi was the government's emissary on board.

The operation of getting under way in the steel steamer, instead of calling for all hands to man the capstan, run aloft to make sail, and hustle about the decks hauling on gear, was conducted without great labor and without noise except for the whirring of a manless windlass and the hum of a great cable coming in speedily. I was charmed by the prospect of a cruise promising so little hard work. Our principal duty while on watch at night was to get the ashes out of the firerooms through the ventilators, and even this was done by machinery, as was the operation of the steering gear.

In spite of many improvements, the ship rolled excessively even in a moderate sea, and turned out to be so dangerously unstable that after our cruise the masts were shortened and the yards removed. She was, after all, an experiment, and mistakes discovered in her operation led the way to the larger and better ships of the navy to come.

After a five-day passage we arrived at the island of Haiti, and we remained at Port-au-Prince until the middle of March. The ship then proceeded to the near-by British port of Kingston, Jamaica, and moored at the dock to load coal. Watching the performance of this grimy task, I was homesick for the spotless wooden vessels that never needed to pause in their voyages to fill the hold with tons of black and powdery lumps. The work of loading was done by Negro women, who carried the fuel aboard and stowed it in the deepest bunkers. They were an impudent lot, and physically strong almost beyond belief. The soft coal was shoveled into round baskets, each holding about ninety pounds. With the basket held on her head, arms braced on hips, clay pipe in mouth, and perspiration trickling down and grooving the coal dust, this human beast of burden marched to the staging on our sides and dumped her load into the chutes. The male lords and masters of these slaves fought and gambled, frolicked and sang on the dock, and spurred the jaded and lagging women to renewed efforts.

As night came on, the restlessness of the lawless element on a warship at dock made itself felt. There was a furtive shifting into clean clothes, many whispered conferences, and exchanges of money. The brief twilight of the tropics had barely fallen when the first of the ship-jumpers slipped over the side.

The executive officer, Lieutenant Leutze, was a strict man who spoke with a German accent. He was the son of a famous artist, and was what we termed a "mustang" officer, who had come into the navy from the merchant service during the Civil War.[1] He took no

1. With respect to Eugene Henry Cozzens Leutze, the term "mustang" is inappropriate. He was appointed to the Naval Academy in 1863, graduated in 1867, and was retired as rear admiral in 1909.

measures to prevent the crew from leaving the ship, and he was not permitted to land armed men in this foreign port to hunt for absentees; but the jumpers were noted and marked for severe punishment on their return. Searchlights were trained on the gloomy coal piles, and as men scurried across the dock some of them were recognized and their names written down. Some dropped over the bows and swam through water where during the day we had seen sharks; thus dangerously will a man sometimes gratify a sudden impulse for change. Quarters were sounded at frequent intervals in order to learn who was absent from muster—a great annoyance to the law-keeping folk who stayed aboard.

The next evening a group of the ship-jumpers gathered on the dock and, ranging themselves abreast of the gangway, flourished bottles and shouted to us to come ashore and join their good times. Those who could still carry a tune taunted the officers with a snatch of song:

"Many times have you hungered round my cabin door—
Hard times, hard times, come again no more!"

Our ship was not overmanned, and we were glad that when we drew away from the docks we had regained most of our shipmates, who when their money had all been spent sorrowfully came back to duty like ill-behaved children. But on their return many of them managed to smuggle rum aboard with them. There were many ways to circumvent the watchfulness of the authorities. Liquor was hauled through the ports from native boats, and dead chickens ordered for the messes were filled with live firewater in bottles. As the drinks circulated between decks, men ordinarily conspicuous for good sense and leadership remembered and renewed old quarrels. One man, who in later years I was happy to be able to count as my good friend, roamed the forward part of the ship, ax in hand, seeking someone who had offended him ashore. We had steamed back into Haitian waters before the crew was straightened out and the men had settled down to the regular round of drills and cleanliness.

When we again reached Port-au-Prince we found in the harbor

the American first squadron of evolution, commanded by Rear Admiral Walker, whose flagship was the *Chicago,* the new "pride of the navy." Beside her lay the *Boston, Atlanta,* and *Yorktown,* and later we were joined by the beautiful wooden corvette *Kearsarge* of Civil War fame. The notorious *Enterprise,* present on detached service, made ours the most formidable fleet that the port had seen since the British and French navies had battled in former days for the possession of the rich island, which both sides had lost.

The landlocked harbor was sultry and crushingly hot, and this caused much suffering and sickness among the crew. The admiral gave orders that no work was to be done about the decks between the hours of ten and four, and the time passed slowly. We loafed about and watched the Haitian gunboats and transports moving the ragged troops that were ordered from place to place to get into combat with the revolutionaries they were fighting at the time. The gunboats were poorly manned, and the crews drilled not at all. One afternoon when the natives were firing a salute for our admiral, one of the mismanaged guns blew a rammer and the two arms of an unlucky gunner into the bay.

It was here in this port that I witnessed my first torpedo practice in the navy. The deadly weapon of naval warfare today could hardly have had a cruder beginning. A long boom, used to secure the ship's boats in port, was lashed fore and aft on the steam launch, with one end extending far over the bow. At the forward tip of the boom were secured some tins of high explosive, which were to be set off through a ramming contact with an enemy ship. It seemed apparent that any charge that would do marked damage to the vessel of a foe would be suicidal to the crew of the little launch whose task it was to explode it. In practice this "bomb-on-a-ram" was detonated by driving it into a channel buoy, wreaking havoc on the fish of the harbor, but fortunately not injuring the men of the launch.

Many corners of our ship, above and below, on the orlops, under the bridges, in lamplighted storerooms and sun-blistered tops, served during those dull days as studios where art was abused by those who made a profitable business of tattooing their shipmates.

Sometimes these "artists," when they lacked customers, would practice on their own arms and legs. Often, however, even a beginner could find any number of volunteers when he wished to exercise his skill with the inky needle. One little Tartar named Tony, a subject of the Russian Empire, had an ambition to cover every inch of his body with colored views and mottoes, although he was already a walking picture gallery. He was the only person I ever knew who had sunbursts tattooed over his eyes, cleverly designed to conform with the leathery wrinkles on the rest of his face. He had anchors on the lobes of his ears, and there was enough ground tackle marked on his body to hold an armada. Many of the scenes depicted would have caused his arrest if they had been exposed to public view in the United States; and Tony would certainly have been barred from the mails. His skin was so dark that only the deepest red and blue shades would show. If the ambitious artist could not find a piece of skin on Tony that was still unmarked, he was welcome to prick in a dagger, serpent, eagle, or burlesque queen over some design that was already to be found there; it was all the same to Tony. He seemed immune to the pain, and did not wince while receiving jabs that would bring tears to the eyes of apprentices and cause knots of agonized muscles to bunch up under the sufferer's arms.

It is said that the practice of tattooing is more than a mere barbaric wish to mar one's body with childish designs, and that among soldiers and seamen it is an almost instinctive attempt to identify the body so that it cannot be disfigured beyond recognition and thus come to an unknown burial. If that is true, some of the men of the old navy would certainly have been recognized even had a mine exploded under them. Many men had crosses and other sacred symbols marked on them so that if they died in Catholic countries they would be interred without question in holy ground. A famous Japanese tattoo artist of the period specialized in scenes of the Crucifixion and had done some of his most pious work on the broad back of one of the vilest seagoing rascals I have ever met. Other men besides Tony were covered with black and red designs on all parts of their bodies: stars on foreheads, half-moons on cheeks, nude ladies on shoulders and chests. Some of the full-rigged ships I have seen on a man-o'-warsman's back might well have been displayed on wood or canvas. One petty officer had anchors on the back of each hand and stars on every finger, and spent many a payday for diamonds to wear as a contrast to the ink (he was a moneylender, and could well afford the display). Many a seaman had the words "HOLD FAST" pricked on his fingers, one letter to each digit; there was an old superstition that one so marked would never lose his grip when working aloft.

One old fellow, a cockney survivor of the Civil War, bore on his back a map of the world in two globes. He carried in his outfit two mirrors that were used to point out to curious listeners the places where many of the incidents of his adventurous career had occurred. There were bright flags over the names of many ports not ordinarily visited by American man-o'-warsmen. Two red flags flew over Liverpool—that was where his wife lived. Other red flags marked the homes of unmarried acquaintances. One flag showed where he had received the gash on his cheek, and another where a broken bottle had almost severed a hand; still another flew over the port where he had been wounded by an Austrian woman (this was a personal matter, he would explain, and did not appear on his naval record). The North Pole had an English flag over it, but the South Pole was hidden from sight, marked only by the jutting flukes of a buried anchor. His personally conducted tour of the world was filled with highly lascivious comment. . . . Several years later I met this man in London during the Queen's Jubilee. He had retired, had got religion at the Bethel Mission at Cob Dock in New York, and had married the lady missionary. Every bit of objectionable tattooing had been removed from his body, which was then covered with sacred scenes and inscriptions.

During the hot days on the *Philadelphia* in Haitian waters, the boredom of the crew reached such a stage that many men had new designs tattooed over the old ones, and fashions changed rapidly. Some of the more expert workers—notably a tall, redheaded seaman named Ellis—executed lovely effects by shading and blending colors of sea and sails and sky. I received my share of hideous pictures on my arms and legs, because it was the style to do so. Paradoxically, I would have been a marked boy if I hadn't been thus marked, for everyone did it.

I have often wished since then that someone had advised me against the savage and foolish practice, which was unhygienic and highly painful as well. It cannot be denied that there is some fascination in the custom, but because Africans skewer their nostrils with human bones is no reason why civilized people should copy them. Among our officers on the *Philadelphia* was Chaplain Parks, the first Catholic priest to become a navy chaplain. He was a fine man, but so far as I know he never lifted a hand to mitigate the dangerous possibilities of tattooing; nor did any of the other officers. The attitude of many naval officials and the sense of certain paragraphs of the Navy Regulations implied that, upon enlistment, a boy gave himself to the government body and soul. Therefore, a plain ukase from the Secretary of the Navy would have prevented the vile practice of tattooing, but such an order was never issued. It has always been a marvel to me that an epidemic of cutaneous diseases did not follow some of these orgies of tattooing, with its indiscriminate jabbing of needles into skin and blood.

Our mission at Haiti having apparently failed, we departed and on May 6 arrived at St. Thomas on the passage home. The great haste we were in may have been due to the fact that one of our officers, Lieutenant Allan G. Paul, was seriously ill. I hoped he was too ill to know that at St. Thomas we took on three hogsheads of ice for the preservation of his body in the event of his death. He died two days out, while we were driving north. His loss did not affect the fo'c'sle as the passing of one of the crew might have done; possibly we would not even have known of his death had it not been for the icing of his body on the quarter-deck. But the loss of the officer and the attempts to preserve his body brought from the old-timers many a story, weird and even horrible, of death at sea. A very old fellow claimed he had been on a ship that brought a dead admiral from Hong Kong to Boston; the body was barreled in alcohol, and some of the crew didn't draw a sober breath all the way home.

"Did you get any of that alcohol, Carrigan?"

"Gwan, ye blaggard—didn't I say he was an admiral? Sure it's me that's particular in me tastes!"

To make greater haste and forestall the melting of the ice, I was detailed with other unlucky apprentices to relieve the slaving coal-heavers at trimming the bunkers. After a day or two at that job I was ready to declare that the men of the new navy who fired the great boilers were the most important and least appreciated toilers of the lot. Sweating in the torrid bunkers, so filled with black dust that the lights overhead could hardly be seen, I learned also a great pity for the women of Jamaica or any other folk in the world who had to perform such labors. The dust was taken in with every breath; it seemed to be absorbed through every pore, and it penetrated the very soul.

During the short time that I spent on the *Philadelphia,* I heard rumors that the frigate *Lancaster* was being made ready at New York to serve as the flagship of the Asiatic Station. All this fired my ambition to return to sail. I felt that were I to be transferred back to a ship of wood and canvas, I should be released as from a prison. The sides of a steel ship sweated and felt cold at all times; and it seemed to me that the innumerable bulkheads and compartments had been planned with the idea of breaking up the crew into many parts and that this destroyed the chance of close friendships among the men. I couldn't find the reason, but it was a fact that the men were not nearly so happy as they would have been under sail. This may have been because we were not so steadily employed in useful seamanlike work, nor did our labors develop the self-assertive qualities brought out by work aloft. There was also little boat drill, for the *Philadelphia* had a steam launch, which provided no chance for heartening exercise at oars.

The *Lancaster* was said to be a beautiful ship, but it did not need a sight of her to hurry my application for transfer to her. I would have applied just as eagerly for service in any sailing ship, even the *Enterprise* with her current reputation as a "bloodship." Perhaps the destination of the *Lancaster* had more than a little to do with my desire to join her. She was going to China! We spoke of that part of

The *Lancaster*.

the world as we would of the scenes of the *Arabian Nights*. It was a navy man's playground, and no matter how often a sailor might have cruised there, he was always hopeful of going back. For a sea-loving lad it meant a year or more of leisurely sailing from port to port, from country to country, through four-sevenths of the world's oceans. It meant a wonderland where a sailor's dollar doubled in value and where any pleasure on shore could be charged to one's laundry bill. In the golden age of our navy, China was the golden paradise.

I was a happy boy when, at New York, I was given in charge of a midshipman who conducted me to the berth of the lovely frigate. She was a real ship, the *Lancaster,* with her shiny black sides reflecting the ruffled waters of her berth. Some of her spars were bright with yellow paint, while others showed their virgin pine grain under the oiled surfaces. Brightwork sparkled, and snowy white sails were furled in holiday bunts held with harbor gaskets. As we climbed over the side, the young officer remarked that he'd be willing to sail as a seaman to the Orient if he could go in that ship.

The *Lancaster* was rated as a sloop of war and was built at Philadelphia in 1857. During the Civil War she had served as flagship on the Pacific Station. She was 235 feet long and had a beam of 45 feet, but her crew numbered 333 men and boys and 36 officers. As armament she carried ten 8-inch smoothbore guns, four revolving cannon, and two 6-pounders. She had a 1,500-horsepower auxiliary engine, but sails provided her chief means of propulsion. I received a station billet assigning me as Number 313, detailed to the starboard mizzentop, to the topgallant yard in making and furling sail, and to the crosstrees when handling light yards and masts. Later, as I grew heavier, my stations aloft were shifted to lower altitudes.

On the *Philadelphia* I had met an ordinary seaman named August Biel, a tall, blond fellow who had roughed it for years in the merchant service. His stories of hardships and bucko mates had made me feel pleased that my lot had fallen among the easier ways of the navy. I now learned that he had preceded me into my new ship, and that we were to make the China cruise together. An invitation to pass my last liberty in New York in his company was eagerly welcomed.

We had no trouble securing permission to go ashore together; officers and crew seemed to be in harmony, and signs presaged a contented voyage. At the Brooklyn Bridge, a common meeting place for navy men, we were joined by my friend's father, who had also been a sailor. His experience with rigging had been utilized to build up a good business in furnishing the New York Fire Department with rope life nets, which he was also kept busy repairing. As we strolled about the city, the old man spoke in a homely and practical way of the dangers to be found in Chinese and Japanese ports. So kindly were his remarks and so effective his illustrations that I wished every one of the boys on our ship could have been there to hear him; his talk would have been of infinitely more use to them than a heap of the platitudes uttered by the average chaplain.

At midnight, tired and hungry, we stepped into a decent restaurant on Broadway for supper. The manager bowed to my companion's father, but regretfully stated that the rules did not permit him to serve any man in uniform. Mr. Biel deplored the ruling, his son swore sailor oaths, but all to no avail, and hopelessly we drifted off toward the Bowery. The incident stuck in my mind as one more offense against the dignity of the law-abiding naval men ashore; and the remembrance of it was to keep me in China and away from home for a year longer than otherwise would have been necessary.

When a man-o'-war left her home port for a cruise that would extend over a period of years, her storerooms were filled with tons of government rations: salt pork, beef, pickles, hard bread, tinned mutton, rice, coffee, flour, and sugar. Among these were no common delicacies such as tea, chocolate, fresh vegetables, or butter; and in order to add such things to our table, the crew were permitted to commute their ration into cash, with which the paymaster purchased the extra supplies. Also, every man contributed a certain amount of his pay to his mess for the purchase, while in port, of fresh meats and fish, soft bread, and vegetables. One man of the mess was designated as caterer, or "belly-robber," and was entrusted with the duty of buying for his comrades.

The caterer selected by our mess of fourteen men and boys was Peter Schwartz, an ex-apprentice and captain of my top. He was a fine confident seaman and an equally confident gallant ashore, claiming to know all the gamblers and dance-hall girls in every port. One of these brazen ladies came aboard several times to see him; and one afternoon as we were making ready to sail for the Orient, after she had affectionately taken leave of him, Schwartz said to one of his messmates:

"Gee, Jinny looks good to me! But she ought to have a nicer coat to wear."

"Why don't you buy her one?"

A curious look came over the caterer's face. "Now that you mention it, maybe I will! I have to go ashore this evening anyway to buy our sea stores. Will you let me have that five dollars of mess money?"

Dressed in his flashiest rig, wearing a prized neckerchief that I had purchased for five shillings in England, Schwartz went ashore with all our money. Not long after, he sent us a message that he was looking for a fine coat for Jinny and wasn't coming back. He was decent enough to warn us to get some sea stores or we might get hungry on the Western Ocean.

The captain permitted each of us to draw another ten dollars on our accounts, and this was hurriedly exchanged for necessary provisions and paid out on bills that Schwartz had run up on the mess. As for me, I managed to get leave to make a final trip to the city to search for the defaulter. My messmates had instructed me what to do in case I found him: I was to call a policeman and make charges against the rascal. Chiefly I wanted to get back that lost neckerchief.

From the Battery to Fourteenth Street I could find no trace of the vanished Schwartz, but at last I located Jinny in a barroom. My kerchief was sadly spotted with beer and gin. I asked her to tell me where the sailor could be found.

She blew cigarette smoke through her nose. "I haven't seen him for days," she lied, "and when I do, hell itself will look good to him! Sit down, honey, and tell Charlie to bring us some drinks!"

Discouraged, I wandered back toward the bridge. As I dropped my penny in the turnstile and started to walk across the great span, an officer in uniform jumped from a horse car and waved familiarly to me. It was gray-haired Gunner Chard, who had served with us at Newport and had later been sent with the flagship to Barbados.

"Can you come with me up to Bellevue Hospital?" he asked, after our greetings had been passed. "They've got one of our men there, and at my home in Flatbush I got a message that he wanted to see me. They may allow me to take him over to the naval hospital, and there's where I'll need your help. I'll make all the explanations for you if you are late getting to your ship—she won't leave until morning, anyway."

"Mr. Chard, I'd go a long ways to be with you, so that I might ask you some questions about a shipmate of mine, old Tom Dunn."

"Good Lord, boy," said the gunner; "why, that's the man I'm going to the hospital to see!"

Chapter XIII

OFF TO THE ORIENT

As we hurried across the deserted City Hall Park, Chard said: "Ain't you the apprentice who wrote to Tom from the training ship? I thought so! Well, you can just feel good about that, because it freshened up the old fellow and made him happy. Though, of course, he didn't lack chums in his own ship."

"He was always a good friend to me, sir, when I needed one. I heard about his trouble from Tim Walsh, a prisoner who came home on the *Portsmouth* with us. I was worried about Tom."

"You might well have worried, son, for if ever a man was unjustly hounded on a naval vessel, Tom was that man. I shouldn't say this about an officer, but God forgive me, I'm not a bit sorry for the way that young snob feels about the whole business now. Your man Walsh couldn't have heard the rest of the story—only a few of us know that.

"One day while we were down in the West Indies I heard Ensign Thompson telling some of the other youngsters about his Academy days, and about the generosity of the senator who had fathered him. 'You know,' he said, 'I assumed the senator's name. That's news to you, eh? My real father was a mustang officer; and if he hadn't been killed in a drunken brawl down in South America he'd now be ranking our admiral. His name was Winfield Scott Galvin.'

"I couldn't believe my ears. This blustering nincompoop, the son of an officer who in his day was one of the most popular men in our navy!"

Mr. Chard snorted. We climbed the stairs to the elevated platform and sat on a bench to wait for our train. It was late, the night was warm, and few people were about.

"This fellow didn't seem surprised," went on the gunner, "when I walked up to him and asked if I might speak to him in his room. With a wink at the other officers, he agreed. His roommate happened to be out, and we had the place to ourselves. He sat down, crossed his legs with a superior smile, and lit a cigarette. He's a tall fellow with olive skin and black hair, good-looking in a dissipated sort of way; but I had never liked him, and had spoken to him only when I had to. 'Well, what is it?' he said. 'Shoot!'

" 'Is it true, Mr. Thompson, that your father was Lieutenant Winfield Scott Galvin?'

" 'Sure,' he said. 'Although I guess it's nothing to shout about. You were shipmates with him in the old days?'

" 'Yes, and I'm proud of it. And I'm ashamed of you!'

"He snickered. 'Hear, hear! I never met anyone before that knew him. Pretty wild, wasn't he?'

" 'You met no one that knew your father,' I said, 'because you chose to sail under false colors. You needn't be ashamed of your right name or the man that gave it to you. Many people remember your father—our captain, for instance. And then there's Tom Dunn. You never mentioned your right name to him, did you?'

"He bristled right up. 'That fellow would be the last I'd talk to about anything! Only the other day the captain gave me merry hell about him. He's been sending his allotments to some tricky dame down south. The miserly old beachcomber will get me in bad yet—'

" 'Belay that!' I said. 'It's about that old beachcomber, as you call him, that I want to speak to you. The knife cut he carries in his shoulder he got while trying to save your father from death. It was Tom Dunn, the old miser, who has been sending money to your mother every month for more than twenty years. When he didn't contribute to your fund for boat races and theatricals, it was so he could send the money to her!'

That ensign's face was a sight to see. His cigarette dropped from his mouth and started burning a hole in the rug. 'My God,' he said, 'don't joke with me!'

" 'I wouldn't waste a joke on the likes of you, sir,' I said, and started for the door. But he grabbed me by the hands. He was frantic.

" 'Come back, Mr. Chard!' he shouted. 'Please, don't leave me now! Tell me that you're making this up—that I'm dreaming—' The change in him was really pitiful.

" 'Oh, damn you,' I said. 'It's up to you now to do what you can to square yards with the captain and—Tom Dunn. Beachcomber, I think you called him!'

" 'I will, I will,' he cried. The color had begun to come back to his face, and there was a look in his eyes and something about the quirk of his lip that for the first time reminded me of his father."

Our train thundered into the station. When we were settled in an empty car, the warrant officer went on.

"My boy, that was one of the most miserable half hours I ever passed. As he came to realize the whole thing, that young officer—he is still really little more than a lad—began sweating blood. The humiliation must have been misery for him, but it was good for his soul. His first thought was that at least he could make up the money part; but I told him that I was much mistaken if Tom Dunn was the kind of benefactor to accept the return of a cent. He was sobbing on his bed blanket before we were through. 'This will mean the end of the navy for me, Mr. Chard,' he said. 'I could never face the officers here, or on any other ship. To owe my education to that old man's sacrifice! Really, sir, without that money he sent us I could never have gone through the Academy. Why didn't I get some hint of this before I started nagging the poor fellow? I admit it; I didn't like him, and I don't know why.

He struck me as so old-fashioned, and yet he knew so much more aloft than I did. I'd order him to do something and he'd do it, leaving me with a feeling that I had been challenged and beaten. But now I don't matter—it's him that matters, and I'll do anything I can to show him how I feel.'

"Well, I didn't want to be hard on him. 'Let's leave it to the captain,' I said. 'So far as I'm concerned, there's no need to tell a soul about this but Tom himself.'

"With that, we went to the skipper. Pretty soon there was the usual hail, passed from deck to deck. 'D'ye hear there? Thomas Dunn to report to the commanding officer in his cabin!' The whole world knew that Tom was up for something again. He was working on a sword mat for the main rigging, and as he gloomily went aft, his shipmates passed him such remarks as: 'It's that snotty Thompson again, Tom. Just saw him going into the cabin. He'll get you yet!' 'Don't talk back to him, old man. You can do the rest of your time standing on your head, and then tell them to go to hell!'

"As Tom entered the cabin, the captain astonished him by pulling out a chair and telling him to sit down. Then the captain motioned the marine orderly to leave, and the four of us were alone. Tom stared at Ensign Thompson, wondering what new persecution might be in the offing. He was still more disturbed when the captain spoke to him with a smile on his face. The skipper is usually pretty cold and official.

" 'Dunn,' he said, 'some strange news has come to me today. Mr. Chard here tells me that your officer friend down in South America more than twenty years ago was Lieutenant Galvin?'

" 'Yes, sir.' Tom looked at me reproachfully, but I shook my head.

" 'In that case, I want particularly to commend you on the fine thing you did for his family. I wish I had earlier known all the facts I know now—' But Thompson, all nervous and white-faced, jumped up and said:

" 'Captain, will you please permit me to tell Dunn the rest of it?' He walked over to the old seaman and faced him. 'Dunn, I want you to forgive me if you can. I would like you to forget the past, and to call me your friend from now on.' He held out his hand, and the two stood there for a moment with hands clasped. Then he went on: 'Because Lieutenant Galvin, your good friend, was my father.'

"That knocked Tom over as nothing else could have done. He let the officer's hand drop and repeated in a whisper: 'Your father! Never!'

" 'Yes, Dunn,' put in the captain. 'His father. It was Mr. Thompson's mother you've been sending money to all these years.'

"The ensign tried to smile. 'And I'll never forget it. I'll pay back to you every penny it cost you to help me to become an officer.'

"Tom repeated: 'To help you become an officer!' After a moment he said: 'No one would expect any payment for that!' A narrow look had come into his eyes. But the ensign did not notice how chilly was that reply.

" 'Yes, I know that. But when you retire, perhaps. Mr. Chard, you'll convince him, won't you, and allow me through you to make allotments to him as he made them to us?'

"Tom just stood there in a daze. His eyes wandered from the captain to me, and then fastened on the young officer. 'No, sir, I shall never take a cent from you, sir.' He turned to the captain again, and saluted. 'Is that all, sir?'

" 'I'm sorry you take it so hard, Dunn. Yes, that is all—except that I'm going to leave it to you whether or not this affair need be made public.'

"Tom roughed up, and said in anger at the door: 'Please don't think for a moment, sir, that I'd ever want any of my shipmates to know about this!' He threw a pitying look at Thompson and was gone. The captain looked surprised and hurt. He didn't understand the meaning of that answer. But I did."

The train came to a stop at our station, and we hurried out on the platform. "But what about Tom?" I asked. "Did he finally forgive the ensign?"

"He should have, boy. That young fellow has become a different man. He's made a lot of good friends since then, forward and aft.

Most everybody on the ship is proud of him. But Tom was too broken up to notice the change. So many years of sacrifice, and then— Well, nobody knows but Tom himself what it meant. He went ashore that same night, and somehow his old weakness took hold of him. He cracked all to pieces with the drink. The captain restricted him for his own good, but last night he jumped the yard wall, and now this call from the hospital is the first we've heard of him since. The captain asked me to get him under care in our own hospital as soon as possible. Tom is too old a man to be able to stand much of that sort of life. Well, this is the place. You'll see your friend mighty soon now."

Up the steps of the great hospital we walked, emerging in a brilliantly glaring hall, where nurses in white smiled at my companion wearing the broken gold stripe of a warrant officer, while others looked askance at my own plain uniform. The girl at the desk summoned a young interne, and Mr. Chard made known his errand.

The medical man dropped his eyes. "I know the poor old fellow you mean. He wouldn't say anything to a soul after he sent that message to you. He left no word for anybody."

"But—you mean he's—"

"I'm sorry, but it's true. He passed away just a few moments after we sent for you."

We were stunned. Neither of us had suspected that we might be hastening to find a dead man. Woodenly we followed the doctor to where a shrunken old figure lay stretched on a marble slab. Tom Dunn's face looked peaceful, as if he had forgiven all trespasses against him and was now himself forgiven. It was comforting for us to remember that we had been privileged to know Tom Dunn and to have lived at his side.

Gray-haired Gunner Chard fumbled in his wallet, and drew out the medal of honor that had been bestowed upon him by Congress years before as a mark of conspicuous bravery. With a shaking hand he laid it on the knot of the dead man's neckerchief.

"Tom Dunn," he said, "we are proud to have served with you, and we say: 'Here lies a shipmate!' "

The *Lancaster* shifted down to Fort Wadsworth in the lower bay on July 10, and three irksome days were spent loading ammunition. Eleven hundred 8-inch shells of various types, with their powder charges, were taken on for the main battery. During those days we ate all our meals cold, and it was a court-martial offense to be caught smoking. All of us were anxious to get to sea.

On the thirteenth—a bad day, in the minds of superstitious sailors, to start a voyage—everything was ready. The officers who had remained in the city during the loading of powder were back on board. The launches and cutters were hoisted, the accommodation ladders pulled in, and the last of the sea stores heaped in the gangways. On the quarter-deck the navigator and his gang were soaking the log line and checking the marks for the run of more than ten thousand miles. At our mizzen truck flew the white-starred blue flag of Rear Admiral David B. Harmony, who occupied the luxurious port cabins with his retinue of servants. He had his own staff of officers, a band, a coxswain, and even a printer, whose press was bolted on the starboard side of the half deck. Each man who "belonged to the admiral" assumed an air appropriate to such an exalted position, and expected to be treated with more deference than his rating actually deserved.

The cables came in, the auxiliary engine turned over, and the *Lancaster* plowed through the Narrows. Behind us loomed through the haze the Statue of Liberty, bidding us farewell—for how long? Some of us would never see America again.

We steamed for the first forty-eight hours, drawing heavily on our scanty supply of coal. Quickly the crew straightened out and lost their land kinks; men got acquainted with other men who must work side by side with them for thousands of sea miles. It was good to be afloat again. The smell of the ocean, of steaming coffee, of tarry ropes—these were incense to us, and the familiar sounds of sucking pumps during the dogwatch, the rattle and bang of dropping mess tables, and the wrangling of top captains were like music to our ears. We of the deck and the tops lived in a little world of our own, and aloft we could discuss our new officers to our hearts' content and look down with pitying contempt on the unfortunate worms destined to remain under the watchful eyes of their superiors on the decks below.

Out of the northwest came a welcome wind, and the trill of the boatswain't pipe stung the watch to action. "Lay aloft topgallant and royal yardmen!" Boys and men jostled for the sheer pole, scrambled up the converging shrouds, and, panting, hauled themselves through the lubber's hole. "Aloft, topsail yardmen!" The topsail men followed, and the straining rat-lines vibrated with the shock of a hundred active men. "Loose sail!" "Man the topsail sheets and halyards! Stand by! Let fall!" "Sheet home! Lay down from aloft!"

Then: "Hands lower the smokestack!" The blackened stack was telescoped into position below the deck. We had shaken off the domination of steam and had spread our snowy wings at last. Back on the heaving deck, helping to straighten out the gear, I gloried in the feeling of being once more under sail, feeling the draft of the great main course and hearing the creak of sheaves and blocks. "Watch on deck—coil up your gear! Pipe down!"

In the second dogwatch all hands stood at the nettings, heard the white-faced chaplain read from the Book of Psalms, repeated the Lord's Prayer, and then by numbers each man of the watch received his hammock. He went below to sling it on the hooks and immediately returned to the deck to relieve the other watch, so that no station was left unguarded at any time.

The night came down swiftly, bringing rain. The fore- and mainsails gustily filled and alternately collapsed with cannon roars; the headsails fluttered uncertainly, while the deck force stood on their toes, expectant and ready. Far out beyond our screaming eagle figurehead and the plunging battle ram, high above the white-maned waves racing with the ship, the fo'c'slemen were fisting the jib; others, helped by the foretopmen, were bending on a foretopmast staysail. Aft, worried officers, with gold-striped coats pulled on over sleeping clothes, paced the deck. They were dubious about the new men of the crew but had no fear of the old ship, for she was doing her best and everyone was proud of the the way she leaped through the night like a living creature.

Even idlers who might have been snug in their hammocks came up to feel the world's commotion. We backed them into the dry shelter of the hatch hoods, making them keep clear. Go below, you soldiers—this is a time for seamen! Pull, boys, just one more swig at that forebrace! Aye, now, belay that!

The day dawned clear and sunny, with a fine drying wind off the starboard quarter and the tacks close aboard. Now the real beauty and power of the ship was revealed as she fulfilled the driving uses for which she had been built. She was sturdy and solid in her lines, as a frigate should be. Because of her engines she was not as lofty as older ships of her tonnage, but she was well proportioned nonetheless. Now, at the outset of the voyage, she was bright as oil and paint and polish could make her. On the lower and spar decks, the waterways and hatch coamings were painted a spar color; all other woodwork, except the decks, ladders, and gratings, was pure white. The masts were spar color to lower caps, as were the yards and other spars; the upper masts were shellacked natural wood, and the truck funnels were black. Outside, the vessel was black and even at sea was kept shiny with oiled rubbing rags. The visible copper of the hull shone from burnishings with sand and canvas; the boot-topping at waterline was red; and from bow to stern ran a bold stripe of white in line with the chains. No men ever built a better ship than the U.S.S. *Lancaster.*

Life aboard, during the first leg of the cruise to China by way of the Cape of Good Hope, was not onerous, except for the hunger of our mess, shorn of its stores by the absconding Schwartz. Could epithets break bones, our erstwhile caterer would have had his troubles wherever he was. We had to depend for bread and vegetables upon the generosity of some of the other messes. Fortunately, I had discovered on my first day aboard that the captain's steward was none other than John R. Bell, the little colored man who had greeted me on my first day in the *St. Louis.* He was genial as ever, and I don't know what our mess would have done without Bell and the food he provided us during the time of need.

Every morning at sea we had gun or other drills, and in the first dogwatch the entire ship's company exercised with sails or spars, so that we would be a highly efficient crew of seamen when we arrived at the Asiatic Station. At times the navigator's division took charge of the ship as if she were going into battle, while all the other officers and men marched in double column about the spar deck and performed every military evolution possible in that limited space. Headed by a sixteen-piece band, followed by our buglers and drummers, the men of the hospital and pioneer corps, the marines, and three companies of infantry and artillery, every man trying to keep his place in line while the deck swayed and pitched, we must have been a stirring sight when one day we passed close to a clipper ship that was heading for home.

Once a week, in clear weather, all our bedding was triced up in the rigging,and then the ship looked as nearly like a washer-woman's back yard as a fine ship could look. The airing could not be done, of course, at times when a sudden change of weather threatened. I sometimes wondered what might happen to any unlucky fellow who tumbled overboard when every part of the rigging and decks was covered with open hammocks, mattresses, and blankets.

Whenever we met a bit of nasty weather, or ran into head winds, in would come our square sails, up would go the smokestack, and under steam and steadied by trysails and spanker the vessel would plug along at about five knots. The use of auxiliary power made the duties of the deck force somewhat easier, although there always seemed to be some task to keep us on the jump.

I had long ago given up hope of hearing chanties sung to speed the work of a man-o'-war. This tradition of the sea, so dear to the thoughts of landsmen, may have had its place in the merchant service of my time, but never did I hear the voices of naval men raised in raucous salty lays. We pulled at cables for hours, ranged tiers of chains along the decks, sweated at braces, without benefit of a cheering song; we slaved aloft on many a cold night, but all in absolute silence except for occasional harsh taunts from the captain of the top or curses from the mastmen below. When we manned the capstan bars we heard an occasional "Heave and pawl, boys, heave and pawl!" but never a word of "Stormalong" or "Reuben Ranzo." The power of song that we lacked we made up in numbers and massed strength. Our chanties were the whistle of wind in the rigging and the sigh of wheel ropes, the creak of timbers and the piping of mess gear. Nor did we ever hear the poetic word "larboard," except sometimes during a dogwatch when the darkies let it slip into one of their crooning songs. The word was officially banished from our navy in 1846.

We sighted the heights of Madeira on August 10, 1891, and under steam and sail rapidly approached the island. In darkness we crept in, and a little after midnight dropped anchor in the harbor of Funchal. The morning light touching the vineyards on the high mountains, and the shallow triple-keeled surfboats that came out to us, recalled the place to my mind with a sudden feeling of familiarity.

Not yet, however, could we revel in the delights of shore. Stages and bosun's chairs were whipped over the sides, and from these precarious perches the seamen covered every inch of the outer hull with rags dipped in thin oil paint and rubbed the copper boot-topping with sand. The next thing was to scrape the spars, blacken the rigging, and set it taut. Men were then detailed to break out the ridgeropes and awning stanchions from the hold, and the awnings from the sail lockers. Before noon the ship was a flash frigate again, in harbor trim with a stay-awhile look. Then the boatswain was pulled ahead of the ship in the dinghy, from which he bawled instructions for squaring the yards with the precision of perfect seamanship, his critical eye and shrill piping keeping us pulling at braces and topping lifts for the better part of an hour. Satisfied, he reported to the first luff, and together they circled about the ship in a whaleboat. After they returned from that inspection and no complaint was made, it was a certainty that there was not a blemish on the sides of the *Lancaster*, that the sails and yards were squared and trim to an inch, and that there wasn't a fag end of shameful Irish pennant dangling anywhere.

We could go ashore.

Chapter XIV

THE LINE AND THE CAPE

At Funchal our chaplain was relieved of duty and sent home, where he no doubt retired on a comfortable salary. He was an anaemic consumptive whose proper place was anywhere except among the rough-living officers and men of a sailing vessel. He had been seasick all the way, and to see him standing on the pitching quarter-deck in full view of all hands, forcing his devitalized body to earn his pay, was agonizing. He was not missed from among us, for during his month aboard the *Lancaster* he had never, so far as I knew, spoken a single word to one of the enlisted men of the crew.

His pay was ten dollars a day, which was about as much as any of the younger apprentices received in a month. Many a boy was heard to remark that he would cheerfully read the Psalms every evening and perform the other duties of Holy Joe merely for the privilege of "sleeping in" once in a while until six bells. Some of those boys, as a matter of truth, could have done as much good as ever our chaplain did. It seemed to me then, as it does now, that when the real purpose of a chaplain on a man-o'-war is squarely considered, any man who made the effort to claim his shipmates' respect and affection could have worked as much real good as a dozen gold-braided sky pilots to whom a quarter-deck face came naturally. A simple man of God who could help the members of the crew to write letters home, to console them in sorrow or adversity, to represent them at "the mast" in an understanding way, to guide them on shore to places that were good and ways that were decent, to take charge of the sports, and to be accessible at all times to the humble Jack in trouble—that was the kind of naval chaplain that we might have had. Instead, too often we found an imperious officer flaunting his presidential appointment, jealous of his seniority "numbers," and even further apart from sympathy with the crew than any of the other officers.

On Sunday mornings, after quarters, church was rigged on the *Lancaster*, and the call was sounded: "All apprentices attend divine service!" Everyone was expected to attend, of course, but for the apprentices there was no choice. After we left Madeira our commanding officer took over the sermonizing. He was one of those captains who would give you the limit of punishment with an air of paternal sorrow, and many a resentful boy's faith in Christianity was weakened by hearing his lord and master preach forbearance and kindliness on Sundays.

It was good policy for the officers to be seen at services, for the captain liked to talk to his men through the officers; he did not have to unbend so much, and dignity was not strained. The advice he gave was good, if trite, when he kept within the limits of ship life. His topics were cleanliness, patriotism, the evils of theft and slackness in duty; he rarely ventured to talk of the higher aspects of religion, and when he did he sounded affected and hypocritical. I wished often that he would surrender his pulpit to his little steward Bell, or to someone of the stamp of my shipmate Biel's father. And there was a lowly sailor buried in a Brooklyn cemetery to whose advice I would have eagerly listened had he been spared to offer it. I yearned many a time to break away from tiresome prayers and to be free to loaf on deck with my mates, to write in my log, or to paint water-color pictures of every ship we sighted—pictures lacking in any hint of perspective, but having the sailorly merit of showing in clear detail the run of every single shroud, stay, or shred of gear.

In Funchal Harbor, customs officers in boats had closely watched our ship, intent on permitting no tobacco or other contraband to reach shore without duty being paid. For all their watching, these men did not prevent two Portuguese stowaways from getting aboard; and shortly after leaving the port on August 22, these ragged and dirty wretches were found on the berth deck. They were clothed and put to work helping the cooks, and soon made themselves quite at home in the ship.

We beat southward with variable and shifty winds until the first of September, and then proceeded under steam for fully a week until we met the northeast trades. Thereafter we enjoyed fine weather for many days of southward sailing.

As we approached the Line, old-timers of the crew could be seen busily preparing costumes of dried seaweed and spun yarn, and whispering together in anticipation of initiating the rest of us into the realm of Father Neptune. In accordance with age-old tradition, on the day we crossed the Equator the ship would be turned over to the men and a heavy-handed ceremony would be performed on the neophytes. The shellbacks made a thorough search of the ship's record to get a correct list of men and officers who had never before crossed Latitude Zero.

The navigator on September 10 posted the ship's noon position as 0° 36′ N. That evening we lay almost on the great imaginary circle belting the earth. The crew stood at its stations waiting for their hammocks, and the captain had finished reading the Lord's Prayer. The ship lazily swayed her three flaring masts, and a booby bird circled the trucks and alighted on the starboard foretopgallant yardarm, disturbing a sleepy lookout. In the soft hush of equatorial twilight, from over the bows came a hail:

"Ship ahoy!"

The executive officer, Mr. Gilmore, answered through his trumpet: "U.S. Flagship *Lancaster!*"

"Where are ye bound?"

"Asiatic Station. Who hails?"

"Neptune, sir; he and his minions are coming aboard."

The officers smiled; the captain nodded, and Mr. Gilmore gave the order: "Bandsmen, go below and get your instruments. Bear a hand!" Nearly every bandsman was expecting the next day to undergo operations at the hands of the boarding party, but they came back to the deck quickly enough.

Now came across the headrails a spectacular train of performers. Foremost among them was Neptune, whom we could recognize as the coxswain of the gig, a short, squat personage dressed in a robe of canvas festooned with seaweed. Under his arm he carried a huge conch shell and in the other hand a neatly made trident of iron. The band struck up "Hail to the Chief."

With great dignity the buffoons marched aft, while we tried to guess the identities of the ringleaders. Neptune's consort, Amphitrite, with a crown of spun yarn and Manila, wore a long dress covered with barnacles and crab shells; it was hard to believe that she was one of the oldest quarter gunners, who had sacrificed his treasured mustache for the occasion. Then came Dr. Dippy, armed with his syringe; the secretary, with his logbook under his arm; the judge, the lord chamberlain, the barber with a large and wicked-looking razor, and a sextette of shaggy black bears, bodies covered with thrum mats and each carrying a huge stuffed club. Last of all, as if he had run hard to catch up with the procession, came Davy Jones, in the queerest rig of all. He was nearly naked, except for a skirt of seaweed and rope yarn, wild hair and whiskers, and a smile painted across his face.

Reaching the quarter-deck, Neptune addressed himself to the officers there assembled, headed by the admiral. To admiral and captain he spouted a few lines of doggerel, paid his respects to the other officers in another verse, and ended with the words:

"Now on the morrow I will return—
Though it blows a gale you can't leave me astern.

I know that tonight you'll be crossing the Line,
So be ready to meet me at the hour of nine.
I wish you good night, with a blessing from me,
For I and my wife must return to the sea."

The bears danced about, brandishing their clubs at those of us who would soon fall into their clutches, and thumped on the decks as they sang an improvised ditty to a Gilbert and Sullivan tune. As they ended, Neptune's secretary handed the executive officer a separate subpoena for each man and boy to be initiated in the morning. Then His Majesty, followed by all his retinue, marched forward and disappeared over the bows one by one as they had come, while the band played "A Life on the Ocean Wave." That night, sometime in the midwatch, our ship took us with a mighty roll across the Equator.

At nine o'clock in the sunny morning came another hail from Neptune, the ship was hove to, and our visitors again came over the bows, the bears licking their chops in eagerness for the rough fun to begin. The king and his wife were hauled aft on a decorated gun carriage. The clever acting of the troupe was impressive, especially that of the man so fittingly selected to play the part of Neptune. His name was Gamaliel Talleyrand, and his father was a minister in Vermont. He himself was about five feet tall, with chestnut hair going gray, and silky sideburns down his jaws. The rest of his face was seamed with a thousand tiny wrinkles. He was a splendid seaman and in his youth had fished off the Banks. He played several musical instruments, and like so many of the men of the older navy he had read well in good books, and aptly quoted the Bible and the poets on occasion.

This man took his seat, on a dais erected on the bridge, with all the suavity and high decorum of a real emperor. Before him, from the bridge to the mainmast, a spare topsail had been stretched, filled with sea water to a depth of some three feet. About him were grouped the people of his court, and as the secretary called out one after another the names of the men to be initiated, the victims, escorted by bears, appeared to answer the dread summons, from which there was no appeal. Each trembling neophyte took a seat on a swivel chair, was bombarded with questions, and when he opened his mouth to answer, a bitter pill was inserted and a paintbrush lathered with soap, tar, and slush was wiped across his face. Then the barber began shaving with gusto. The barber was a berth-deck cook, a huge Hollander named Jurgenson, clothed in a long gown splotched with red paint; and bloodthirstily he plied his big hoop-iron razor across many a tender face, until he sometimes brought blood and at last had to be admonished by the ship's surgeon. He was a quarrelsome man and used this chance to repay many a grudge. Newly shaved men prayed for an opportunity to be revenged on him.

When the barber had finished his ministrations, the hapless initiate was given a shove backward into the tank, where he was mauled by the bears until they were satisfied that he had enough. My friend Biel happened to be one of the bears, and when I came up, quite sick from the nauseating mess I had swallowed, and half-drowned as well, he grabbed me, handled me with pretended roughness, and hauled me out on the deck and into the enviable position of holding a certificate to announce to the world that I had crossed the Line and thenceforth would be granted the freedom of Neptune's kingdom.

Great pains had been taken to get an accurate list of those to be initiated; but, as was to be expected, there were several recalcitrants who would have evaded the ordeal if they could. Foremost among these was Moynahan, a ship's corporal. He was a rowdy from New York's East Side, a handy man with his fists and reputed to be a deserter from an earlier enlistment in the navy. He had loudly claimed to have crossed the Equator on another ship, but his papers failed to prove it; if he had been initiated under a different name, he could only substantiate this by showing himself to be a deserter.

When his name was called and Moynahan did not appear on deck, the bears went off in great glee to summon him; but they could not get at him. The corporal had gone to the brig, and with a pair of hand-irons snapped through the staples of the door had barred himself within. Grinning, he defied them. "I threw the key out the porthole," he declared. "If you don't believe me, there's the open port to prove it!"

When this action was reported to Neptune, His Majesty addressed himself to Captain Seeley:

"Captain, as one who has done me the honor to be baptized by me in days gone by, will you grant me a favor before I return to my home in the deep?"

"Certainly, Your Highness," replied the officer grudgingly, with a glance at the genial admiral beside him, whose condescension alone had allowed the celebration to advance thus far.

"Then, sir, permit my lord chamberlain to put another handiron on the door of your brig."

"Your wish is granted; but in order to log such confinement properly, what number of days do you specify?"

"Till the end of the present cruise!" Amphitrite put her forefinger on her lips and simpered. But Neptune interposed:

"Be your sweet self, girl. Five days, captain, thank you, and—"

"Yes, Your majesty?"

"Please, will you make it bread and water?"

"Bread and water it shall be, my man!" shouted the admiral. "No fellow, by Jove, has a right to take exception to the amusing ceremonies you have so handily conducted. Five days' solitary confinement, bread and water, for disobedience of orders."

There was much quarter-deck laughter, and all hands forward joined in merriment at hearing how Moynahan had got his just deserts. Then the officers, who by paying tribute in liquor and cigars could escape manhandling in chair and tub, took the performers below, where many a toast was drunk in wardroom beer.

At last Neptune and his men lined up at the mast to say their farewells. "Sir," said the monarch, "I beg to report the completion of my duties, and I return the ship to its former authorities."

The executive officer returned his salute. "Talleyrand," he said, "the officers and crew are indebted to you for a most pleasant day. But before you go below, there is one more task to perform. We have a man on board who claims he crossed the Line five years ago on the U.S.S. *Ossipee.* But after investigation the commanding officer has discovered that this man was in a naval prison at that time." He turned and pointed a finger at Jurgenson, the demon barber. "Have you ever crossed the Equator before?"

The Dutchman smirked uneasily. "Yaas, sir, I was on merchant ship." We knew he lied, for he was no seaman.

"Have you papers to prove that?"

"No, sir, but—"

"No exceptions have been made today. Call all hands to witness punishment, boatswain. I hope, Talleyrand, that you will order a good shave for Mr. Barber!"

Thus was justice done, and the harsh Jurgenson hoist on his own petard. After this last initiation, we were once again a well-regulated naval vessel, and the enlisted man's brief day was over. But down on the berth deck, in the stuffy brig, a ship's corporal clamored for release from confinement. For him the joke had been carried far enough. He demanded to be taken to "the mast" for a hearing, he threatened to write to the Navy Department; but all clamor fell on deaf ears, and when he was told that the admiral himself had ordered his punishment, he had to admit defeat. On the fifth day of his incarceration, he found the key to his cell attached to the hand-irons with a canvas tag on which was written in red ink: "He laughs best who laughs last. Better luck next time!—*Neptunus Rex.*"

Moynahan was thus freed, but he did not forget. And so flared a feud between the corporal and the coxswain which had had its beginnings long before. Fortunately their duties kept them several decks apart; but all of us knew that the time would come when the enmity of the two would have to be resolved by nothing short of blows.

Soon after we had begun to mark our position in south latitude, a Norwegian seaman named Frederickson balanced his six-feet-four of bone and brawn on the slender backropes under the bowsprit and landed a harpoon so adroitly in the back of a porpoise that we had to believe him when he said he had spent many years on a whaler. The fish was fully eight feet long and weighed more than four hundred pounds. The head resembled that of a pig, and so did the flesh. The admiral and captain selected choice steaks, and then, like prize money in wartime, the catch passed from wardroom to steerage, to warrant officers and chief petty officers, and what was left came to us. The meat was a welcome addition to our messes.

On September 23, well below the Equator, we were becalmed and took the opportunity to hold the prescribed quarterly target practice. For many hours we steamed in a circle around the target—a sail raised on a floating cask—and finally demolished it with some well-placed shots from the Hotchkiss 6-pounders. For the greater part of the day we were close to a majestic clipper ship, her slatting canvas spread to royals and skysails, staysails and drivers, all set to catch the first puff of breeze. She was, like us, China-bound.

In these latitudes the weather grew colder every day, and our peacoats and oilskins were carefully overhauled. All the day we were accompanied by flocks of Cape pigeons, man-o'-war birds, and albatrosses, some of these last weighing thirty or more pounds and having a wingspread of fifteen feet. There were also large flights of stormy petrels, or Mother Carey's chickens. Some of these were caught with hook and line, much against the advice of head-shaking superstitious older men. That night it blew a gale, and we reefed topsails to the tune of "Boys, I told you so!" All our toil aloft was blamed on the scamps who had caught the birds.

You know, every old sailor that dies at sea, mark you," said old "Sinner" Flukes, a veteran of the merchant service, "comes to be a white gull or an albatross, depending on where he went over the side. Wicked souls turn to dark birds."

"That means only the old fellows?" I asked.

"Yes; the kids and apprentices, they come to be Mother Carey's chickens."

"But all those birds are kind of dark, aren't they?"

"Sure. That's the law and justice. But after a while any sailor, no matter how bad he was, gets to heaven. I don't believe in any Fiddler's Green or the like. That idee may be all right, of course, for them that can't rid themselves of sooperstition."

Evidently we were not in for a prolonged spell of bad weather, seafowl or none, for on the following day we were bowling along again under full sail, with the mizzen topmast staysail extended out to port in the shape of a stuns'l. Even then our hurrying ship could not outdistance the credulity of sailor minds. As we drove farther toward the Cape of Good Hope, the old story of the Flying Dutchman was revived:

> "Sailing always without gain,
> Leagues on leagues as sailors reckon
> Flies the undying Vanderdecken."

Whenever a southern fog enveloped us, we stared into its shadows, seeking in vain the mysterious phantom ship of legend.

As we approached the Cape, the gambling instinct which, along with superstition, has always had a prominent part in sailorly character, was sharpened by the formation of various betting pools based on the time at which we would drop anchor off Cape Town. Each pool consisted of twenty-four men who were awarded by lot a number indicating one hour of the day or night. Bets could also be made on whether the starboard or port anchor would be the first one dropped. This was an equal gamble, because no one could foresee which anchor would be needed, depending upon wind, weather, current, or the whim of captain or pilot, who of course were not in our confidence.

The approach of payday likewise whetted the appetite for gambling. This was strictly forbidden to the men; but since the officers themselves spent most of their waking hours off watch at playing cards, little effort was made to detect similar recreations forward. It was up to the master-at-arms to prevent it if he could, but as the Jimmylegs was reputed to be the owner of a gambling house at Norfolk, there was little to fear from his vigilance. Games might be carried on anywhere in the ship and even up in the tops, but the berth deck, the boiler room, and the coal bunkers were the chief places of resort. Between four and eight bells in the evening, the regulars grouped themselves about their recognized bankers at Honest John, Big Six, Stud Horse, and roulette. Lookouts were stationed at each of the hatches and all other entrances to the berth deck. If one of these signaled the approach of an officer or one of the ship's police, all illicit pastimes ceased and the evidence was covered with deucy-acey boards, checkers, or games of casino. One ingenious gambler's spy used to run a sewing machine industriously, stitching endless rows on scraps of cloth and halting only when danger was near—a hint which the gamblers took at once. Some of the men who had worked hard to make extra money doing the tasks of others would quickly lose all their earnings in a few days of the gambling frenzy. By the middle of the month, most of the spare cash of the ship's company would have found its way into the monk-bags of the lucky and professional few.

We had now been sailing five weeks from Madeira without sighting land, or any vessels except two sailing ships. On October 2 we resorted to the use of our engine, and a week later we made our landfall and came to anchor in the port of Cape Town, South Africa. On the log the distance from our point of departure was entered as 6,666.6 miles. The decimal, I think, was the result of some turnings suggested by the pilot to make the series of sixes complete. We had been forty-one days at sea, without fresh food during nearly all that time.

Next morning we were about to get up anchor in order to warp in to the dock when one of the sudden gales peculiar to this port swept down from the mountains to the southward, forcing us to drop both our hooks again, and the cables became fouled. After much hard work by the fo'c'slemen our hawse was finally cleared, and we were moored with our stern to the dock, with nothing between us and a new continent but a narrow gangplank and an easily acquired liberty pass.

Among the first to be sent ashore were the two boy stowaways from Madeira; but one of them returned, and was formally enlisted as a landsman. This was nothing unusual in the days when half an American warship's muster might be of alien birth; today, that same man could be made a part of our navy by nothing less than a special Act of Congress. At Cape Town a number of the crew deserted; it seemed that they considered the discipline of the *Lancaster* to be too strict for them and the drill too frequent. The vacancies were quickly filled by foreigners who were attracted by the beauty of our ship, and who rightly supposed that, with such a large crew as we had, the work would not be hard.

The town gave us a genial reception, for the place was filled with British sailors and soldiers, and the kindness of the civilians to their own men was extended to us. We were invited to their games and sports, welcomed at the theaters and the best eating houses, and received into their many barracks and even in some homes. Visitors came aboard the American ship, to tour the clean decks and to ask many a question about our navy and "the States."

One such conversation led to an invitation from a lady and gentleman for me to visit their farm near Johannesburg. On my arrival there I found that the "farm" was a large fine estate, where I was introduced to the sons and daughters and urged to spend the night. Next day, returning by rail to Cape Town, I was overhauled by a shipmate who dragged me to a near-by tavern; to refuse would have been considered an insult. Here we found a group of our lads in befuddled gaiety, alternately hugging and threatening a band of British tars. Interminable stanzas of "God Save the Queen" were howled out, and at last one of the Englishmen asked us to sing "The Star-Spangled Banner." We were fairly graveled, for not one of us knew the words; but the Britishers obligingly sang it for us.

Everything was brotherly as could be until a Russian barged in and howled for brandy. A limey told him to drink ale as his betters did. He refused. A mug was forced to his lips, but our roaring Karl Witt pushed it aside.

The Englishman looked surprised. "Strike me top light, Yankee, this bloomin' foreigner's got to drink our ale!"

"I'll strike you for fair!" howled Karl. "It's a free country, ain't it?" He sank a blow on the other man's teeth, and immediately was floored by a heavy glass thrown at his forehead. Gorman, captain of our maintop, tackled the thrower, and in a moment half a dozen men were mixing it on the floor, and the air was full of swinging chairs.

The barmaids ran screaming into the street shouting for the police, who came quickly, batting skulls right and left. In a trice the fighters were taken into custody. As they climbed the granite stairs on their way to the jail, grinning with delight at having released the violent feelings pent up during many weeks at sea, Karl Witt with his neckerchief tied about his head marched along with his arm around the Russian's neck. Gorman came behind, with cheek cut and dragging one leg, but helping to carry an unconscious Englishman.

"God save the Queen!" he cried. "For fighting or fun, none can touch our Bluttish brid brothers of the sea!"

Chapter XV

CHINA COAST

We dropped our moorings at Cape Town late in October. As we sailed out, a quick southeaster sprang up, mantling with white folds of clouds the flat top of Table Mountain, draping it in a tablecloth of mist. That was our farewell to the lovely African city. Now we resigned ourselves to the long passage east and north through the Indian Ocean.

One of our few diversions was listening to the band. Each evening, weather permitting, they assembled with stringed instruments about the wardroom hatch on the gun deck. Every man of them was by now known to all the crew, and his musical merits or failings were fully discussed fore and aft. They were improving with daily practice during times when we had gun or other ship drills (at sail drill, bandsmen and marines were called to the ropes alongside the deck force). From their positions around the hatch, the musicians during their performance could not fail to see, below, the officers seated at their long and well-filled table, being served by white-clad Chinese messmen with bottles of wine and beer. Thoughtlessly I once asked the bandmaster why he always called for stringed instruments in the evening. He answered that when his men, after a meal of cracker hash, had to stand for hours gazing with watering mouths at the vivacious scenes of festivity below, to try and play wind instruments was out of the question!

Most nights the weather did not allow such gaiety on the decks. We had made little northing before we entered a zone of bad storms. There was much hail and snow, and usually fog as well. It was not unusual for us to turn in at eight bells of a night of pale darkness with light sails drawing nicely, only to be hauled out half-asleep after two hours by a clamor of pipes, bugles, and drums, and stagger forth to be drenched with scud and hail and labor ankle-deep in the flow from the waterways. Then it was "Man the t'gallant and royal clewlines!" "Let go your sheets; clew up!" "Lay aloft and furl t'ga'nts'ls and royals!" Up into black pandemonium we would crawl, and out on the yardarms, sometimes before the braces had been belayed—a breach of orders as well as a foolhardy act. Then, at the word "Reef courses!" we would lay down to assist the fo'c'slemen, carpenter's mates, quarter gunners, and many another idler stretched out on the great lower yards to stow for dear life, while the ship rolled us almost down to the leaping crests of ocean.

So far on our voyage we had not lost a man, and old-timers knocked on wood in the hope that this luck would continue. But one morning in the Indian Ocean, running before a steady breeze with the sea moderate, the sky filled with wondrous color, and a flood of sunshine drying the decks after a field day of scrubbing, the ominous call rang through the ship: "Man overboard!"

Walker, one of the apprentices detailed as striker to a "quarter-growler," had fallen out of his port while trying to remove the tompion from a gun. He was seen to sink, and had not reappeared.

It is almost incredible to conceive how a ship of more than two thousand tons, forced along at ten knots by three towering peaks of canvas, could be halted in her progress so quickly as to seem as if she were turning on her heel and bringing up instantly at a standstill. To do this, every man of the crew had to act handily at his particular post. Our light sails were swiftly clewed up and halyards were let go by the run. Sheets were let fly, clew garnets jerked up and thrown over pins, and braces were checked and hauled in hand over hand—all done without confusion or any noise except for the slatting of the head sheets and the clumping of their blocks on the rail. In a few moments the ship was without perceptible way on her, and a lifeboat, fully manned, was bobbing a hundred fathoms astern. "Who was it?" "Poor Walker!" "Can he swim?" No, like many another of his shipmates, he could not.

A crew jumped into the second lifeboat, and lowered away. The lad must be found! Men who had never spoken to Walker now mentioned him by his Christian name. "Poor Lawrence, I saw him scraping his gun carriage only a few minutes ago." "Why, he asked me for a chaw of tobacco just before he dropped!" "Why in hell don't they keep the ports closed at sea, anyway?" We were overcome with remorse that we hadn't been kinder to Walker, lent him our soap or swapped liberties with him.

Reluctantly the captain gave orders to recall the two boats. They came alongside, one of them with a still smoking flarebuoy on board, and were hooked on to the falls. To the rhythmic thunder of hundreds of feet, the sad crew began to walk the boats inboard.

It was only the habitual composure of sailors at work that prevented those boats from being dropped "on the run" when Walker or his ghost calmly marched up the main hatch ladder and saluted the quarter-deck. As if nothing much had happened, he reported his return to the ship. He had sunk deep, he said, and when he came up had just time to grab the Jacob's ladder that always trailed astern. He had climbed through the captain's cabin port, gone along the deserted decks to his bag, shifted into dry clothes, and now thought it was time for him to return to work. From an unobtrusive member of the crew, Lawrence Walker leaped into the limelight and was the hero of a day.

One evening a short time later, when one of the bridle ports had been bucked in by the heavy seas, I sat with old Steward Bell on his sea chest by the knightheads, watching the repair work of the carpenter's gang. I had been talking of Walker's escape, and the little Negro was telling me of harrowing experiences on one of the old ships, when so many of the crew were suffering from scurvy that even the cooks and stewards had to stand deck watch. I asked him:

"Don't you ever get tired of the sea, Bell, and the discipline of a man-o'-war?"

"No," he answered; "if you like your work, you won't easily tire. I feel that I shall keep going to the end, and that is the best way. I will end my days at sea; that will be less trouble for everyone. I shall never die on shore. I'll be buried deep in the sea I love, in clean water."

"Why, how can you know that?"

"Don't you ever feel that certain things are bound to happen?" Often the old man talked in that strain, and as he talked his faded eyes would shine with light. I wonder now if he really could have had a presentiment of the manner of his death, and the burial at sea he was to have with the eyes of the nation on him.

"As for the discipline of the navy," he continued, "that is something felt only by those who look for trouble. I never have known anyone's discipline, because I discipline myself."

"But how about those men who were thrown in the brig on the *St. Louis* the first day I met you? Was it right to punish them when they were doing their best to obey orders?"

"I wouldn't like to say; but I never saw any good come of criticizing what our officers do, or deploring what is past and done. Such happenings might be good to weed out the people that are easily discouraged. Remember, you boys here are making a new navy."

I found it hard to agree with him there, for it had already seemed to me that the usual result of such arbitrary punishment and injustice was to force out the good and hopeful men without eliminating the undesirables and peace-disturbers. I changed the subject.

"How about your people, Bell? Wouldn't you like to be with them all the time?"

"My people! I would, yes, of course; but it is a question if they don't see enough of an old colored man for three months at the end of every three years."

"What do you do at home?"

"Well, in the first place, I get up at six o'clock as usual, and nobody has to dash a pail of water against my window to make me do it. At eight o'clock I hoist a silk flag on a staff I put up some years ago. Then I have my dahlias to attend to. One of the boys—"

"Your boy, John?"

"Ye-es, one of my boys, God bless him. He is in college now. He sounds colors for me on his cornet. Then I visit some of my friends in the afternoon, and in the evening I attend my lodge. The three months seem no longer to me than some midwatches do to you."

At this point we were interrupted by some of the workers with chain hooks and tackles. I learned later that Bell made his home with the family of a naval officer to whom he had been body servant during the Civil War, a man who had lost his life in a daring action. That officer's home was Bell's home; that officer's widow and her children were the old Negro's "folks."

In all my "square-rigger" days it had been my lot to be detailed to the after parts of the ship—either in the main- or the mizzentop or in the afterguards. The perversity of human nature was exemplified in me by a constant longing for sailor experience well forward. The booms and the head gear held for me a peculiar fascination, and the sea, looked at from forward, ahead, and from both sides, possessed a charm lacking abaft the beam. The extreme forward part of the ship typified progress, movement, and action; the slender head booms, reaching out, and up, and over the blue of the sea like a gigantic hand, penciled on moving clouds our hopes and longings with the restless flying jib boom end.

Early one evening I left my companions, the waisters, skylarking amidships, or at their cards and deucy-acey boards, and, sauntering forward, leaned over the headrails, wondering how it would feel to take my hammock out there and spend just one watch on the protecting meshes of the flying jib netting. To ride there, alone, up and down—now so near the sea as to feel the spray and to hear the whisper of the swirl about our ram; a moment later to be high above the creaming crests, swayed toward the Milky Way. I chose to think that there I'd be far in advance of the officers and other people aft on their way around the globe, showing the way to the three towers of canvas and cordage so eager to tumble the ocean to foam. A sailor cannot be real unless he can feel for and be of his ship.

The sun had just disappeared behind a shimmering horizon as if in apology for a strenuous day, its golden cloud rims promising a better one for the morrow. The churning swirl of foam ever about our cutwater, with pearly drops dripping from the bobstays and oily flashes of sea on the lee side as the towering mass of canvas forced the ship ahead, thrilled me as the ship lunged and tossed her head. The dolphin striker made deep scratches in swells of halting seas, and dolphins themselves kept an exact distance ahead of our ram, always escaping being trod underfoot as the ship playfully shook her foamy mane.

My waking dreams were interrupted by a big fist between my shoulder blades. I cried out in pain, and looked around. It was Karl Witt, the belligerent of days ashore.

"Why the Tevill you not come here when we have clear hawse to make, you lazy afterguard!" he asked in pretended anger. He gave me to understand that he was at a loss to know what attraction I could find in the forward part of the ship. I could not explain to him in smooth sentences, but he understood. As for himself, he told me, nothing could be better than the after part of a ship, as far as he could get away from the constant noise under the bows, the gurgle, the roar and hiss, the thunder and poundings. He mentioned the fights of the foretopmen and the odors of the heads. It was the quarterdeck for him, where everything was clean and fresh, and where he could hear the band. He loved music.

Karl was a German. Had he been much older than I suspected him to be I would have believed him the original of the boatswain in a well-known novel I liked to read. Like "Jemmy Ducks" in *Snarleyyow,* his short, well-knit form had the neck of a wrestler, and he was quite a man from midships up; below that point his legs seemed to have been forgotten in the making. They were so short in proportion to his girth that none of the paymaster's sizes of trousers would fit him. His eyebrows were thick and furry. He was bald except for a fringe of blond hair over his ears. He had enormous fat hands. His eyes were blue and always kindly on board ship; but on shore after a few drinks they took on a steely glint. He had a sparse mustache covering fine white teeth which gripped an expensive meerschaum pipe. He was a mass of muscle, a man whose presence would be felt on the foreyard when reefing or furling in a gale.

Karl had a better education than might have been expected in one who claimed never to have been in any school. He wrote a copperplate hand. It was from this old sailor, who had learned fortitude from the sea, and not from any book, that I learned the why and wherefore of many things nautical that I had not become familiar with in my own parts of the ship. He was the one to explain to me why the bight of a chain under water was a catenary. While talking on this subject, the word "cat-o'-nine-tails" came up, and he informed me that the fine picture of the Savior on the cross that was tattooed on his back covered the wales and scars he had received as a boy in a cruel flogging. As that sort of punishment was abolished in the United States Navy in 1847 I assumed that he had met the ignominious treatment in some other service, but the good fellow was silent in that particular.

On our starboard hand the last glow of the sun framed in gold the clouds of silver and purple. And then the sky closed in on the sea, and on us. The lamp trimmer, a Yankee with narrow face and withdrawn chin, had placed his heavy charges of green and red in their places for the night and clamped them down, and the cathead watches had been stationed. Silent men gazed intently ahead and abreast.

At this point MacFarland, who was Karl's opposite number on the station bill, joined our group. He had just finished a private lunch of sardines with his latest favorite among the boys, and was wiping oil and crackers from his whiskers with a hand swab. He took his pipe from his cap, and scowled in all directions. He was looking for a stray bucket belonging to his wash-deck gear. Aside from their everlasting wrangling about the ownership of swabs, squilgees, and other gear, he and Karl got along very well.

A private marine, one of the few who was tolerated by the sailor force because he knew how to drink with them on shore, and often turned his head at duty post when he should not have done so, stood by, taking it all in. He had been on duty as admiral's orderly that morning, and was peddling tales about the admiral's habits. Ned Mack, captain of the foretop, standing by, put in an oar. He told us of an admiral on the European Station who had drilled his entire squadron hard a whole day, and for what! Not because he had had trouble getting his socks on, but because his wife called his attention to the fact that he was trying to get both socks on one foot.

Karl Witt laughed, and punched MacFarland in the ribs. That little fellow always walked away when his German partner started horseplay, and swaggered along the deck. As the Scotsman went away he sneezed fitfully, and Karl explained:

"I don't know if that fellow gets more satisfaction from pulling hairs out of his nose than he does from the sneezing that follows. It makes him carry on like a regular snuffer."

Spiros, the armorer, a short, wiry, black-haired baseball enthusiast, had joined us. He smoked Manila stogies, and seemed to possess an inexhaustible supply which was drawn upon by the gunner and even some of the commissioned officers. He offered one to Mack, and it was refused.

For once Spiros did not talk about baseball. Something had led him off that track; it was something that was said about married life. It was like pulling a trigger:

"Maybe you fellows don't know that I once was spliced. It didn't take, and the contract was a poor one. I tell you, boys, there's no such thing as a good cruise in a home where the husband isn't the skipper, or worse by a damn sight where there's two skippers. It won't go. I earned the money to fit out a nice place in Connecticut, with bamboo chairs from Manila and all kinds of gewgaws from every hell'ngone place, but when I started to give orders I had no crew to obey me, and even if I wanted to obey my own orders there was another there to tell me how I must do the thing myself. Yes, sir, fellows, I must have been drunk when I got spliced. It was hell. If I wanted to go out into the park, my mate wanted to stay home. If I said I was tired, she'd get all rigged out and stand at the door waiting for me, and she wouldn't say one word, just look, and tap her toes. She claimed when I was home from a cruise it was her time to rest. It was the first time I ever did any cooking, or there wouldn't have been anything to eat, and nothing suited the mess I was cooking for. One day I up and told her she should have gone to the store for her door mat and not to a minister, and I shot out the door with her after me, and I haven't seen her since. Shore's all right for them that's born to it, but it's no place for a flatfoot."

Besides the berth-deck cooks, marines, and an occasional bandsman, there were others of the crew who preferred the forecastle section to their own parts of the ship, especially when the wind-starved sails aft in warm weather failed to cool them off. Sitting on coils of rope, on the edge of hatches, and on flaked sheets near-by were men washing clothes in the precious fresh water saved from the morning watch. From starboard the apprentice on cathead watch was hauling his blanket out of the sea. He had tied it to the end of the flying jib downhaul and towed it overboard to rinse it. He had left it overboard too long, or had misjudged our speed, with the result that he found what wool was left in it bunched in a lump at one end of the blanket. It meant a month's pay to him!

The moonlight was streaming down our decks, after silvering the yards and tops above. Faintly, from far below came the refrain of a darky song. Karl rapped his pipe gently against the billboard, saying:

"Here comes Gorman to know what you are doing in this vulgar part of the ship. I feel as if I had been to a prayer meeting tonight. Thanks for coming forward. Bedamn if any of us can tell what's the best for us."

My captain of the top, Jim Gorman, with his usual worried look, as if charged with responsibility for the entire ship, first spat carefully to leeward, and then informed me that I had the wheel from ten to twelve o'clock. He and Karl called each other "turnpike sailors" and other loving expressions, some of them unprintable, until eight bells struck, when there was an immediate stirring on every part of the deck. Karl gave his shipmate a prod in the ribs:

"Shove off, you barnacled, dirty-bottomed beachcomber, and make your regular trip."

New officers came up the after ladders, and the forward hatches were jammed with men hurrying up and down.

"Starboard cathead, bright light!" from the rasping throat of the man who stood beside our group, and opposite the contralto of the apprentice boy with:

"Port cathead, bright light!"

The boatswain's mates in the gangways whistled and bellowed:

"Call the watch! Relieve the wheel and lookouts!"

Men bade each other good night; the idlers who stand no watches went below singly and in groups. The men on deck were mustered and, the night being fine, all braces taut, and the gear clear for running, even the watch on deck soon became quiet, sleeping or dozing under tarpaulins and covers.

I hurried below for a drink before my trick at the wheel. Under the hatch hood sat a shriveled fellow from New York's East Side whose brown skin was gashed with scars. I paused and listened with others crowded on the gratings:

". . . had no money left, but I had to eat, don't you see. So I went into a nice restaurant on Forty-second Street and had a fine feed. When I was finished I fished a cockroach out of my pocket and dropped it into my coffee. I set up a holler, and I said I would lick the manager. I pretended the roach made me sick, and they soon had me out of the door, and were glad to get rid of me that way. That worked every night for a while, always in a different section, but one night I was going to try it again when some feller in the other end of the room starts to squeal, and I heard him holler that someone had dropped a cockroach into his coffee. Now, gee, fellers, two of us couldn't work the same game in the same place. So I walks over, and I said to him, so the manager could hear me:

'My good man,' I says, 'ain't you puttin' up a stiff holler, especially as it's only half a cockroach, anyway?' I says then to the manager: 'See here, sir, I know this feller, and I'm an officer on his ship. I'll see he gets bread and water for this,' and both of us walked out and didn't pay for our dinners. But I had to ship over the next day, as there's no use of workin' where they'll steal your stuff."

Thanksgiving Day was spent miserably in the Indian Ocean; it was a day of squalls and sleet that prevented the program of sports planned by Lieutenant Quinby. On December 7 we entered the Straits of Sunda, and here orders were received to proceed to Batavia for coal. Anchored in the lee of the Dutch guard ship, we refueled without going ashore, and were not even allowed to eat the fruit temptingly held out to us by bumboatmen, so unhealthy was the reputation of this North Java port. The following Sunday we were close to Singapore and turned to early in the morning to get the ship in harbor trim to the old sailor's growl:

"Six days shalt thou labor and do all thou art able—
And on the seventh, holystone the deck and scrape the cable."

On our way into Singapore Harbor that evening we fished two Chinese out of the sea. We could not learn how they came to be swimming in the gulf, but probably they had stowed away on some steamer that had passed us, and had either jumped or were forced overboard. They told our interpreters that some other natives with them had drowned.

At our moorings in Singapore the decks were besieged by an army of tradesmen—bearded Malays, white-robed Indians, grinning Chinese—who would sell you silks, silverwork, diamonds, sapphires, or change your money into clinking Mex dollars. They came alongside in fifteen-foot sampans, each with projecting horns over the stern and eyes carved on the sharp, tapering bows. The boats all appeared to be identical, with the same sleepy boatman living in each. The boats had two seats for passengers; on one side of the cockpit holding the helmsman was a thwart under which rested a portable stove with a simmering pot of rice and fish. Near at hand was the boatman's bowlless pipe and tobacco box, and above his head were stowed the spear-shaped oars, a lateen sail, and the straw mat on which he slept. With the merchants there came aboard an East Indian fakir who entertained the bluejackets with many an eye-deceiving trick.

We left Singapore four days before Christmas, with a deck-load of coal and our gangways filled with live beasts and noisy fowl that would be slaughtered for a rare holiday feast. But again the weather broke our hopes of leisurely enjoyment of the occasion, for most of Christmas Day was spent aloft taking in sail, reefing, making sail, and taking it in again.

Two weeks later we dropped our hooks in the mud of the busy free port of Hong Kong for a long stay. The ship was immediately surrounded by hundreds of sampans bringing little Chinese girls to solicit our laundry trade. These lively, slippery, and not unhandsome native maidens, in their embroidered jackets and trousers of blue, red, and yellow, clambered over the heads of the astonished marines at the gangway ladders and swarmed through every open port to the gun deck. Each girl carried her own visiting cards—poorly printed and quaintly worded:

> "Marry Yung, washerwomans and Men clothers."
>
> "Kum Kwick, No. 11 Aberdeen Street, Wanchei. Washerwoman most handsome and patchwork done most shortly."
>
> "All Choy—the iron rust can take out."

Of course each customer was invited to visit ashore, where "joyment could be had, also lotry tickets." A glance at the hands of the dainty girls, and an appraisal of their silks and ornaments, caused one to suspect that these little imps did very little laundry work themselves. They had their own coolies to gather the clothes and carry them to the boats.

Our bunkers were at once filled with coal, and as soon as the muck had been removed we scraped the ship inside and out, removed paint, and again overhauled all the standing rigging. It was surprising to me how much that wire rigging could stretch under sea conditions. The ship was then repainted, and the decks were calked by native workmen.

The admiral and his entire staff boarded a steamer to Japan for a tour of inspection of other ships of our oriental fleet. We sighed with relief, believing that this meant cessation of drills for a time.

Liberty money was served out to those who were not under punishment. It was handed to us with a flourish. "Here it is; take it. You'll never find an easier place to spend it!" Some of the first men to go ashore made a week-end trip to Macao, an island in the Canton River where the Portuguese government had crowded into a space of two miles more viciousness than could be found in any other area of its size in the world. Men of our ship who should have known the facts said that the Bowery was a Sunday school compared to Macao.

In the crowded streets of Hong Kong were to be found large numbers of seamen from British, French, German, and Japanese naval vessels, and merchant seamen of many nations and English soldiers as well. The man-o'-warsmen sometimes drank together and often fought together in an international melee—all except the Japanese. As soon as a fight started, the little Japanese mysteriously melted away. None of them ever were escorted to jail by tall, bearded Sikh policemen. Most quarrelsome of all seemed to be men of our ships who had formerly been in the British navy. Many a good battle was started by a *Lancaster* man of English birth who sneeringly referred to an English naval man as "an 'owlin' bleddy limejuicer."

The feud between Moynahan, of our berth deck, and the gallant Talleyrand, the little coxswain of the gig, which had been aggravated by sundry doings on the Equator, had not been settled at Cape Town because the berth-deck bruiser had not been allowed ashore at the South African port. Everyone confidently supposed that things would therefore come to a head at the first liberty port in China, and they were not deceived. Both men went ashore on the first day, Moynahan several hours earlier than his enemy. Talleyrand and some of his gig's crew searched Hong Kong from the head of the docks to the top of Victoria Peak for hours, without luck. At last, as it was getting dark and 'ricksha lamps were being lighted, the ship's corporal was sighted in a British hangout near the race track. As he saw them enter, Moynahan shouted to his

British companions: "There's the hammered-down, unfidded bootlicker I was telling you about—the scummy runt!" and jumped to meet his enemy in the middle of the room.

Battle would have been joined at once, but a fuddled Britisher interfered by striking at Talleyrand from the side; whereupon Moynahan, resentful at this intrusion into a private fight, immediately attacked the stalwart Briton. In a flash the room was riotous with men who slugged away at anyone in sight who wore a different uniform, and the gig's crew was fighting back to back with the aggrieved Moynahan. The barmaids screeched, bottles and mirrors crashed, and Chinese coolies peeked through the doors with a stoic gaze born of centuries of nonresistance. At the piercing call of a whistle, a band of turbaned Sikhs rushed in and quelled with clubs the bitter battle, which flared up again and again until most of the bluejackets on both sides were prostrate.

When the last ember of combat was quenched, our men carried Moynahan into the street. He had been laid out by a bottle hurled by one of the Britons. At his side knelt a repentant Talleyrand, wiping the blood from the wounded man's face. "What did the murderin' brutes do to ye, shipmate?" he asked again and again. "Never fear, shipmate, we'll take you aboard with us and cool your poor head, shipmate!" Thus ended a *Lancaster* feud.

The crowning exploit of the cunning Talleyrand took place in Hong Kong Harbor not long after the departure of the admiral for Japan. The captain was on the warpath, and junior officers took care to keep out of his way as he stamped about the quarter-deck while the executive followed him placatingly with the ship's reportbook in his hands.

"The way the rum is coming aboard this vessel is a disgrace!" the old man roared. "We'll have a change if I have to stop all liberties to do it. Soon we'll be the laughingstock of the Asiatic Station. By heaven, I think we are already, after the sail drill yesterday. Sail drill! This ship looked like a bumboat in distress!"

"I admit, captain," said the executive officer, "that it does look as if we were connected by pipeline with some distillery. But I think we will soon have some information that will help us to put a stop to it."

"Well, see that you do. And when you find out what boat is running the stuff, and I have proof, nobody connected with this scandal will escape, no matter who he is—not even if he's an officer, sir! Now, I'm going ashore to the U.S. Consulate to see about those reprobates of ours who are in jail. I wish we could leave them to rot along with the Englishmen they've been fighting, but I suppose we would only have to pick up men that were much worse. Damn it, some of my best topmen are stuck ashore—Malia, and O'Brien, and that other Irishman, O'Donnell. I missed them yesterday when we had that parody of a sail drill. We'll have to get them back if we want to look like a ship again. I'm glad the admiral is in Yokohama and doesn't know about any of this yet."

Calling his coxswain, Talleyrand, to bring round the gig, the captain went ashore. Meanwhile, the chief master-at-arms sought out the executive officer in his cabin, a prized privilege he had when there was any secret information to divulge. He found the first luff in an evil humor after the dressing-down he had been given by the captain. But after the conference, a delighted look had come into the executive's eyes. He could hardly wait for the return of the gig.

As the captain's boat approached the ship, and four side boys were piped to the starboard gangway, the first luff and his chief of police stood eagerly awaiting its arrival. The commanding officer had barely reached the deck when his subordinate saluted and said, bursting with his news: "Captain, I have full information that a certain boat is running this rum every day. When that boat is ordered astern to the Jacob's ladder, one of the crew brings the jug aboard over the rail at night—and by glory, even in the daytime, if no one is around, they bring it right through the cabin port of your cabin, sir! And that boat, sir, is the captain's own gig!"

"Be careful what you say!" admonished the horrified captain. "How can you be sure of that?"

In answer, the executive signaled to the lurking master-at-arms, who rushed down the gangway ladder and leaped into the gig, almost capsizing it in his haste. He snatched the boat cloth from the backboard of the boat, and disclosed in the rear of the transom a ship's bucket filled with floating ice, in the middle of which bobbed a slender, long-necked bottle. Waving this evidence triumphantly, he rushed breathlessly to the deck, but not before Talleyrand, the coxswain, with a courteous "Please permit me, chief!" had solicitously wiped the drippings from its sides.

Jimmylegs could hardly speak with excitement. He felt that he had at last won the reputation of being the most vigilant ship's policeman in the American navy. Handing the bottle to the officer of the deck, he shouted down to the gig's crew: "Come topside, every one of you, you rum bloats! Thought you'd put one over on me, did you? Well, here's where you hit a reef!"

The captain was still unable to comprehend the situation. "What is the meaning of this, Mr. Gilmore?"

"The facts will soon show themselves, I think, sir," said the executive, attempting to remain calm and judicial. "I have already sent for the surgeon on duty, and a number of marines as well." The marines were already there in the background, loaded down with hand- and leg-irons for the culprits.

The captain called one of his servants. "Inokichi, bring me a tumbler. Master-at-arms, see what the stuff in that bottle might be!"

"It's swanky," volunteered Talleyrand, standing by the gangway with his eye on the marines.

"Silence there!" commanded the captain. His confidence in his pet coxswain was shattered. "You speak when I ask you. Now, master-at-arms, what is the verdict?"

Jimmylegs sniffed and tasted, at first sagely, but then with a more puzzled air. Then the doctor took a try.

The captain was impatient. "Oh, come, come! Make up your minds—is it alcohol?"

"No," said the doctor. "I don't think it is. It tastes slightly sour, but not unpleasant." He turned to Talleyrand. "Is there vinegar in this?"

"Yes, sir," said the coxswain. "Good clean ship's vinegar, with water and plenty of sugar. Swanky we call it. It keeps us cool when we are working at the oars. Everybody on board ought to drink it all the time, sir. We like it in the gig because we know it's better for the stomach than what rum or other spirits would be." The members of the gig's crew smirked in agreement.

The master-at-arms stood crestfallen, rattling a pair of useless handcuffs in his pocket. The captain was thunderous. "That will do, men. Go forward!"

Talleyrand, however, remained at salute.

"Well, coxswain, what is it?"

"Sir, captain, did we do wrong in bringing that swanky aboard?"

"Why, not at all, coxswain; but hereafter you will keep it under the bow end of the boat, and not in the stern sheets."

"Aye, aye, sir; thank you, sir. May I bring the pail with the ice aboard?"

"Yes, coxswain; and I want to say that I am sorry for the unjust suspicions brought against you and your crew."

"Oh, that's all right, sir; we all make mistakes!" With that, as the officers turned away, Talleyrand ran down the ladder and quickly returned with a pail filled with liquid and ice. Holding it high in air, he disappeared below.

That night, deep down on the berth deck, Talleyrand and his merry pals mixed a strong rum punch and handed it around in mess bowls to their friends. "Here's another to the gig's crew, for they're all jolly good fellows!" "And here's to the skipper—a jolly good fellow to let us bring the stuff aboard!" "Did you hear him tell the luff to have his Jimmylegs keep his hands off the captain's boat crew in the future?" "Here's to Jimmylegs—good old Talleyrand brought this aboard right under his sniffin' nose, and it almost burnt his whiskers! The old brig-filler is sure on the rampage tonight!"

Talleyrand had been tipped off that morning by a friendly shipmate that the gig was suspected and would be searched on its return from the first trip. Therefore, the bottle that usually brought the rum aboard through the cabin ports was filled with the weak sugary mixture, and the forbidden liquor was dumped into the pail of ice, which was covered by the boat cloth to protect it from splashing salt water. The newly invented scheme of smuggling was carried on for some time, and never was brought to a halt by detection. Talleyrand and his "swanky" became a China coast legend.

Chapter XVI

LIBERTY DAYS

Born as a scuttle-butt yarn, the whisper soon spread through the ship that we were to be visited by a member of the British royal family. The truth of the rumor became assured when a date was finally set, and an edict proclaimed that shore liberty would be canceled until the function had been logged as a past event.

Great preparations were made for the visitation. We cleaned and scrubbed the ship until we ached, and used up many tins of scoojie-moojie on canopies, cutlass hilts, and elevating gear. Many were the remarks, all unflattering, that could be heard regarding royalty in general and this young prince in particular.

As a signal honor to the visitor, we were called upon to perform the difficult evolution of manning the yards. So rare was this ceremony in the American navy that our boatswain consulted beforehand with men of European ships in the harbor, to make sure that all would be done according to custom. When at last the royal entourage was seen to shove off from the navy dock (after exercising the highborn prerogative of keeping us waiting in suspense for more than an hour), and bands on ships nearer the shore began to play, we hauled out our lifelines, which had been stopped down to the brace bands, and pulled the lines taut and parallel with the yards, arm-high, from lifts to inner rigging.

"Lay out!"

Out we laid, keeping time to the rhythm of our bugles, walking barefoot over the furled sails until the shortest man on each yard had reached the stiffened lift, which he grasped with his outboard hand, facing forward. The next man held the shoulder of the first, interlocking arms around the lifeline; and thus did every man on the yard as far as the slings, where the tallest men were stationed. Although we had no rehearsal, the whole effect was smartly obtained. I was on the maintopgallant yard, having been transferred to the main from the mizzen some time before; and from there I had a chance to reflect on my good luck in obtaining an easy, though lofty, position. The ship pitched a trifle in the rough waves of the bay, making it necessary for us to sway forward with the motion of the vessel. Not only on the three masts, but also out to the topping lift on the spanker boom and even far forward to the flying jib stay, several hundred men stood, straight and stiff, paying honor in this old dramatic fashion. Salutes boomed below us as the flag of our noble visitor was broken out at the foretruck; neighboring ships also saluted, and many guns were fired from the forts ashore.

We remained in our unnatural, rigid positions until the prince and his party of high army and navy officers and shore officials had gone down into the cabins. Then at the command we laid in, pulled on our shoes, and hurried to quarters. There we were inspected by the royal visitor—and he was inspected by us. To my mind there was nothing striking about the fellow's appearance. We had ensigns on board our ship, such as Eberle with his soft brown beard and blue eyes, who were more than a match for him when it came to handsome looks. Place the prince on our fo'c'sle in any morning watch, I thought, stripped with the other men who were dashing salt water on each other, and you would never be able to pick him out from the others because of any visible superiority.

As the visit drew to a close we were ordered aloft again, and once more we manned the yards, clinging between sky and sea like marionettes until the visiting boats had shoved off and the smoke of our last salutes had drifted down the wind. The pomp and circumstance were over. We breathed a sigh of relief and looked forward to a welcome letdown in work and drills after all this flummery. What was better, we knew that a general liberty would be granted to all hands.

One afternoon I drifted into the native bazaar, teeming with coolie life and the usual battery of letter writers, fortunetellers, and eating booths. The air was full of steam from snail pots, chestnut boilers, and the hot vapors of itinerant barbers and corn-doctors. I strolled about among the thousand sights and stenches, watching youngsters roll firecrackers and marveling at the adroitness of a young girl using fingers and feet on a native loom.

Attracted by a ring of Chinese, I paid five sen for an elevated position where I could look over the bare heads of the crowd to the center, where a dirty and almost naked juggler was holding them spellbound. He placed an empty two-quart tin on the ground and chanted over it, whereat the tin filled with a clear liquid. He lifted the vessel to his ear, keeping it level, and the liquid disappeared. Next he swallowed two iron balls which we could see ripple down his throat. He leaped into the air, and as he touched the ground the balls could be heard to click. Later on, in Shanghai, the same trick by another street juggler resulted in loss of control of the balls, and the performer died in agony.

Now another fakir, equally dirty, took the place of the first, and removing one of his many coats stretched it out on the ground. A rusty knife hung from his broad, embroidered belt. Two native women assisted him, continually chattering in shrill tones. With them was a little boy who, wearing nothing but a loincloth, shivered in the cold wind from the bay. Red candles and joss sticks sputtered and smoldered within the circle. The performers banged upon a brass gong, a pair of cymbals, and a drum. Above it all rose the strident screaming of the women.

I didn't share the eager interest of the rest of the audience that showered down hundreds of square-holed pieces of cash, and was about to leave when the fakir dropped his drum in apparent rage, seized the little boy, and threw him to the ground. In motions too quick for my eyes to follow, he drew his knife and seemed to thrust it into the boy's belly. The feigned terror of the two women, and the sight of welling red blood, were dramatic and shocking. In spite of the calmness of the crowd, I was moved to look about for help. Across the street stood a Sikh policeman, impassive and unconcerned.

Suddenly one of the women picked up the boy, held him over the flame of the candles, wiped off the red stains, and stood him on his feet. The boy opened his eyes dazedly, but appeared completely unharmed. Then the crowd thinned.

As they drifted off, I glanced again at the policeman. He was ordering off a foreigner in ill-fitting garments—a beachcomber, by the look of him, but there was something vaguely familiar about his movements. I hurried over to where he was standing by a veranda post. He knew me as I knew him. It was Jim Durgin, of my *St. Louis* days.

But this was surely not the handsome, careless Happy I remembered! His once powerful frame seemed shrunken. His skin was sallow and blotched with deep spots; most of the thick and curly hair I had remembered was gone except for a wisp here and there. Some of his teeth were missing, and he spoke with difficulty.

We went to a restaurant where I knew we would be able to talk undisturbed. Happy did not want to eat anything, but I prevailed on him to take some soup and soft bread. Then I heard his story.

Durgin had been sent to one of the ships of the White Squadron soon after I had left the receiving ship at Philadelphia. He was shortly advanced to a fireman rating, with a small increase in pay. He kept up his correspondence with Doris, the girl who had played the church organ on the guardo; the two planned to get married as soon as the boy's enlistment had expired. Doris's father was port engineer for one of the steamship lines serving South America, and could get Durgin a shore job.

"What happened then, Happy?"

"Oh, hell!" he muttered, and his bloodshot eyes filled with tears. "Don't call me Happy any more. That's all over."

He had gone ashore in New York, he said, with Red Jackson, who knew the places where they could enjoy their liberty without getting kicked out because of their uniforms. They took a room with a woman who did laundry work for their captain. The old lady was a shrewd one and had her eye on Jackson as a sheet anchor for her daughter Nellie in the event of trouble. And trouble, it appeared, was never more than a cable-length from that young but worldly-wise girl. Jackson hung about her closely for a while, and then was suddenly gone. "He was declared a deserter from the ship," said Durgin, "and of course I didn't keep the room alone."

He stared up at the mat ceiling and the lacquered beams of the dingy eating place, his face raked with the guns of hopeless despair.

"We stayed at the Brooklyn yard too damned long. I didn't go ashore often because I was trying to save some money. Once I went down to Philly to see Doris, and I was able to tell her I had been promised the rating of fireman, first class. We were both happy to think that the time would pass quickly and then we would be able to get married. O God!

"One day on the ship I was hailed and told to go to 'the mast.' I had just come off watch, and was grimy with oil and coal dust, but there was no time to wash up. On the spar deck I found the captain talking to my former landlady. Her daughter stood there, too, and some of our other officers and the master-at-arms. Soon enough I heard the charge. The girl was going to have a baby, and I was accused.

"I denied it, of course. But the captain—you've heard of old Hallelujah—had his mind made up. He hadn't heard a word about Jackson and his doings. He looked at me through his thick glasses, and pointed at a paper in his hand. It was my enlistment record, and I knew he was looking at the old black marks set against me that evening on the *St. Louis*.

"'You started out as a first-cruise man by using insolence to your commanding officer!' he accused. 'A hard case, ain't you? No wonder the people ashore put up signs to try and keep you away from decent folks. Taking advantage of a young girl and her old mother! I wish I could have you flogged!'"

The knuckles of the boy's clenched hands showed white. "I swore I had never had anything to do with the girl, and I begged her, right there before that crowd, to tell the truth. She herself would make no charge against me—but that harridan of a mother of hers tended to all that. The pompous old baboon of a captain saw a good chance to preach all the things he'd never thought of practicing himself—God damn his fussy and hypocritical soul! He laid the whole thing at my door without a qualm, and then proceeded to flay me alive. Take my advice, Bunny—get out of the service while you can, or sooner or later you'll fall afoul of one of those sneering tin gods who think you are dirt, and he'll break you as he broke me!"

"Go on, Durgin. Did they make you desert? Did he actually believe you were to blame?"

"He did. He wouldn't listen to me, but that dirty woman's word was all he needed. And according to him, there was only one thing to do. He sent his orderly out on Sands Street for some papers. He had me put in the brig to be sure I'd be there on the next morning. When that time came, he had the chaplain of the navy yard marry me, right there on the gun deck, to a wench I'd never had a thing to do with! Then I was told to draw a month's pay, and get ashore with my family, and enjoy my honeymoon! The officers laughed at that. The devils in hell must have been laughing too."

"But why did you consent? Surely they couldn't force you to go through with it!"

"Ask yourself what you would have done." He shook his head wearily. "It came as a command, a command to a subordinate from an officer who never had to give reasons. Also, I was afraid that I would be locked up all the time, so that I couldn't desert, skip out, and hope that time would prove my innocence. But something in me was killed after that morning on the deck. The old woman was crafty. She took me back to the house ashore, and I drank the stuff she poured into me. For days I was dead to the world."

The color came and went in his face, and he seemed to have aged as he talked.

"You can guess the worst. I was married to that girl, and how could I know what I was doing? Her life had left its marks on her, and it left its marks on me. Look at my head—look at my skin! My eyes are covered with film, and I can hardly see. I had glasses, but someone stole them on my last ship. The girl was incurably sick; and the arbitrary power of one old man and the scheming of one vile old woman made me share her curse.

"I never went back to my ship, even to get my clothes. I was afraid of what I might do to that chaplain and that captain if I saw them. I deserted; I'm a deserter right now. When the child was born, the red hair and features of Jackson mocked me. I didn't dare go home to the farm. It seems like years ago that I signed on with my first tramp steamer. But I got sicker and sicker. I couldn't keep on at the boilers, and was shunted to the deck force. I had no warm clothing, and this lung trouble started. I'm no good now, and all the shipping officers know it. I've been on the beach here for two weeks now, and all they do is tell me to move on, to get out! For God's sake, if you ever see Doris when you get back home, tell her you know I'm dead. Maybe I am dead right now, for all we know!"

I tried to give him what assurance I could; but I knew that there was no hope of getting him back into the navy, even if he would have consented to try. Any officer on the *Lancaster* would have been duty-bound to bring him to a court-martial if he found out Durgin was a deserter, and then the boy would have been returned to the United States for years of imprisonment. He would not even go aboard for treatment at the ship's sick bay. But he promised to wait for me while I could go to the ship and return with the money and clothing he needed.

Bell, the captain's steward, remembered Durgin kindly, and generously gave me money for him, as did Sinner Flukes and Bugler Gannon and many another. Two of the men went with me ashore again, and we carried a clothesbag full of warm garments and two pairs of shoes. When we reached the place where I had left Durgin, he had gone.

We walked up and down the water front, looking into the haunts of merchant sailors, in the offices of compradors and shroffs, in boardinghouses and gospel missions. When our time was nearly up and we had to return to the ship, we left the money and clothing in the care of our Consulate, where orders were given to the U.S. marshal to find Durgin if possible and to take care of him. But a week later, when we sailed for the north, nothing had been heard of the boy. A year later, again in Hong Kong, we inquired about him. He had disappeared. We gave him up for lost, and I never saw Happy again.

The *Lancaster* remained at Hong Kong too long for the good of her crew. The decent pleasures of shore had long been exhausted, and we huddled on the ship through a cold spell lasting many days. Usually the water of the harbor was rough, the wind sweeping violently across from Stonecutters' Island over Kowloon Bay. During the bad weather the natives would not venture out in their boats, and our boats' crews were assigned to labor at the cutters and whaleboats, on each day of duty making dozens of torturing trips at the oars. At one time there were more than sixty members of the crew confined to their hammocks by sickness, and this, together with the loss of the men on liberty as well as an unusual number of liberty-breakers and some deserters, gave us all double duty to keep the ship clean, perform routine drills, and work the running boats.

We were not sorry, therefore, when we hove up the anchors on April 12 and headed for Japan. Almost at once we steamed into the teeth of a gale that made us seek shelter in the lee of Turnabout Island. Thenceforward we had much bad weather, of the wet and sleety sort to be expected in the Formosa Channel at that time of year. It called for fiendish labors aloft, much fussy trimming of the yards and rigging, and freezing watches at the bucking brutal wheel. Often I had time to ponder Durgin's story, and to compare my grueling lot with that of the officers who caroused in the warmth of the wardroom below while I stood with the stolid Norwegian Laag at the helm, almost frozen to the wheel gratings. In my jumper I carried a letter filled with bad news from home. My hopes of a return to school upon the expiration of my enlistment, and possibly a course in college, were dashed. I might take a chance on shore in some foreign port, but there I would be unknown and without friends. Would I drift into the ranks of the beachcombers, as my shipmates predicted? No white man could hope for a decent job in a treaty port, they said, for the labor of natives and Eurasians was too cheap.

Formosa Channel continued to kick up bad weather and misery for all hands. Many times we were roused out of our dreams in wet hammocks by the bellow of "All hands reef tops'ls!" After standing by the braces would come the order: "Clear away the bowlines!" "Tend your lifts and halyards!" followed immediately by the liquid swish of the topsail halyards as they spun around the lignum vitae hardness of the kevels, radiating nasty cold wetness to eyes of tenders who watched coils as they emptied themselves out of the halyard racks. What certain members of the crew did in the meantime was perfect adjustment of braces at every mast to suit the temper of the gale. I never heard the word "adjustment" applied to this work, but what other word describes so well the many niceties of tautness here and slackening there, a suiting of the angle of each yard—first to spill out of the sail the blustering wind threatening to shake the cloths out of the bolt ropes; then to guard against straining of the masts, raked aft from the perpendicular. A badly tended brace might result in lifting the head booms out of their seats and cause many hours of work in setting up the rigging when the storm had passed. There were indeed many adjustments to think of, and if the men tending the topsail yard lifts did not slacken them with proper care the devil would surely be on liberty up there for a while. A topsail yard, with a wet sail, straining and thumping at its sheets, with impatient men clinging to jackstays and footropes, meant many tons of weight. In times like this no man had more responsibility than a mastman; at other times he was practically a nonentity. I never envied a mastman his duties or his pay, and my plans for the future did not include the possibilities of that kind of work, especially on a dark night with the deck canted first one way and then the other, the mastman's legs spread across coils of rope, and all hands shouting for his attention at the same time.

During the same watch the reefed foresail would be wet to the yardarm, the decks a welter of loose gear that whipped itself into the waterways and down the scuppers. The power of the wind truncated the sea with the weight of mountains. The moaning in our top hamper was like a dirge, and the weather backstays twanged with the tensity of a violin string. On the following day there might be little wind, but a nasty sea, keeping everything topsides wet and the interior of the ship stuffy like a tightly closed house in damp weather.

We were hove to one night, some days out of Hong Kong, and it was my trick at the wheel from eight to ten. It was miserably cold; the ship shook from stem to stern as the seas pounded at her yellow pine breasts. A wet sleet dashed the weather side of my face, ran down my neck, and found the last warm place on my body. Occasionally there appeared a stingy segment of moon from behind torn clouds. I tried every expedient I knew to keep my teeth together, but they would chatter. There was no exercise, for with the ship hove to, steering of the *Lancaster* was not difficult. I just watched the older man on the weather side and gave him a lift when he decided to bring her head up a little. Our great double wheel was immediately abaft the skylight which afforded daylight and air to the wardroom two decks below. Just beneath our feet on the gun deck stood a marine orderly reading a novel by the dim light of an oil lamp. I wished I could change positions with him, in his warm, dry clothes, and in his security from wind and snow. I was truly so miserable that I envied a marine!

The ship's clock hung on a bulkhead where the marine stood. Every half hour he put down his book, slipped on a rubber coat, and came on deck, where, standing by the wheel, he reported the time to the officer of the deck above us on the bridge. Before the messenger could reach the fo'c'sle and strike the bell the orderly was back to his book.

A sea hit us abaft the beam and flooded the deck, sousing us two at the wheel and threatening to lift the gratings on which we stood. I could feel the ship sag to leeward. Laag, the square-set Norwegian opposite me, shook his broad shoulders and never moved his gaze from the binnacle light. I could feel the man's masculine strength through the wood and bronze of the wheel. Nothing in this world could disturb the equanimity of that man, I believed. Like a ship, he moved tranquilly through a confused world. That sea was past; it could do no further harm to us, so why look after it! He was the most saving man on the ship, and one of the most respected. He was a Hercules in strength, impeccable in morals, and no one would think of tempting him to take a drink. He was blond, gentle-voiced, with a straggling flaxen mustache that stood out white against his weatherbeaten face. His clothing was irreproachable always and adhered strictly to regulations, perfect no matter what the weather. Silent, circumspect, and obviously free from all bothersome difficulties of a man-o'-warsman's being. Nothing was ever denied the man by his officers because he never made any requests. He was a foreigner, yes, but he, "Froggy," a Frenchman, and some few others, formed the real backbone of our personnel. Strangely, though, Laag's arm never sported a "crow," or rating badge, and I never heard the man laugh out loud. I could not help admiring the skill with which he wrested a living from the sea.

On the berth deck, fourteen feet below us, I could see the wardroom table spread with dishes that moved within the prescribed squares of the storm fiddles when the ship rolled heavily. Dinner was over for them down there, and I had watched every course. Dessert was being nibbled at daintily. There were dishes of large raisins from Spain and boxes of chocolates from France. There were many bottles and glasses. My eyes fastened on a cherry pie, with breakers of whipped cream dashing over it. How long since I had tasted a piece of American pie? My supper had been cold canned mutton and tea, five hours ago. The Chinese boys had retired to their pantry so that the officers could continue more freely with their celebration of the birthday of one of their number—a man from a line of officers who graced the pages of our naval history. The officers had been drinking together for some time and were sounding happier and louder with every bottle, which opened with a pop heard above all other noises. They laughed and at times burst into song, one of which I had thought was the property of men forward:

> "Strike up the band, here comes a sailor;
> Cash in his hand, just off a whaler.
> Stand in a row, don't let him go,
> For Jack's a cinch and every inch
> A sailor!"

The officers, whose shouts of laughter came through the thick skylight and could be heard above the screeching of the wind, enjoyed themselves unrestrainedly in a way forbidden me and my companions. My thoughts ran in a bitter vein, and emotion got the better of me. Why was it all right for them to drink things that would mean punishment to us? At this point one of the celebrants called to the marine above to lift the gun-deck skylight: "Let's have some air; it's hot as hell down here!"

My teeth sounded like reef points tat-a-tatting against a flapping sail in a calm sea. "Hot as hell down there!" No wonder, with a tankful of fine champagne on top of a rich dinner, and the air fogged up with the smoke of smuggled cigars. Burn me! As a belch of cold mutton threatened to nauseate me I closed my eyes to curtain the sight of the warm scene from my mind. A cold, rubber sleeve brushed my hand as the marine orderly saluted the officer of the deck:

"Four bells, sir!" At last! The bell rang two, and two.

"Relieve the wheel and lookouts!" from the officer of the deck and repeated by the boatswain's mates.

It had started to snow, and it lashed our faces like stinging whips. My relief helped to twist my fingers from the spokes. At first I could hardly move, and I feared I had frozen to the gratings, but I had just stiffened there through inactivity and sleepiness. When I did move my legs, an intense stinging sensation telegraphed my body from port to starboard, and I staggered forward to the sound of laughter and a wavery singing of improvised words below, some inelegant expressions having been added. After all, forward or aft, a bottle of gin and we're all the same under the skin.

The next night, when I went below to my hammock, some stars shone between small wind clouds, and we were again sailing full and by, with the weather leeches trembling. The wind was moist and friendly. I fell asleep thinking of Happy, not as I had seen him ten days before but as the handsome shipmate on the *St. Louis,* with a future bright before him and a lovely girl waiting for him. But in my sleep his face faded into leering, diabolical features more clearly defined than the pleasant face I wished to retain. And it was from among a nightmare of such faces that I was roused a few minutes before midnight on to a flooded deck to go on duty with my watch. Again the ship was hove to, and we were laboring in heavy seas.

We came to anchor in the beautiful landlocked harbor of Nagasaki, in the southern part of Japan, on the twenty-first, and there the ship was coaled by hundreds of Japanese women, young and old, streaming aboard with laden saucerlike baskets. Three pleasant weeks were passed in our first Japanese port, which seemed remarkably clean in comparison with the native sections of Hong Kong; and the people were so smiling and polite that we did not learn for some time how deep or shallow might be the smile of one trained from birth to bow affably to everyone. On May 10, 1892, we passed up the wonderful Inland Sea to the great industrial port of Kobe, where Captain McCormick awaited our arrival to relieve Captain Seeley. The officer who had brought us safely halfway around the world was just an officer to us forward, and we would have missed any one of our topmates more than we were to miss him.

The United States ships *Marion* and *Alert* were in port with us, and at that season all vessels had to be constantly on guard against sudden gales from seaward. Frequently we had to send down our light yards and masts, secure everything, and stand by with steam pressure up, in case we had to get to sea hurriedly to prevent a disaster such as that at Samoa.

One of our boatswain's mates was Mike Donnelly, a graduate in 1864 of the Schoolship *Sabine.* After cruising in her for a year along the Atlantic coast he had shipped in the famous *Hartford* for a three-year cruise on the Asiatic Station. In these waters, in January, 1868, he had witnessed the loss of Admiral Bell, Lieutenant Read, and ten enlisted men when they attempted to land in the surf at Osaka. The admiral and his men were buried at Kobe and, on Decoration Day, John Bell (who remained as steward to our new captain) and I went with Donnelly to place flowers on their graves.

The old boatswain's mate informed us that on the same cruise of the *Hartford,* during which they covered 47,000 miles, they lost twenty-nine officers and men. One of their officers, Lieutenant Commander A. S. Mackenzie, was killed while skirmishing against savages on the island of Formosa. This man was the son of the commander of the brig *Somers* who, in 1842, had ordered a midshipman, a boatswain, and one seaman to be hanged from the yardarms for attempted mutiny—the only record of mutiny ever to stain the pages of American naval history. Even here the facts were far from obvious, and as the midshipman happened to be the son of the Secretary of War at the time, there may have been a clash of personalities that would have rendered the justice of the sentence questionable, although Mackenzie was exonerated on a charge of murder.

We returned to Nagasaki on June 10 for another long stay. Our visit this time was marred by much cold and wet weather. One morning I found posted on our bulletin board the following effusion of a fo'c'sle poet:

"Dirty days hath September, April, June, and November;
From February until May the rain it raineth every day.
All the rest have thirty-one, without one blessed gleam of sun—
And if a month had two-and-thirty, they'd be just as wet and twice as dirty."

While we were in port, our friend the *Marion* arrived towing a small ship ignominiously by the nose. It was the U.S.S. *Palos,* and she aroused our curiosity and amusement, for she was the smallest ship in naval commission. For years the tiny steamboat had cruised up and down the Yangtze River. She had a corporal's guard of marines drawn up on deck to salute the admiral, but so small was the crew that when she reached her moorings the corporal dropped his sword and ran to let go the anchor. The *Palos* spent a brief while in dry dock before returning to her accustomed and important patrol on China's great river.

At Nagasaki we saw with interest the lovely observance of Bon Matsuri, a Japanese feast day in honor of the dead. On the night of August 13 the tombs of all who had died within the past year were hung with colored paper lanterns, while the families and friends of the dead gathered in the cemeteries to honor the departed ones with offerings of food and drink, while recounting all their virtues. At about two o'clock on the third night, the lanterns were gathered up by the memorial throng and carried, like thousands of dancing tiny stars, in a brilliant procession down the mountainsides to the shores of the bay. Each lantern was then placed in its own little boat of woven straw, cargoed with fruits and flowers. The straw sails were trimmed to the morning breeze, and the tiny vessels bearing the bright burning spirits of the dead were gently borne out toward the sea, burdened with remembrance.

The time had come when shore liberties were due all the good-conduct men, as well as the poor fellows who "hit the beach" every ninety days and were on probation between times. In spite of an unusual number of drunks appearing daily at "the mast," the ship passed a creditable admiral's inspection, and men of the first conduct class were granted a forty-hour liberty every three weeks, from Saturday to Monday. This gave me an excellent opportunity to extend my trips inland, to bathing resorts where an American dollar was a real fortune, and to distant temples and other sights mentioned in the guidebooks.

With my topmate Karl Raddatz, a German boy from the merchant ships, I spent one long liberty in a small sailing boat, cruising out to sea and touching a number of little islands whose natives had never seen an American bluejacket. We boarded a junk at sea to beg some fresh water (something we should not have done), and landed at a lighthouse to buy fish and other provisions. That night we slept on the beach of an island outside the harbor, Papenburg or Takaboko, which the Europeans also called Massacre Island because, some three hundred years before, thousands of native Christians were butchered there and thrown into the sea. We returned to the narrow quarters of the ship with real regret.

Once some of the liberty men were ashore, it was not always easy to get them back to the ship. At the U.S. Consulate there was a marshal who had a special zeal in apprehending deserters and returning them on board. He never stooped to compromise with a defaulter for half the reward money—he wanted it all, and therefore the liberty-breakers had a profound dislike for his methods. One of our petty officers, named Farley, was captured by this marshal and taken out to the ship in a native boat. When they were within a hundred yards or so of our port gangway, Farley leaped from the sampan and swam to the *Lancaster*'s bows, to come in through the bridle port and give himself up. The marshal, who was a man of some bulk, had jumped to the rail of the sampan in a futile effort to catch his prisoner, and in so doing capsized the boat. He couldn't swim, and his shouts and those of the native boatman startled the harbor, until one of our whaleboats rescued them. It wasn't necessary to inform the marshal that he could not collect his reward because he hadn't personally delivered his man; but his anger knew no bounds when he found he had to settle with the Japanese wherryman for the loss of his cookstove and boat gear.

The *Lancaster* man who undoubtedly had the most pleasure from his liberty at Nagasaki was an old fellow named Briggs, a cook. He made pastry on his own account for private sale to shipmates, and invested the profits in lucky gambling. When he went ashore he might have had as much as five hundred dollars stowed about his person. Virtuously he avoided the water-front saloons and secluded himself in a vine-bowered cottage up in the hills behind the coal piles. Here he surrounded himself with a large retinue of native servants, including a number of pretty little geisha girls.

The cottage was stuffed with the finest food and drink, and Briggs embarked upon the life of an oriental potentate.

Rumors of his gay life reached us, and as days passed and he was long overdue to return, it seemed as if the flagship would sail lacking one excellent cook. The ship's people could not reach him, for Briggs was a likeable fellow and free with the yen, so that the native officers were not willing to turn him over.

Our first anchor had been fished and brought aboard; its mate had left the mud and the engines were beginning to turn when the quartermaster reported that many boats showing American flags were leaving the docks and heading toward us. A Japanese in uniform was frantically waving a U.S. ensign.

The captain stood at the port after rail with the admiral, and his eye was caught by the flags.

"Admiral," he said, "that is probably the United States senator who arrived this morning on the Canadian Pacific steamer. He must want to go with us to China."

"All right, captain. Hold the ship for his arrival, and be ready to accord him the honors."

"Yes, sir. Mr. Gilmore, call the guard and the band!"

There was a scurrying of uniformed men up and down the ladders, bugle calls rang out, and side boys were piped. Meanwhile, out from the docks streamed a nautical parade composed of almost every sampan in the harbor trailing behind a large boat carrying a Japanese brass band which was making a brave effort at "The Star-Spangled Banner." As this foremost boat came into view of the captain's field glasses, he turned savagely to the executive.

"Dismiss the guard, sir. Get under weigh at once. Admiral, it's that damned ship's cook I thought we were going to leave behind!"

At once the remaining cable clanked around the capstan with angry thumps as our engine began to turn over. Sure enough, in the stern sheets of the largest boat sat Briggs. Surrounded by streamers of tissue paper and innumerable flags and branches of trees, our cook made his kingly progress over the water. With all the impassive dignity of a great potentate, and with a gold-embroidered cloth draped over his shoulders, he sat surrounded by many lovely maidens who, at a word from their lord, posed prettily for our benefit. Several of the girls who were corked to look like Nubian slaves opened bottles reposing in iced pails, while another beauty cooled the nabob's brow with a large feather fan.

The deserter's complacence was quickly dropped, however, when he noticed that our ship was forging ahead, further and further from the gay procession of sampans. As if awakening from a dream, he threw off his golden cloak, pushed his attendants aside, and urged the oarsmen to pull for their lives. Our accommodation ladder had been rigged in, and the cook lost his final shred of dignity when he leaped to cling to one of the cleats of the sea ladder. He had not yet crossed the gangway and was still free of the ship's discipline. Clinging precariously, he smiled up at the captain on the bridge, and with a final surge of munificence put his free hand into a pocket and pulled it out filled with the last of his money. With a true sailorly gesture he scattered the last of his fortune among his former retainers in the boat, and then scrambled aboard to face a court-martial and the loss of much pay. But he had taken his fling, and thoughts of his only liberty in Japan would console him for the rest of his life among galley ranges.

Several years later I passed through Nagasaki on my way homeward. Few of the people there remembered the name of our ship, and fewer still the name of our admiral. But hardly a one of them had forgotten Briggs, the cook, and at mention of his name many an eye lightened and many a Japanese face broke into a reminiscent smile.

Chapter XVII

FAREWELL TO SAIL

We arrived at the mouth of the Yangtze River of China on October 5. There at Woosung we had our first view of the famous U.S.S. *Monocacy*, a side-wheel steamer which had represented our country on the great river since 1866.

Woosung, the port of entry to Shanghai, seemed to me a dirty, disagreeable spot that caught the full force of gales from every direction. It offered merely one great vista of mud, lowland flats, and more mud at the mouth of the Whampoo, a river with low clay banks on each side of a swirling lane of yellow water. It was from this place that some of us received our first liberty for Shanghai, and our party was taken in the launch up the twelve or more miles to the city—a three-hour run. There was no railroad in that section of the Middle Kingdom, because the Chinese objected to such devilish means of transportation and claimed, moreover, that the tracks, ties, and poles might disturb their sacred dead. The land between Woosung and Shanghai looked like one vast graveyard, apparently covered with brick or wooden mounds enclosing the coffins of natives.

The cosmopolitan appearance of Hong Kong had in a way

prepared me to see the fine streets and substantial modern buildings of Shanghai, but nonetheless when we landed at the modern wharf I was astonished at the tall beautiful buildings of granite and marble opposite, and the great banks and plateglass show windows that lined the side of the Bund. I knew, however, that all this was the work of the foreigners, and lost no time in engaging a native guide who promised to show me a bit of the real China. In company with one of the apprentices, named Barr, I was rolled in a 'ricksha through the commercial sections of the International Settlement and the French Concession. In the native city, walled high enough to prevent entrance except through massive gates, we left our conveyances and, crossing the narrow street, plunged from West to East, from modern progress to ancient tradition, from enlightenment, efficiency, and science into filth, degradation, and shackling custom.

The streets of the native quarter were narrow and dirty, with many deep ditches of open sewerage over which hung the carcasses of butchered goats. The house walls were lined with beggars as thick as flies, sunning themselves and currying each other like monkeys and exposing their self-made sores. My companion was skylarking about and cracking jokes with the stolid "Chinks," as he called them, here slapping a coolie on the back and there chucking one of the painted girls under the chin. Sullen glances meant nothing to him, but in the courtyard of the yamen we passed some heavily barred cages of prisoners, and something Barr said caused one of the occupants to spit at him. Foolishly, he became angry and started out to find someone to whom he might make a complaint.

While he did this I wandered into the incense-laden dimness of a great temple. Suspended in its dark upper regions was a large model of a Chinese junk. In the wings of the main building were hundreds of idols, with prayer mats and jars of joss sticks in front of each. I strolled about the temple for a short time only, but when I got outside Barr had vanished, after leaving with our guide a message that he had gone along to the south gate and would see me on the dock in the morning.

When we turned back through the streets of one-storied shops I was glad to reach again the comparatively cleaner air of the French settlement. The scenes I had left, in spite of a few artistic tea-houses, a goldfish hatchery, and several wavy walls of curved glossy tile, were steeped in ancient filth and stench. As we passed through the high gate I noticed a tall white man who was talking fluently in Chinese with some of the pottery vendors, from whom he was purchasing quantities of their wares. Seeing my uniform, he smiled toward me and asked if he could help me in any way.

He was an American, he said, and as he volleyed me with questions in a pleasant way I could not help feeling attracted to him. Where did I hail from? How did I like the navy? He seemed to be well acquainted with our admiral and some of the other officers. The Chinese about him showed him great respect, and he was the only person I had met who was able to bring a smile to their sober faces. This gentleman said he was surprised to find that I had visited the native city, and told me that many foreign young men born in Shanghai had never ventured so far into the old town as I had gone that day. After a brief exchange of words I watched him drive off with real regret. I could not dream that this chance encounter would have its effect upon my future life in the Orient.

The city of Shanghai could be reached from the sea only by having the ship cross a wide bar of mud at Woosung. At this time, the moon, the tides, and several other conditions were just right, and the *Lancaster* was able to cross the bar with depth to spare, anchoring off the Bund on the fifth of November. Barr, the apprentice, returned to the ship on time, but looking tired and worn. With a lackluster air he dropped the bundles of curios he had purchased, and turned in as soon as he could. His hammock swung next to mine on the gun deck, and that night he rolled about feverishly. He went on the sick list the next morning and was transferred to a hospital on shore. Ten days later he died of black smallpox.

No doubt Barr had picked up the infection in some of the dark holes of the old city on the day he wandered there with me. What kind quirk of fate had separated me from him in the lee of the temple? I shivered to think that I too might have been caught in the talons of that dread disease. We buried the boy in the foreign cemetery, laying his body in a cement-lined depression that was its only protection from the water-soaked earth of the riverside.

Our ship and everything in her was at once fumigated with sulphur. We were then ordered to make a healthier port or to cruise at sea, so that the contagion might be checked. But when we reached the bar at Woosung on dreary New Year's Day, there was not enough water to permit our crossing. Day after day we tried to pass the soft barrier. Lighters came alongside, and most of our coal and stores was transferred to them; this helped some, but not quite enough. The guns were then all rolled aft as far as they could go, and the entire crew was crowded to the stern. This maneuver lifted our bow over the bar, but the keel aft was stuck fast. We then moved the guns and ourselves far forward, and over we tilted into the deep water.

Now everything had to be taken aboard from the lighters again. To reduce our weight further we had dropped both anchors, and could find only one of them at the buoys. Our diver force tried in vain to find the lost bower amid the soupy waters of the river. We had decided to leave it behind when a native, who dove with large stones held in his hand, recovered the ground tackle for us. His primitive skill succeeded where our up-to-date methods had failed.

It was not until February 5 that we got clear of the Woosung region with its high winds, cold rains, and squalls. Another boy was taken with the sickness, which showed that we had not entirely left it behind; but he recovered, and when at last we reached Hong Kong we were given clearance papers to show that once more we were a healthy ship.

We sailed out of Hong Kong one day for target practice off the rocky coast. As we were shifting into working clothes, Apprentice Croghan, of the foretop, dumped a textbook of Ben Pitman shorthand out of his bag. Noting my curiosity regarding a subject unfamiliar to me, he lent me the book at once. Perched on the gratings of the main hatch awaiting my turn at the guns, shaken by the booming of our smoothbores, I dug deeply into my first lesson at abbreviated writing. I was no longer concerned with the hits and misses at the target, or even the scores of my own battery, and it was with reluctance that I laid down the book when I was ordered to my post as captain of the starboard Hotchkiss 6-pounder. Nothing else had so touched my interest as this fascinating study, and within a week I had reached a stage where I lay in my hammock at night trying to transpose my thoughts and the speech I heard about me into hooks and curves, dots and dashes.

The executive officer, noting my preoccupation and struck by the novelty of study aboard ship, gave me encouragement, permitting me to practice under the flickering light of the half-deck lamp near the printer's press, even after taps in port or during my watch below at sea. The navigator furnished me with paper from his storeroom, and from the ship's writer I got some pencils. Bugler Gannon volunteered to read to me, and my first dictation was his slow and careful reading, from beginning to end, of Rider Haggard's novel *She*. My lessons were so painstakingly acquired that, although progress in speed was barely perceptible, the notes were so clear and legible that even today they can be read like print. As lesson after lesson was mastered, there grew in me the assurance that I should follow the business of reporting, as Charles Dickens, that pioneer in shorthand writing, had done.

The boy to whom I was indebted for my start on this new tack in life was a tall, ungainly, good-natured fellow of the sort that was inevitably called "farmer" on board ship. He was slow but methodical, and was never ruffled. After I had made some progress with my study of pothooks and dashes, I asked "Pop" Croghan if he had ever learned it himself.

"Sure," he replied. "I almost went through the book in college, but what's the use of learning something that takes so much effort? You can get a buzzard [a rating badge] in this man's navy without rattling your brain extra hard. I should worry."

"But wouldn't shorthand help you on shore when your time is out?"

"Maybe. But so long as I have shipped in the navy, why

shouldn't I take things easy? I'll be content to take what's in store for me here. Perhaps some day I'll be a bosun and have a cheese knife at my side and a command of my own. That's what I'm heading for if they let me. If not, then give me a p.o. rating forward, and I'll be happy."

Pop was destined to keep pace with his ambition, for some years later he had reached the rank of boatswain and was able to wear a cheese knife, or officer's sword. On February 5, 1910, the U.S. Tug *Nina*, under his command, left Norfolk for Boston with a crew of thirty-five men, and on the way disappeared at sea without trace. Her loss was one of the saddest disasters to befall the new navy. The *Nina* was the eleventh ship in American naval history to be lost with all hands; the first was the privateer *Saratoga* in 1780. Of all those ships that sailed to meet a blind ocean grave, none was commanded by a man more capable than the overgrown boy who carelessly declared that day on the *Lancaster* that he would be content with whatever fate had in store for him.

A time-honored ceremony in our navy in those days was general muster, which was held once a month, usually on the first Sunday. This function was preceded several days earlier by the most vigorous cleaning and overhauling of the ship that a hard-worked crew could accomplish. The holystones were roused out and every inch of deck was scrubbed down to the grain. Many reasons for the origin of the nickname of "holystones" were to be heard forward. One was that the scrubbing blocks were used so much on Sundays and holidays. Bob Lindsay, a sea poet, had a better one. He claimed that at the time of the Reformation in England, when the Church of St. Nicholas at Yarmouth was despoiled, the carved stones of many monuments were sent to the British ships for cleaning use. Another reason given was that in Queen Elizabeth's time one of the Commandments, or a passage of Scripture, was cut into each stone. Still another idea might occur to anyone who for the first time heard the kind of language used by the sailormen as they hauled a heavy stone to and fro—many of their words had a distinctly Biblical flavor.

During the overhaul, the running gear had to be perfectly arrayed, or flaked and flemished down; tacks and sheets were laid out in the waterways in neat figures and designs; halyards were coiled with a geometrical nicety in their spindled racks. Standing gear was glossy and taut, and all braces were snugly secured to their pins. All ironwork and every inch of served wire rope was tarred down with rags soaked in "Stockholm," a brand of shiny black tar. This stuff could easily be removed from face and hands by the use of navy butter, and the cooks had to be watchful when the work of tarring down was going on.

The work itself was not hard, except that afterward the sailor had to "ride down the upper stays." He would sit in a bosun's chair and descend along the stay, drawing one rag-filled hand after him. If the rag was gripped too hard the liquid would weep out and rain black drops down over the decks, the boats, and anyone unlucky enough to be standing below. The process was accompanied by the disagreeable task of slushing masts. Every part of the topmast from heel to hounds that was touched by the sliding tub, and the topgallant and royal masts as far as the funnel, was scraped with knives, and then slushed with tallow or grease. The topgallant masts were usually left in place for this operation so that the backstays, the shrouds, and the fore-and-aft stays remained taut and could be ridden down for the final touch of tar.

When the fatal Sunday arrived and the ship was thought to be in perfect order, the men would clean up and haul from their bags the best apparel they owned, and after a preliminary inspection by division officers would seek their quarters. Then the captain, with his retinue, visited every part of the ship. With a solemn air he rubbed his white gloves over the beams and carlings and across the bottoms of scouse kettles in every mess. It was: "Put this man on the report—that paintwork shows streaks!" "That gear should be stowed better." "Boatswain, can't you see that the bunt gasket of our main royal is not square?" The ship's writer was kept busy entering the names of offenders; the messengers ran for this person and that; the bugler sounded one call after another, and the boatswain's mates passed the word from deck to deck. Every man's heart fluttered with fears, and never more than during general muster did the ship justify the title of "floating madhouse" that some disgruntled old-timers occasionally bestowed upon her.

The most trying ordeal was still to come. Even the boatswain, who sent forth the tremulous call "All hands to general muster!" looked unhappy. The captain and his officers, standing on the deck according to rank, maintained their dignity as best they could while swaying to the roll of the ship. Opposite them the crew was arrayed by divisions, flanked by the marines and the band with their shiny helmets and brass buttons. The executive officer then read the Articles of War—which, it seemed to me, were designed mainly to impress upon the hapless enlisted men the danger of not kowtowing always to any person in officer's stripes, and the dire vengeance to be expected by a poor fellow who might "pusillanimously cry for quarter" in battle. After one had heard these articles read some fifty times, certain sentences were impressed sharply upon the dullest mind.

The paymaster or his clerk now began reading the full muster roll, beginning with the chief master-at-arms, the ranking man of the crew. Each man answered his name by saluting and calling out his rate. He then passed alone around the capstan, in full view of a thousand eyes, and disappeared forward; and so on down the line until every last trembling apprentice and coal-heaver had run the gamut of the officers. General muster as a monthly naval ceremony has been abolished for some thirty years. I doubt if there ever was an excuse for the custom except possibly in a suspicion by the navy pay office that the commanding officer of some ship a century ago was collecting the pay of men discharged by death or desertion. It was an awe-inspiring ceremony, and when the old men spoke of general muster it was in a tone of reverence. It was usual for them to figure the unexpired portion of their enlistments by the number of "walks around the capstan" they still had to serve.

When we sailed from Hong Kong to Nagasaki on April 5, 1893, the wife of our admiral accompanied her husband on board, and there she remained until I left the ship. To have an occasional glimpse of a woman at sea was a novelty even then, and I think it was soon after this that the presence of officer's wives on warships was prohibited. We did not envy the afterguards who took care of the sacred quarters aft. The fear was great that they might talk too loudly, or let loose an occasional swear word, or drop a squilgee handle on the deck. Mrs. Harmony was a little woman, gray-haired and kindly, but whenever she appeared on the spar deck there was an immediate exodus of officers and men to other parts of the ship; and for an enlisted man to be addressed by her was more terrifying than it would have been to receive a dressing-down from her august husband—who, after all, was a mellow old sailorman who liked peace and quiet as well as anyone.

The presence of the admiral's wife on board proved a hindrance to the admiral's habit of wetting his whistle. His steward asserted she kept him under strict surveillance, but on a nice afternoon the old man would bring Mrs. Harmony on deck, lead her to a big chair in the lee of the spanker, out of the draft, and then he would order one of us boys to secure her with the end of a brail in event of a heavy roll. Even so, sometimes he would say: "Here, lad, take another turn around Mrs. Harmony!" When she could not free herself without help the old man would go below. At the foot of the ladder stood the steward, ready with glass and bottle. I believe the good lady knew all the time what he was up to, for one day she smiled and almost winked.

We rarely saw His Lordship, as the admiral had been christened because of his labored British accent, unless the helmsman steered badly or there happened to be an unusual amount of noise above the admiral's spreading quarters aft. But old storm eagle that he was, he was sure to smell a gust of bad weather when it was still far in the offing, and up he would come to see out the worst of it. We thought this foolish of him when he could have remained in the warmth and comfort of his cabins. This habit he had of prowling about on deck was to lead me into a paralyzing personal encounter with our squadron commander.

One midwatch, when we were plowing a path northward through the angry swells of the Formosa Channel, drenched in cold squalls, there was a short lull in the furious blinding rain, and the weather hammock cloths were triced up to give the men at the wheel some protection from the stinging wind and scud. Some of us maintopmen huddled into the nettings space to keep warm, and with the insouciance of young sailors were soon asleep. The rising of another squall caused our mates to draw the cloths over us to keep the nettings dry.

It was about two o'clock in the morning when the old admiral came on deck to prowl, sniffing the air as he went to the weather side and thrusting his hand under the cloths over the nettings compartment. Looking for damp nettings was one of the old man's hobbies. He was as surprised as I was when, groping about for dampness, his fingers tangled in my salt-coarsened hair. Calling for a lantern, he pulled me out. Shaking off sleep, I almost gave myself up for dead when I saw who my captor was. In a voice that could be heard high above the thrumming of the wind, he shouted to the officer of the deck: "Quinby, oh Quinby, theah's a chappie in the nettin's! And the nettin's are all *wet,* sir!"

The old man seemed more displeased at the wet nettings than at finding a boy off his post. But he couldn't punish the nettings, and so he ordered me on the report. While the captain gave me six days of extra duty, I could see he was still amused at the admiral's version of how he had captured me. The real punishment came in after years. Whenever I joined a new ship, or visited one on which some of my old acquaintances were to be found, some waggish sailor would be sure to greet me, mimicking the port-wine voice of the good old admiral: "Quinby, oh Quinby, theah's a chappie in the nettin's!"

The punishment for my first recorded offense on the cruise was to serve extra time helping the painter. This man was a dark Spaniard, with pointed black mustaches, crisp curly hair, and piercing black eyes. He gave all his instruction in whispers, and his particular vice was an excessive use of red pepper, which he breathed up his nostrils like snuff, and spread over his food as well. I soon learned to "sling a handsome brush" and to do finicky lettering, and my services were appreciated so greatly that when I had served my extra time the executive informed me that the painter still had plenty of work ahead and that I should continue to help him in my spare moments. "And when you feel like taking a nap in the nettings again," he wound up, "you'll get credit for the time you are putting in." When my enlistment expired, the government owed me for many days of extra duty, for which I have so far failed to collect.

I was up in the mizzentop one evening, stealing a chapter out of a dime novel which we were not supposed to read. I lay flat, and unobserved, looking down through the lubber's hole, glorying in the peace and quiet of the quarter-deck. The starboard side, being the weather side, belonged to the captain, who exercised his legs in a short walk from taffrail to mainmast. The executive officer and navigator consulted charts and sailing directions on the bridge, and the officer of the deck was forward making his rounds. On the port side were the wardroom officers, walking up and down, or congregated in groups, smoking. At the starboard gangway were the four warrant officers and one of the pay clerks.

There was a loud noise of throat clearing below the admiral's hatch, and his white dome appeared like a full moon on the horizon. The captain saluted him and hurried over to the lee side. The wardroom officers crowded down their ladder to the gun deck. The admiral walked a few turns, slowly. He had the gout. At sea his position was not a gregarious one, and no doubt his missed the intimacies with other officers. Personally, I would have talked to him. I would ask him why he clipped his aspirates from words beginning with one, and why his manner was so brusque now that it was no longer necessary for him to inspire fear. He said something to the captain across the deck, and this was a signal for the latter to cross to the admiral's side. Now they walked together.

I felt fortunate in my own position. If I had disagreement with one of my topmates I could visit some other part of the ship, and among the four hundred men I could find kindred spirits. I could chat with friend Bell up in the warm eyes of the ship, or hobnob with O'Leary, a carpenter's mate who spent much of his time off watch at the port gangway.

The poor warrant officers—how difficult it was for them to find a place to sit and smoke without stepping on someone's rank. Such is the discipline of the sea: inexorable laws prescribed by centuries of rule and tradition in our service and that of Great Britain. I wondered why the warrant officers did not swallow their pride and talk with the crew, fraternize with the captains of tops, or the chief master-at-arms, who was so near their own station. These warrant officers who had crawled to their positions through the hawsepipes were the most unreasonable in their demands for observation of naval etiquette.

On April 13 we sailed into the harbor of Nagasaki again, a port which, with its familiar hills and smiling people, was beginning to seem quite homelike. Ten days later we arrived at Kobe and anchored in a bay filled with foreign merchant ships, some of them harbor-bound, awaiting the release of crews who were in jail ashore for refusing duty.

Here at this port there was an alarm of fire on shore one afternoon. The quick hungry blaze showed fiercely against a background of brown hills. The fire was in the European section, a foreigner's house, built less of paper and flimsy than usual to native houses. There was no need for a call for volunteers, as a fire is ever a gala happening for a man-o'-warsman—if the fire is ashore. A working party of us tumbled into a cutter, with leather buckets, axes, and that stand-by of all sailormen, rope and plenty of it. The flames were crackling merrily when we arrived, as if amused at the feeble attempts of native pump-and-bucket men to douse it. There being no building immediately to leeward of the doomed house, we just stood by and watched the servants of the former home make a crazy to-do over a few things they had saved. The petty officers of our party proceeded to the nearest saki shop for some native beer. The ubiquitous police were there, quiet, their silence matched by the complacency of the crowd. The children, so many of them, stood respectfully behind their elders, aghast to see destroyed such things as they themselves could not hope ever to possess. There was 'ricksha men, some in rags, hauling brightly dressed yoshiwara girls; maidens, geisha girls, graceful, smiling. Under their elaborate, perfumed hair dressings their faces were painted like dolls.

Across the way, at a public bathing place, the doors were crowded with patrons, girl attendants, the rubbers, the government officials. Everywhere there were burgees of bunting and calico, just as every day—nothing special except the fire.

A landing party of a dozen men from a German man-o'-war arrived at this time, under charge of a two-striper. In clipped words he ordered his men to lay out their gear, connected the hose from their small force pump to one of the vats in the bathhouse, detailed his rope-and-ladder men, the bucket passers and wreckers. He tried to tell the authorities in mixed German and Japanese what he wanted them to do, but the natives stared at him. Then he aimed atrocious pidgin English at us, with no effect. He was a short, insolent sort of man, with close-cropped hair and mustache of straw color. An old native, who had been quietly and efficiently directing the bucket tenders, approached the Prussian. Toothless and aged, his eyes were mere slits in a brown, wrinkled face. He had large white characters painted on his blue frock. He bowed low before the lieutenant, and said in a gentle voice: "Please-s, s-sir; I als-so s-spik little Inglis-s."

We laughed, but the German boys stiffened in their white mustering clothes. The officer confined his further orders to German. Feeling the need for action, he commanded his force to turn to with crowbars and wrenches. They piled upstairs in the house we considered to be in no danger, and we could hear a ripping and splintering of wood, with now and then a protest from the owner of the house. It was a modern place, and soon a tin tub, with its wooden casing, was shoved out a front window onto the bamboo roof of the porch, while we cheered the wreckers with shouts of encouragement and promises of leather medals. We did envy them, for next to saving anybody's house from fire we would have enjoyed wrecking one. The bathtub was heavy and crashed through the flimsy roof, narrowly missing some of the Germans who were carefully bringing a mattress and some bedding down the stairs. A large mirror followed the bathtub, then came a patent toilet and a trunk filled with ladies' clothing, which slipped from a parbuckle sling they hitched around it. Men walked through the house with bricks from a cookstove in the rear, and piled them neatly in a black square. A servant would not let go of a pigskin trunk, and she was brought out on top of it. "*Na, na!*" praised the officer; "*Sist's gut gethan!*" There being nothing of value left in the stripped home, the Germans drew up at attention as the last embers of the fire winked at the setting sun. And we winked, too, at the ruddy, soiled, and perspiring German boys, who almost dared to smile in return. They were patient, well-disciplined, and put up with our jokes as we watched them replace some of the things they had removed. We parted with them on friendly terms. English man-o'-warsmen were so different. I don't know why, except maybe the fighting was usually started by our own gang. They repaid us in kind—words, then blows; then police and jail, just like that.

On May 1 we sailed for Yokohama, reaching that eastern Japanese port on the second day. At the end of the month, on Decoration Day, the ship's company paraded to the foreign cemetery, where memorial ceremonies were held beside the fine monument erected in honor of the dead of the U.S.S. *Oneida;* and afterward some of our G.A.R. men, headed by John R. Bell, went to Ikigama to decorate the graves of other men lost in the same disaster. Later I made a trip with my shipmate Biel to the town of Kamakura, where we marveled at the great Diabutsu. This is an immense figure of Buddha, made entirely of bronze and dating from about the year 1250. It is fifty feet high and contains a temple inside; the circumference of one thumb alone is more than three feet.

My twenty-first birthday was rapidly approaching, and I had decided to quit the navy. The latter days of my enlistment were to be saddened by the tragedy that struck my young friend Karl Raddatz. This German lad who had come out of the merchant ships to the comparative paradise of the American navy, and whose one ambition had been a clear record to smooth his way some day to a commission in the service of his adopted land, had greatly changed in the past few months. No one could help seeing the difference in him, and in the way he carried his formerly strong and healthy body. One day he had almost tumbled off the yardarm while furling sail at sea. He seldom went on shore now, and he had become morose, seeing to avoid his former friends. At the first chance I took him aside and asked him what was troubling him. He cried without shame as he told me. Some months before, in one of the vice-ridden treaty ports, he had taken a disease of such a nature that he refused to report for the sick list, and doctored himself under the advice of older men as ignorant as himself. A rash had broken out on his arms, and he suffered with sores on his legs and hips. His teeth ached so that he could no longer eat our ship rations, and his cheeks were sunken and pallid.

I advised him to put himself under medical care at once, so that he could be treated and released from duty aloft, where his aching joints caused him much suffering; but he was sure that the record would prevent his re-enlistment and bar him from any future naval advancement. "God, how I wish I could live this cruise over again!"

On the afternoon of Saturday, June 3, the wardroom officers gave a luncheon on board at which many ladies from shore were present. Some of the guests may have requested a sail drill to amuse them, for, although by rights it was a sailor's holiday and we should have had the afternoon free, we were roused out and ordered aloft. The royal yardmen were already up the shrouds, and at the next command, "Lay aloft, topgallant yardmen!" Raddatz and I sprang into the port main rigging, and together raced from shear pole to futtock shrouds. The German boy was usually more agile than I, though much heavier, and ordinarily got into the top ahead of me. This time he was slower. I heard him puffing as if at the end of a long trial of endurance.

As I pulled myself through the lubber's hole, the puffing ceased. I heard cries from the deck, quickly followed by a dull sound as the boy's body hit the pump in the port main chains. When I looked over the rim of the top I saw several men swimming toward my shipmate, whose body floated limply some distance from the gangway. Willing hands hoisted him over the side and laid his broken form in the waterways. A call was sent below to the wardroom, where our surgeon was helping to entertain the visitors. By the time he had changed his clothes and reached the sick bay, Karl Raddatz had passed on to a place where there are no re-enlistments. That day I furled my side of the topgallantsail alone.

As a messmate of Karl's, I stood one of the deathwatches that night. The body had been placed on a mess table on one side of the half deck, and I sat on a chair as far away from it as I decently could. The hour was between one and two o'clock in the morning. There was not a sound or sign of life aboard the ship except the tramp of the quartermaster overhead, the gentle lap-lap of water below the open gun port, and the yawn of a drowsy marine sentry at the cabin door. I was sunk in thoughts of our loss, and pictured how different the lad's life might have been if he could have been with us during our last night in New York and could have heard the wise admonishments of Biel's father. Or perhaps if our chaplain, left far astern in Madeira, or the captain who succeeded to his duties—if they had taken an occasion to offer timely cautions regarding the shoals they knew lay ahead of a boy in a Chinese port . . .

My reverie was terrifyingly interrupted by a rustling sound from the table where the body rested. My eye was caught by the movement of something under the flag that draped the corpse. I cried out, and the marine came running. In horror we approached, and my heart almost stopped beating when a dark form leaped at me. It was a ship's rat, which jumped from the table and flashed down the ladder to the berth deck. I slept little for the remainder of that night.

The next day the members of our mess went ashore to listen to a minister from the foreign colony read a funeral sermon. He said nothing of the useless waste of a young life that had come to pass through ignorance and through the blindness of trusted advisers who might have prevented hell on earth instead of preaching empty pieties. So we laid away a good shipmate.

The time had come to strike out for myself. I had finished my contract with our government, convinced now that I had entered the navy through the wrong door. I loved that ship, the weathered *Lancaster*, and my many friends on her, men who growled often but whose loyalty never failed. But the time had come to part. On June 14, 1893, I signed a waiver of consular aid should I in future find myself penniless in a Chinese port sixteen thousand miles from my home place. When I doffed my uniform and was landed in Yokohama, I carried an honorable discharge, a new pigskin trunk to put my new suit in when not wearing it, a ticket to Shanghai, enough board money for a few weeks, a fair amateur knowledge of stenography, and five years of experience in the American navy. In an honest appraisal I was inclined to think that the naval experience was the least valuable of all my possessions.

While awaiting a steamer to take me to China, I happened upon some of my *Lancaster* friends on liberty, and my last night in Japan was spent in their merry company. One of them was old Andy Farrell, a Gloucesterman and coxswain of the first cutter. He was a reserved man who, however, when well set before the wind with a couple of glasses of Scotch under his hatches, could tell many stirring yarns of the navy, going back even to revolutionary times. The two of us drifted about and finally dropped our hook in a sort of native tavern that boasted English barmaids, where American and British man-o'-warsmen were found mingling together and singing with noisy sentimentality. One of our men, spying Andy, introduced him to his English acquaintances: "Here's our best singer, fellows. Andy, let's have the good old song about the *General Monkey!*"

A British petty officer came up and linked arms with Andy. "Come, myte, we're all chums 'ere. Let's 'ave the song."

"All right," said Farrell, "since you ask me for it, although there are more fitting tunes for an occasion like this." Hitching his trousers, he then took off his lanyard and shoved it into the pocket of his jumper, and loosened the buttons of his cuffs. He was clearing the decks for action.

He sang one verse of the old song in his clear tenor, and there was cheering when he ended. Glasses were emptied and someone asked for another verse.

"Lubbers for punishment, ain't they?" Andy asked me in an aside. He gave them another verse. "Now," he said, "I want you all to join with me." Loudly, and not inharmoniously, the combined voices rose until they must have been heard on the ships in the harbor:

"Then yardarm and yardarm meeting,
  Straight began the dismal fray;
Cannon mouths, each other greeting
  Belched their smoky flames away.
Soon the langrage, grape, and chain-shot
  That from Barney's cannons flew
Swept the *Monk*, and cleared each roundtop,
  Killed and wounded half her crew."

"Them's dandy sentiments, me Yankee myte," the British petty officer shouted, clapping Andy on the shoulder. "We surely gyve that *Monk* ship 'ell. Never 'eard of 'er before—French or Spanish, what?"

"My dear old lad," Farrell replied, backing through the door, "my great-grandfather served one of the guns on the U.S.S. *Hyder Ali*, which on April 26, 1782, knocked hell out of the British ship *General Monk*."

There was an eloquent silence; but happily the good humor of the crowd was not broken, and as we left the place we heard roars of laughter. So ended the last of my days before the mast in the sailing ships, the happiest and most carefree days of all my life.

Chapter XVIII

FORTS ON THE RIVER

I landed back in Shanghai to begin my shore venture with a capital of thirty-five yen. On the advice of the man in charge of the mission in the city, I sought out the boardinghouse of Mrs. Brown. This "good, motherly English lady," as the missionary had described her, was to be found in her home at the end of a dark lane leading from Nanking Road in the business section of the foreign city. She was hugely stout and untidy, but I felt committed and innocently handed her thirty yen for one month's board. Our first meal was toast, tea, and a small wedge of cake. All the following meals were about the same, but sometimes lacked the cake.

I spent my remaining cash for a copy of Ballard's *Chinese Grammar* and settled down to study Chinese, as well as shorthand and Spanish, when I was not making the rounds in search of employment. There seemed to be no need for an active young American in the city or on the river, and I was dreading the approach of the day—which could not be far off—when I would be landed on my beam-ends for fair.

On June 22, 1893, the noisy lamentations of my ponderous landlady caused me to look in on her in the sitting room, where she sat knitting socks for some mysterious unknown male. Tears streaked her raddled face, for that day a Reuter cable had been received reporting the loss of two great British battleships off Malta. The admiral had apparently gone mad and given a fatal order of evolution that caused the sinking of his own ship, the *Victoria,* when she was rammed by H.M.S. *Camperdown*. Many officers and men had been drowned, and the tragedy was one of the greatest in peace history.[1]

At our next meal Mrs. Brown showed evidence of having mixed Scotch whisky with her tea, to the disgust of her other boarder, a thin young Englishman who worked in a department store. Rolling her head from side to side, she moaned over and over: "Oh, oh, my dear soul and body, those poor orficers!"

The scanty news that had been received mentioned extraordinary heroism on the part of the crews of the two great ships. I was prompted to protest: "Only a few officers were drowned, I hear. What about the many poor fellows up forward? Their families will miss them as much, or more."

"To 'ell with those bums. I'm sick with thinkin' of those brave orficers." More tears showered down her wrinkled cheeks, and the discussion assumed an increasingly frenzied tone. During it the inoffensive Englishman happened to break a tea cup. He had angered the old lady by siding with me. Imperiously we were both ordered to get out and stay out.

As we departed with our trunks and satchels, my companion laughed and said he would soon sneak back inside and go to bed. Being ejected from his quarters by the old lady was a regular thing, and he suggested that I follow his example. But I could not see it

1. The collision of the *Victoria* and *Camperdown* occurred off Tripoli, on the Syrian coast, on 22 June 1893. Since the vessels collided at 3:45 in the afternoon, it seems highly improbable that the news of the tragedy could have reached Mrs. Brown's boardinghouse in Shanghai before teatime that day, as narrated by Buenzle.

that way, went to the Consulate to make a claim for the few dollars due me, and slept that night on a couch in the marshal's room.

The next morning, nearing the end of my tether and facing the beachcomber's lot, I wandered through the city and happened to come face to face with someone whom I recognized at once. It was the tall, genial American who had spoken to me by the gate of the old town on my first Shanghai liberty. He hailed me cheerily and wanted to know if I had deserted from the navy. Was I still looking for strange sights and adventures?

"No, sir. I'm looking for a job of some kind, and a new place to board."

He laughed when I told him my story, and said that he knew of Mrs. Brown's habit of collecting from her boarders in advance and then quarreling with them. He suggested that I should have remained with my ship—it was difficult for a stranger to get a position in China, and as for clerical jobs, the Portuguese boys, with their willingness to do any kind of work and their knowledge of native customs, filled all demands. "However," he continued, "I am the owner of the Astor House up in the American town. I might use you as night clerk in place of the Chinaman who does the work now. Would you care for the job—room and board and, say, thirty dollars a month?"

I didn't ask whether he meant American dollars or Mex. I accepted at once; and thus through a chance meeting began an association that was to last for two years.

Mr. DeWitt Clinton Jansen, my rescuer, was a native of New York State who as a boy, in the merchant service, had begun a strange career which included journeying as a colporteur in China's interior. He was a student of languages, and could converse in a number of Chinese dialects. He had proved his excellent business ability by making the Astor House the best hotel in the Orient at that time, and he was well known in every treaty port and kindly remembered by the thousands of American and European travelers who had enjoyed his hospitality. He took an interest in my studies and arranged for me to have Chinese lessons with a venerable teacher who had come from Peking to tutor the eldest Jansen boy.

My duties were pleasant and varied, and I was soon promoted to the post of personal guide to the many distinguished visitors from all over the world who came to see the sights of Shanghai.

Time passed quickly, and I had almost forgotten that I had ever paced the deck of a war vessel. One morning Mr. Jansen greeted me cheerily with the words: "Your old ship, the *Lancaster,* is down at Woosung, on her way home! Put on your glad rags, take the houseboat, and go down to say howdy to your old shipmates!"

The big houseboat, which with its crew of six natives had been placed at my disposal, was a fine sailing craft about the size of the U.S.S. *Palos*. As we drove down the river, a surge of homesickness came over me. I could be going back home on the *Lancaster* if I wished—but to what? A return to the navy, or to the deadly routine of industrial life in the States, did not appeal to me as I sat on the deck of my trim little command. She was for the moment my ship, from the brass saluting gun at the stem to the cockpit aft where the lowdah, or native captain, handled the sweep and tended the main sheet. Proudly we rounded the stern of the majestic old flagship in the Woosung tideway and came to anchor abreast of her. Two of my uniformed crew pulled me to the starboard, or officers', gangway, and at the invitation of my former division officer, Lieutenant Sewall, I stepped once more on the familiar deck.

I had not overestimated the effect that I would create upon my former shipmates, nor the heartiness of the greetings that I received. My appearance was hailed with delight by all my old friends. Here I was with a ship of my own, assistant manager of the best, if not the largest, hotel in the Orient, and with no intention of creeping back on the muster roll. They looked up to me; but below, after I had grasped the hand of the best friend of all, John R. Bell, my old doubts were reawakened.

He was, as ever, quietly solicitous of my welfare. Hadn't I better go home with the ship? He would speak to the captain for me and arrange it. I pointed through the gun port to the trim houseboat and the active native crew making things snug for the night. He shook his gray head, and reminded me that most of my former companions were planning to enter the gunnery school, which at the time was the only way open to an enlisted man seeking warrant rank. "But whatever you do," said the loyal old fellow, "you know that you have all my wishes for success."

Some of my apprentice friends were permitted to spend the night with me on the houseboat, and we sat up together until dawn, talking and admiring the luxurious quarters of the boat, the big soft beds and the shining galley and eager servants. At last we had to part. My crew got up anchor, and as our main boom swung out and we drifted upriver with the tide, the *Lancaster's* cables came in. The houseboat flag was dipped as the grand old ship made sail and passed out to sea with her five-hundred-foot homeward-bound pennant of silk trailing from the main truck.

The happy oriental year that followed passed swiftly, but at its end my Shanghai life was brought to a close by the sudden and untimely death of Mr. Jansen, the best friend I had ever found ashore. After that the place no longer seemed the same to me, and I felt the urge to seek fresh fields.

Cocky little Japan at this time declared war on sleepy huge China over the question of Korea, and burn me if I could resist the chance to take part in some of the excitement of that war. Foreigners to serve as instructors to Chinese troops were in demand, and through a friendly customs officer and with a personal letter from Commander J. M. Miller, of the U.S.S. *Monocacy,* with whom I had had many service chats during my night watches at the hotel, where he was a guest, I was put in the way of securing a commission as captain in the Imperial Chinese Army. A German blockade-runner gave me passage up the Yangtze as far as Nanking, where my commission had to be accredited by the viceroy of the province—Chang Chih Tung, a notorious hater of "foreign devils."

One cold Sunday morning I was carried in a sedan chair from the docks up through the city of Nanking to the palace of the viceroy. In the chilly anteroom of the yamen, in company with a German agent for the Mauser rifle, I shivered and awaited the viceroy. But that official was out in the courtyard shoving one-pounder cartridges in the stern end of a "gin-gal," a gun of his own invention, made of cast-iron pipe, held on the shoulder of one man while another aimed and fired it. These crude guns were later manufactured at the native arsenal, and when used in the war were no doubt much less harmful to the enemy than to the Chinese who fired them.

The German and I tried to make ourselves comfortable by heaping charcoal on a bronze brazier in the middle of the stone-flagged room, glancing at intervals through the paper windows to see if the viceroy was nearly through with his plaything. Eventually an aide came into the room, a good-looking young Chinese in a long loose blue robe, wearing a queue which was carried almost to the floor by an extension of plaited silk. He bowed low to us. Not daring to try out my student knowledge of Chinese, I said a few words in the debased pidgin English of the ports. The aide suavely looked at my card and told me in perfect American that the viceroy knew about me and all arrangements had been made. "Mr. Simpson," he said, "who is in charge of the river forts, has instructed me to assign you to Kiang Yin, down on the south side of the river. I have sent for the captain of one of the gunboats lying in the harbor, and he will take you down to the forts tomorrow."

He could not help seeing my embarrassment, but his polished manners soon put me at ease. The aide's name was Ching Tung. He was a graduate of Yale University, had lived in my home town, and was the viceroy's military adviser. He was a competent and kind young man, and we foreigners had cause to be grateful for his many friendly services.

The next day I was landed at the dirt pier of Kiang Yin, about ninety miles above the mouth of the Yangtze Kiang, and there joined my fellow soldiers of fortune. All of them, it seemed to me, bore the marks of ill fortune only; and each was prey to some weakness that made him a part of the world's flotsam. I was the only American. There was one Frenchman, one Russian, two Britishers (one of whom had been a major in the Indian army), one or two Germans, and several Irishmen. Of the lot, only the senior officer, a Dane named Jürgens, carried himself with dignity. He had been a sea captain who for some reason had lost his master's ticket. Jürgens was married to an aged Chinese woman, and on his breast wore an embroidered decoration as large as a pie plate, which the Chinese government had granted him years ago for bravery in their war of 1882 with the French. He was a gloomy man, heavy-laden with the worries of his command.

My arrival happened to fall on a holiday, which the foreigners were passing in drinking and card playing. Captain Jürgens was helpless to check their boisterous antics, and when I asked him for permission to visit the batteries he offered to accompany me, apparently glad of a pretext to get away from the quarters in the temple where we had our meals and spread our cots. As we walked along the fortified embankment he took me into his confidence.

"You are very young," he said, "but I'll be glad to know that you are one who will keep sober, for the others do not. And we may expect trouble at almost any time if the Japanese decide to head up this river. Even among our own troops there are spies who know all that is going on, and an attack might be set for an hour when our officers are off duty and incapacitated. Of all the Europeans on the river at present, few of them are capable of exacting discipline because they themselves are unwilling to obey orders."

I could not help expressing wonder why China employed these foreigners unless they could be of assistance. He explained:

"We are here to maintain discipline if possible, and to prevent graft and extortion. We do prevent padding of pay rolls and falsification of invoices; but as for drill discipline, we depend entirely on native sergeants. The foreign officers, when they are sober, are not a bad lot. They'll borrow anything, from prepared cocoa to your month's pay, and never return a thing; but they'll lend you their last dollar if you need it. Now, tell me, did you learn any of the native dialect in Shanghai?"

I told him of my two years of study. "Hmm. That's the mandarin form. The orders here are never to use anything but English in your contact with the soldiers. Even without the interpreters, they'll understand you. You will be surprised. Mentally, they are the brightest people in the world."

We came upon several deep gun pits of concrete, each containing a 12-inch Armstrong breechloader. From here we followed the shoreline to the water batteries, and then climbed to the top of a ridge which joined the east and west batteries, where a base was being prepared for some modern guns. Here, after issuing some instructions to a native contractor, Jürgens said to me:

"I think I'll give you charge of the two 6-inch quick-firers to be put here. Your knowledge of Hotchkiss and Gatling guns will help you, although you'll find that your men are familiar with modern ordnance used on battleships. Most of the men are from ships of the Chinese fleet at Wei Hai Wei. The guns are on board a steamer expected here tomorrow."

At parade the following morning the corps of instructors were all wide awake, and showed no signs that they had been carousing until dawn. They wore uniforms of blue cloth, with double-breasted coat and peaked cap. On the right sleeve was a dragon worked in gold lace, and the number of coils around the arm indicated the degree of rank. The dragon was shown in the act of swallowing a white silk ball, which represented Japan. Each instructor carried a bayonet taken from a Snyder 50-caliber rifle. After inspection all hands began to drill, under commands called out from the pages of a Brisith navy handbook.

As soon as drill was over, I took my platoon of forty Chinese and went down to the shore to unload from a steamer the unmounted rifles that were to be my battery. I turned the men over to the native in charge of the job of unloading, and watched the operation with interest. The guns and ammunition were put overside into the hands of our men. In spite of much unnecessary noise and apparent confusion, and the way they had of pulling their tackles uphill instead of down and reeving their leads left-handed, they got the guns up on the embankment in quick time. My interpreter, Mr. Lin, informed me that all these men had come from the Chinese navy and were survivors of the terrible Yalu sea battle in which the Japanese had ruthlessly shown their skill in Western warfare by destroying the best part of the Chinese ships and cold-bloodedly sinking the British steamer *Kowshing* transporting

Chinese troops, of which a thousand were drowned.[2] After that battle, since the survivors had no ships left to serve on, they had been transferred to our fort. Few of them were over eighteen years of age. They were clean and neat, real man-o'-warsmen, and I liked to believe that their loyalty was due to patriotism as much as to the eight dollars Mex that they received on the fifth of every month. As Captain Jürgens had promised, they were familiar with up-to-date ordnance, and obeyed any command given them in English.

These troops were smart and tractable. They never became drunk, and their journeys to and from the village were quiet as a church party. But they would smoke cigarettes when handling 200-pound sacks of cordite and gunpowder; and no one seemed to be able to prevent their habit of steeping themselves at night in the fumes of opium. Never were their barracks free of a poppied, headachy smell, and even when we officers took turns sleeping there, some of the worst offenders would manage to do their smoking under blankets. The old first sergeant in charge of barracks would daily ration out to those who were caught a touch of "bamboo chowchow," which meant a severe spanking with a flat slab of bamboo, worn by the native noncom as a sign of his authority.

The lot of these soldiers commanded by foreigners was a happy one compared with that of the ragged, ill-paid native horde camped in the rear of our forts. These volunteers were supposed to receive two dollars a month Mex and to furnish their own subsistence and clothing. But they were robbed of their pay before they ever saw it and had to resort to banditry and terrorism to keep themselves alive. Scattered among the Chinese forces were some ten thousand members of a brotherhood called the Black Flags,

2. Here Buenzle states that the Japanese destroyed the best part of the Chinese fleet and sank the transport *Kowshing* at the battle of the Yalu River. Actually, the *Kowshing* was sunk after a naval action off Asan, Korea, on 24 July 1894. The greater portion and the most important ships of the Chinese fleet survived the battle of the Yalu River on 17 September, and were surrendered at Wei-hai-wei five months later.

coming mainly from the southern provinces. Most of them were starved farmers or peasants who followed the standard of some petty war lord or bandit as a last resort, although there were a number of brigands and pirates among them. Few of these scarecrow soldiers knew the cause of the war for which they were enlisted against the Japanese nation. They were miserably clad, and some of them froze to death on the bare ground during the cold nights of that winter. Their bodies had to be thawed before they could be removed, to be dumped into the river.

We foreigners were virtually prisoners in the forts, for the question of transportation was so complicated that none of us could have gone downriver without permission. I managed to make one visit to Shanghai during my service. I called upon our consul there, and he laughingly assured me that even though I had forfeited my rights to protection by my own country, he had ordered the captain of the *Monocacy* to keep his eye on me whenever his duties took him up our way.

When I returned to the forts I learned that there had been two general night alarms during my absence. One was caused by the detection of a Japanese spy in our cook shed. He was chased to the rear, where the Black Flags caught him and promptly removed his head. We marched our companies next day to view the head, which was exposed in a wicker cage at the top of a thirty-foot pole in front of the ranking general's tent. The other scare was caused by a mob of Black Flag rioters that attempted to take and pillage our fort during a blizzard; they might have succeeded had not a false alarm of Japanese ships approaching from the southward caused the garrison to stand to their posts.

The six months that I spent soldiering on China's river were filled with many a bizarre incident and encounter with odd characters; but this chronicle of life in the old navy is hardly the place for that yarn. One friendship that I made in the forts, however, was important because it was to lead me directly to a sea venture in a sailing vessel, a quest that drew some of our party through the doors of death.

One day as I was crossing the horseshoe ridge lying between our batteries, I noticed one of our new foreign officers, who had been with us about two months, approaching from the other side. Suddenly he halted, crouched down behind a rock, and signaled me to get down also. As I dropped, the ping of a bullet sounded over my head. Keeping well under cover, we approached each other, and he told me that the Black Flags were having target practice down in the basin with their Snyder rifles and gin-gals. Firing on the foreigners, and even drilling them through, was considered good sport by these barbarians, and there would be little chance of catching the guilty man during their indiscriminate shooting.

This encounter led to a close friendship, notwithstanding the disparity in our ages—he was the oldest man in our foreign brigade, as I was the youngest. He was more than sixty; his hair was gray, and under the back of his cap was a long scar in which the blood throbbed close to the surface. His name was M. A. Fabre, and he was called "Frenchy" by the others, although he was an American by birth and France, as he said, was the only part of the world he had never visited.

Fabre entranced me with his stories of life in strange places. He had served under the famous "Chinese" Gordon in Taiping Rebellion days, and had also traded for copra and pearls in the South Seas for many years. He was habitually silent where the other officers wallowed in braggadocio and, unlike the others, never drank too much. He was cynical about himself but tolerant of the weaknesses of others. To hear him talk, one would think that his whole life had been one evil mischance after another, that failure had been his daily meat, and that there was for him only the shadow of a hopeless future. Yet he never repined, but recounted his ill fortunes with a sardonic drollness. On his right forearm were tattoed the letters "*M.p.G.d.*" Whenever he had been betrayed into telling us of one of his many mishaps in life, his glance would fall upon the marks on his arm and he would smile and craftily change the subject.

In his wanderings about the world, Fabre had met a surprising number of American naval men, and when we compared notes it turned out that he had known Jack Robinson and several others of my former shipmates. During one of these talks he happened to ask me if I'd ever known a Sandwich Islander named Frank Aweilu, of Kealakakau.

"I don't remember the name. Why?"

"He was a bright little fellow I had with me on a bad trip. He must be gray-haired by now. Some time ago I wrote to the Navy Department about him, but never received any answer. He and I were shipwrecked on the east coast of Formosa some twenty-five years ago, and buried a bit of money there."

"Then I know who you are! You buried the money in a carpenter's chest—gold coins and pearls too! I knew your man. It's old Kanaka!"

Fabre held up a quieting hand. "So—he spilled the story to you?"

"Yes!" I could hardly hold back my excitement. "Now I know where you got that scar on the back of your head. Your first initial stands for 'Merci.' Merci, the French mate—that's you!"

He got up and pressed my shoulders to restrain me. "Keep cool, lad. No use telling the whole world. But I never thought that Hawaiian would spill the beans to any stranger that came along. Just a sample of my luck, I guess."

"But it must still be there! I'm sure of it!" I told him all I could about Kanaka, how I had made friends with him on my first ship, and how his plans were to forget about the treasure and wait for the retirement benefits that were due him. Merci Fabre thought this over, plied me with many questions about the native and his hopes, asked me whether I thought Kanaka had told many others about the secret, and whether anyone to whom he had spoken might be the sort to go after the treasure. I said that Kanaka had few friends and probably none that would believe his tale, and that moreover he had never trusted his secret to a map. I showered Fabre with a dozen questions in my turn.

Yes, so far as he knew the treasure was still buried on the coast of Formosa in the obscure little cove where his ship had drifted ashore. He had never had the opportunity to seek out the place and try his luck. "It would take money to get the money, boy—quite a bit of it even to start. Then it's a dangerous place if we get caught by an offshore wind, or by the authorities, or by some of the pirates hanging about those seas. Moreover, it's always possible that the chest has been washed out to sea or uncovered and removed by this time."

These appeared to me then to be mere trifling objections. I wanted to embark on a hunt for the buried treasure, and it was not long before Merci had swung over to my way of thinking. I told him that there were two thousand yen in the Hong Kong-Shanghai Bank in my name, and he said that he could add a thousand more. We might never have such a chance again. Gold was lying somewhere unclaimed, and we meant to have it. Gold and pearls—a sackful of pearls! That first night I dreamed that I was passing out a big pearl to each of my friends and bestowing a whole bushel of them upon my sweetheart at home.

Shortly after this, on April 17, 1895, the treaty of peace was signed by Li Hung-Chang at Shimonoseki, where an assassin attempted to take his life. There was nothing left for us to do but resign our commissions. Our places were immediately filled by young officers from Germany, who promptly consigned our troops to the goose step. Captain Jürgens was not able to find a place elsewhere, however, and he remained in the Chinese army. Some years later he ended his worried career in a startling manner. While demonstrating a new type of revolver to a large battalion of men on the parade ground, he suddenly placed the muzzle to his brow and blew out his brains.

Two of us were not at all sorry that our warlike employment was gone. Merci Fabre and I were hurriedly laying our plans to recover a treasure in gold and pearls that had been buried for nearly a quarter of a century.

Chapter XIX

TREASURE QUEST

Merci Fabre and I departed together from the forts and made our way to Shanghai. My enthusiasm for the treasure quest had awakened the sleeping but unquenchable spirit of adventure in the heart of the old man, and he was as keen as I to go through with it. The impulse to seek far-off wealth was stronger in me even than the desire to go home, a desire which had lately been quickened by a letter from my boyhood sweetheart in Philadelphia. It was the first letter she had ever written to me, but our fondness for each other went back to school days, when we had timidly exchanged German romances containing flower buds pressed between the pages. I yearned to see her and my family soon; but first I had to find and seize the Formosa treasure, so that I should not go back to them with empty hands.

After disposing of our uniforms and military gear, Merci and I called at the bank and each of us withdrew one thousand yen from our funds. We entered into an agreement to divide anything we might find into three shares—one for each of us, and one for Kanaka, less his equal share of the expense. Then we set out to comb the port for a small vessel that would take us to the dangerous coast of adventure.

Many interviews with native shipowners convinced us that there was nothing to be had near Shanghai that would suit our purpose and lie within our means. When we heard of a smaller craft on the market at Hong Kong, off we went to the south by steamer. The Portuguese comprador at Kowloon was voluble. Yes, the fifty-foot junk *Fu Kien* was for sale at a wonderfully low price. She could be made ready for sea at short notice. He sounded as if this ship might suit our needs. The junk required only a small crew—a lowdah, a boy cook, and three native seamen. Merci, who had a certificate as a deepwater second mate, undertook to navigate her, and I was to stand a watch. We hoped to reach Formosa, secure the treasure, and run back before the typhoon season to Shanghai, where we believed the ship could be sold for cash more readily than in the south.

The Portuguese representative of the owners took our down payment and spent some of it to get the old tub ready for sea. We lost no time in rounding up provisions and taking them aboard. The old junk, we found, had served as a coastwise native craft around Singapore. She had been rerigged European-fashion, her masts trued up and the mat sails replaced by canvas. The sails were so old that when we tried to make some repairs the twine cut the cloth; but a spare suit of sails was listed in the inventory, and these we found in the forepeak, where the crew had been sleeping on them.

No sooner had we cleared Hong Kong than it became painfully apparent that not only were the sails rotten, but that the ship was leaky and the masts unsound to the core. The spars, which had been liberally coated with varnish to conceal their many defects, soon sprung open to reveal, beneath the rough varnish and putty, huge weather cracks that one could see through. Merci kicked a coil of decayed cordage, but remained cool.

"Just what you might expect of anything I was ever connected with," he said. "I've always found the sea a damned hard, bitter business. Now that fellow has taken our money and merely covered up this tub with paint and putty until she looks like a deceiving old woman. We thought we had a bargain. The sea is a bad thing to face in a bargain vessel, my boy. Well, let's see how long we can stay afloat in her!"

Our course was north and east, and we headed in that direction after reaching the open. It was getting dark, and outside we nosed through clustering junks of cruising fishermen, with flares burning forward to attract the fish. The coast, we knew, was infested with pirates. Merci told me that it was the habit of ladrones to get aboard a ship as members of the crew, and when at a prearranged time the pirate ships swooped down, the men on board would rise and attack the officers when they were preparing to repel boarders. Officers on these routes sometimes barricaded themselves aft behind breastworks, so that they could not be taken by surprise by their own men forward.

The wind had freshened dangerously, and next morning we were flying due north under bare poles, running before it with a heavy sea anchor of old sails dragging from our high stern. It would be impossible in these heavy seas, thought Merci, to try and heave to. The strain had already opened many of the seams, especially those below the waterline where harbor calkers had not been able to reach the strakes. We had to cling all the while to a lifeline strung from mast to mast amidships, or hang on the rail while laboring at the pump—a task that occupied our men most of the time.

In the midst of the worst blow, when Merci and I stood beside the lowdah at the tiller, the grandfather of all combers smashed over our quarter. The three of us were swept against the rail, amid a wrack of loose gear streaking over to leeward. The ship yawed about, and it seemed as though the masts would never stand that jerking strain. The junk groaned mightily and wallowed. There was a moment when I was certain we were foundering and she would never rise again. Then Merci sprang to the helm and forced her stern against the wind. Somehow she rolled free of the sucking waves. When the deck cleared, we found that the forward house had gone overside.

Over into the smother had also gone one of the seamen and the jolly boy cook, nephew of the lowdah. We were helpless to save them. Everything loose on deck had been carried away, but we rushed below and found a crate and a wooden pail that were tossed astern. Without a rag of sail, the junk could not be maneuvered. We had a single boat—a sampan lashed down to the poop—which fortunately had not followed the deckhouse overside, but which we could never have launched in that sea.

There was no time to mourn our losses; and the remaining seamen turned to with us to try and save the lives of the rest of us aboard. Where the house had been, the deck was now an open gash, a well filling with water every time a sea came over us. We hurriedly found a spare sail, and stretched the canvas across the opening, using the sides of a ladder for battens, which were spiked down to the deck.

Fortunately the improvised hatch cover held and the junk did not fall apart beneath us. We expected that at any moment another great sea would poop us and that next time we would not be able to fight clear of it. The storm showed no signs of abating. I remained on deck, fearing the lonely darkness below and shamed by the apparent indifference of the surviving natives and the stoicism of Merci Fabre. I had often longed to face a real storm at sea. Well, here was a storm that I would remember! It was not a gale that would have upset the routine in a ship like the *Lancaster,* with her stanch four-inch planks of oak. But I was not on the *Lancaster* now—I was in a leaky, ancient junk; the seas that looked insignificant from a man-o'-war were now terrifyingly close, and the curling huge waves were still licking over the low rails and sloshing aboard.

We feared to change our course, although we did manage to raise a triangular sail forward and cut loose the drag. The sea remained high, but as the force of the wind subsided we added sail to steady her. For two wretched days we ate our canned food unheated, and the native crew suffered from lack of their hot tea and rice. Merci produced some long stone jars of Holland gin, and we shared a generous ration of this mixed with cold tea. Between whiles we scrambled from stay to stay, hauling taut here and slackening there when the motion of the rickety masts put undue strain on the deck or sides. When the old hooker had all the sail she could carry, we ventured to shape our course eastward, and were surprised at her ability to beat up into the wind. However, the water was steadily gaining in the hold, in spite of all we could do at the never ceasing pump. Somehow we staggered on toward our island of hopes.

Ten days after leaving Kowloon we rounded the south end of Formosa, and started skirting northward, as close to the coast as Merci deemed safe. The seas had moderated, and the need for pumping was not so great. Forward one of the natives sang a shrill tune while another kept time with a belaying pin on the barrel of the winch. In the corner of our cabin sat the lowdah, mumbling between puffs at his pipe, the fumes of which mingled with the spicy fragrance of joss sticks burning before the boat's shrine. Merci and I chatted together soberly, more intimate than we had ever been before.

I looked hopefully at the old adventurer's face. So much depended on his seamanship and on his recollections, now a quarter of a century old, of distances and shore marks. His lost trading ship, the *Mary L.*, had been cast ashore during the night. Was it possible that he could recognize the place where she had broken up? Could part of the wreck still be found, unburied and undestroyed by the elements? Merci felt sure that the disaster had occurred near the southerly end of the great island, and therefore our search might be narrowed to that one rugged strip of coast.

Along a teat-shaped peninsula we sailed northward, scrutinizing the shore until our eyes ached. On our first afternoon of sailing we descried the ribs of a small vessel stranded on a sandy point; but Merci felt sure that we had not yet gone far enough to reach the last resting place of the *Mary L.* The coast was a well-known graveyard of ships, and among its reefs and rock-fanged coves it would be reasonable to expect the bones of more than one ship to be found. In any event, we could not see any safe anchorage near, and there was nothing to do but push on. For several days we beat up the eastern shore.

At last we spied a quiet, hill-enclosed, palm-fringed cove, and dropped our clumsy anchor in shallow water inside a muddy bar. On shore were some scattered native huts, whose occupants pretended to have no interest in our arrival. We took our lowdah ashore with us, and tried to make friends with the suspicious fisher-people and to purchase provisions. These folk, from a village near Amoy on the mainland, did not even know that the war had ended or that their island home had been ceded to Japan as part of the settlement of the conflict.

Carrying a collapsible shovel and provisions for two days, Merci and I set out to walk southward down the coast to where, shortly before reaching our anchorage, we had seen signs of another wreck. When we reached her we discovered what we had not been able to determine from seaward—that these were the remains of a small Japanese steamer. From a high point near-by we were able to look far to the southward, but could not note any landmarks that looked familiar to my friend. We were now convinced that the place we sought must lie to the north of our anchorage.

Returning the next day to the *Fu Kien,* we found that our lowdah had been able to buy some fowls and a goat, and also rice and pork for his men. We celebrated our return with a feast, and after a good night's rest Merci and I arranged with some of the villagers to help our crew to careen the old junk and calk all the visible seams.

Then we started walking once more along the jagged coast, this time to the northward. We were confident now that we could not fail to find the place Merci sought, so long as any trace of the bones of the *Mary L.* remained. We tramped for miles over smooth, pounded beach. At other times the shape of the shore forced us to go inland and fight our way through thick undergrowth of high grass and fern to get around capes and rocky headlands.

On the afternoon of the second day we paused at the top of a high point jutting out into the ocean and scanned the coast to the northward. It was stern and forbidding, and so far as we could see was desolate, except for scattered clumps of what Merci said were camphor trees. We were about to drop down the far side and resume our plodding march when Merci gave a shout.

"There she is—the *Mary L.!* See down there? This is just the kind of place I remember she went ashore on. Some of her timbers are still there!"

We ran stumbling down the steep escarpment. What a rough wall, I thought, to try to scale with a weighty box of gold! We had not brought a rope, or even a sack. I was taking the money home before I found it.

On the ragged teeth of the reef below was impaled the frame of part of the wreck, rotted away and worn by the sea until in some places the rusty bolts were mere slivers of flaking iron. In many spots the skeleton of the ship was covered with sand, and in another year or so there would have been little left of her and we might easily have passed by the spot. A little further along the shore there was an inlet in which we found another piece of the wreck, high and dry. This was part of the transom of the *Mary L.*—some of the letters of her name stood out in etched relief, protected by faded gold leaf, on the wind-polished, sand-bitten wood. Beside it Merci Fabre jumped up and down like a schoolboy, his sixty years forgotten.

"See those hills back there to the westward? Kanaka and I had to cross them, hacking our way through the underbrush, with only a little roll of provisions that we had saved. I had a fever from loss of blood after getting this crack on the head coming through the surf in the dark. We were barefoot, and the stinging bugs nearly did for us. When we got to the west coast, we weren't in the clear by a hell of a sight. The natives wouldn't let us have any kind of boat to try and make the mainland, because we had no money. We had a treasure, but we couldn't rent a skiff! You see, we were afraid to carry more than a few sovereigns with us for fear they might suspect what we had been up to. The people were mighty suspicious, but at last we got a fishing boat to take us over to the mainland, and there we reported the loss of our ship and all her crew except us."

"Yes, yes, Merci," I said impatiently. "I know it must have been terrible. But where did you bury the chest, Merci? Do you think it is still there? Tell me!"

The old man smiled, and waved a quieting hand.

"*Maskee* [never mind], friend. If it's still where we buried it twenty-five years ago,it will be safe for another hour or so. But before we start to dig, tell me—if we get it, what would you do with your share? I mean, of course, if you had it safe on the mainland, in the bank. I'd rather have a handful of oakum than a sack of gold when we need to stop a leak in a sinking ship."

"Why, I'd—Oh, don't talk bosh, Merci! I'd be the happiest fellow on the China coast!"

"Would you? Just because you'd have a little more of a bank balance than you have now? What would you buy with it—a shop, a ship, or a harem? Come on—before we go a step further, let's hear what it would be."

"Well, if you must know, here's what I'd do. With my share I'd buy myself the flashiest little brig-rigged craft on the Pacific. I'd paint her white and have awnings to spread over the quarter-deck in port, and put two breech-loading rifles in the bow for saluting guns. Then I'd like to hire you and half a dozen other old-timers, and we would all sail back to the Atlantic in style."

"Not so dreamy at that. But you're expecting more money than we will find here. As I remember, it was only about ten thousand dollars altogether—just the usual ship's money. You'd soon be up against a shortage."

"Then why not stock up with goods and trade in the islands? You know the ropes there. It would be an investment."

"That's better still, and I might come in with you on a deal like that."

"How about the pearls, Merci? Won't they be worth a lot?"

"Damn the pearls. They're fit for nothing but to give to some woman that will love you about as long as one of those pearls would last in a sea bucket of vinegar!"

"Well, if it's a fair question, what will you do with your share?"

"I never know what I'm going to do; but I know I wouldn't keep it. By and large, I've handled a good deal of money in my time, but I never could hold any of it long, and something tells me I won't keep this windfall either. The stuff is fit only to pass along, and those that keep it the longest are the unhappiest in the end. If I were a wise man I wouldn't need money to make me contented. Only fools are lost without money. Maybe that's why half the world is miserable! Now, you've been on tenterhooks here long enough—let's start to salvage our share of this filthy stuff that keeps the human race in such a tangle!"

Merci rose from the rock on which he was sitting and with exasperating slowness paced inland for about a hundred fathoms. With his back against a ledge he sighted one hand down the shore to the point we had descended. He shifted to right and left, and then moved slowly in a straight line shoreward. Betweeen two of the many pinnacles to the south he ran out on a rocky shelf, over which he scrambled between two swelling seas. On the other side he continued a short distance up a steep bank of coarse sand and pebbles, over some more rocks, and then down again to a quiet little cove entered by a narrow opening from the surf. The place was an ideal nook for hiding a treasure. His recollection seemed unwaveringly true, and I dogged his heels bearing our little shovel.

The old man came to a halt and silently pointed to the edge of a seaweed-covered rock. I flew to work in the wet sand at his feet, digging frantically, so that in spite of my ardor I was soon tired out. We labored in turns, Merci with stolid patience and I with fierce attacks that left me breathless. The shovel was in my hands when it struck a dull slab of rock. I looked up in alarm. We must have touched a hidden ledge—there was no sound of metal or wood.

Merci seized the shovel and probed the sand carefully. Then he straightened up, and there was a gleam in his eye that betrayed his assumed coolness.

"That's the rock we put on top of our dead man's chest," he said.

"Didn't Kanaka tell you we had covered the toolbox with a big flat stone to hold it down against the high tides? He and I could hardly shift it in place. It begins to look as if the treasure is still there!"

With trembling hands I scrabbled the sand and gravel from the edges of the slab, and together we upended it. It was too heavy to haul free, and in working it around we somehow let it drop, crushing in the wooden top of a punky box beneath. It was, without doubt, the chest we had come so far to seek.

I don't know what I expected to find when with the bent shovel we pounded out a hole in the rotten wood of the lid. What we did find was a gurry of dull round coins, crumbling canvas, and stained leather. Among the sodden mass were a number of pea-shaped bits that looked like pebbles, but which I handled with reverent care. Their luster was badly dulled, but there was no doubt that they were pearls. The coins were not as bright as the day they were minted, but anyone could see that they were American eagles and double eagles, British sovereigns, and what Merci called "spiggoty" gold, probably Philippine *centenes*. Among them we saw an old gold watch and two diamond rings that members of the crew had presumably entrusted to the care of the captain of the *Mary L.*

Across the heap of debris we stared at each other in a trance of joy. The salvaged fortune was at last in our hands.

Yet, alone as we were on the naked foreshore, we feared that this was no time to gloat on our luck. It was rapidly getting dark, and if we expected to sort out and stow away our find before nightfall, we would have to hurry. The thought occurred to us both at once, and quickly we began shoveling out the contents of the cache—rotted wood, rusted fittings, sand, and scraps of leather. From the heap we sifted out everything precious, laying each bit carefully on a rock. Then the gaping hole was filled in with rubble and sand, and over it rocks and seaweed were piled.

In a slight depression in the sand, stained with spindrift, the home of scampering crabs, we scooped out a temporary resting place for our trove, wrapped in my only shirt. I sighed as our windfall was once more covered from sight.

"Do you think it's all there, Merci?"

"Roughly, I judge it is. Certainly it is! If any part was gone, all would be gone, for anyone who found it would take it all. But don't forget that we are still a long ways from spending it, my boy. You know, this is more than I've ever had in my hands at once before; but my luck is so bad that I'll be surprised if the devil is away on liberty and lets me spend it. Spend it I will, for I know that if I keep it, the money will send me to hell in a halyard rack sooner or later."

That evening, while we munched roasted crabs and sipped a stew made of tiny oysters boiled in the single pan we had brought with us, we pondered the question of whether or not we should take our lowdah and his crew into our confidence. Merci had considerable faith in Chinese people of the unofficial classes, but after long thought he made his decision.

"I'd trust our own men with the secret, all right; but sure as pot they'd let it leak out to the gang ashore, and they are already suspicious enough of us and what we are up to on this coast. First thing you know, we'd have the *taotai* of this district holding out his paw. Or they might tip off a gunboat to drop down on us, or catch us even out at sea. The Japanese, you know, may have already taken possession of this cursed island, and if they smelled a rat they'd be after us even quicker than the native pirates that work in cahoots with the fishermen. No, I guess we'd better do all the handling of the stuff by ourselves."

Later in the evening he remarked: "We will give the lowdah and his men a bonus when we hit the mainland, and if we can find the close relatives of the two we lost overboard, we'll give them something, too."

We had decided that it would not be worth while to try and make a start of our return that day, and burrowed down in a warm sand pocket near the place where our treasure was buried. Listening to the booming of the surf on the harsh rocks, we fell asleep with visions of our golden hoard dazzling our dreams.

Next morning we were off to an early start and hastened to retrace our steps southward. The return journey did not seem nearly as tedious, and on the morning of the second day we reached the village where our boat lay. Our absence had apparently not aroused the curiosity of our men or the villagers; but Merci thought it best for us to lie about for a day or two before starting back again, thus assuring the natives of an indolent complacency that I was very far from feeling.

The calking of the junk was going on as well as the resources at hand would permit. It was hoped that careening the vessel would force some of the sticky blue mud of the creek banks into the garboard strake and other lower seams, and make her a trifle more seaworthy. She was more and more precious to our plans now, for to her we must trust all our treasure if we were to make the mainland safely.

Two days of negotiations, and we were able to hire a fishing boat, the only one available in the village. It was long and shallow, with a combination of lateen and square sail forward. The boat was steered by a long sweep, with the use of which Merci was familiar, and he showed me how to scull her along. Once outside the bar and around the nearest headland, we squared away and ran up the coast. The little vessel made about the same time that we had made walking along the shore, and early on the second afternoon we came in sight of our secret cove. We had suffered no misadventure, but as we landed in the breakers we were glad to be free of the cramping narrow quarters in which we had been confined.

Our cache was uncovered and found still safely wrapped in my shirt. Quickly it was transferred to a strong little packing box we had brought with us in the skiff. Fingering the coins again to make it all seem real, we slowly covered the lid and buried the box in sand. There was a light southerly wind, and it seemed best to pass another night on the beach rather than try to beat back through the dark.

Daylight found us outside the breakers, with the box of treasure securely lashed under the main thwart. We trimmed our sail as well as we could, but most of the time aided our progress with the sculling oar. The gold was ours now, secured snugly beneath us; and within a week or two, I fondly hoped, it would be divided and I would be off for home. I ventured to say as much to my friend.

Merci spat, and ran his fingers through his gray hair. "There's many a slip still, lad," he said. He glanced at the tattooed initials on his arm, and his face wrinkled in the old sardonic grin.

"Now that everything is almost over, Merci, tell me—what do those letter on your arm mean? *M.p.G.d.* You glance at them so often, they must remind you of something that means a lot to you. If it's not too painful, I'd like to know what it is."

Fabre grinned again. "You think it is a woman, eh? Some great mystery about the girl who spoiled my life, some fine romance. Ha! I am sorry to disappoint you, but there is no wicked lady in my past—that is, no wicked lady to break my faith. No, I spoiled my life quite by myself."

"But what do the letters mean, then?"

"They stand for the one thing I have learned in sixty years: 'Man proposes; God disposes.' Just that, and all that. Nothing is truer in creation, and nothing is proved more often. If you can remember that, you have a treasure that can't be lost. Now, let us find our ship!"

After a day of labor at sail and oar, we came abreast of our harbor. Here we found ourselves wind-bound and faced with beating against the outgoing tide with our single sweep. But at last we reached our junk, still careened on her side with the workmen finishing up the calking job. In the dusk we attracted no suspicious attention as we hoisted our heavy box over the rail and settled it safely aft in our cabin. Thereafter we could not examine it closely, for our quarters were shared by the lowdah.

Next evening, with a high tide and a land breeze, the *Fu Kien* drifted out to sea at sundown and with the aid of the friendly and warm current cleared away from the rocky coast. The villagers had not troubled us, and there were no pirate sails or gunboat smudges on all the horizon. It looked as if all Merci's forebodings were vain, and that for once we would show destiny a clean pair of heels.

The next day, with a breeze on the quarter, we made a long reach and cleared the land's end. Here we squared away and drove for the mainland. But the breeze did not last long, and the following day it left us altogether, sweltering in an oily calm, with the calking shredding from the strakes and the men busy once more at the pump, while the water gurgled in steadily. Under the broiling sun and cloudless sky we squinted at the visible layers of heat on the horizon. Over that way lay Shanghai and safety, but it might take days to reach there. Would the *Fu Kien,* with her spongy timbers and punky sails, hold together for that long?

Soon Merci and I had to relieve the men at the pump. The natives were almost done up, and after a few hours at the grueling work we were in little better shape ourselves. Still we bent at the job, with the water from the pump sloshing over our bare feet, while the snores of one of the exhausted seamen rose from below. The junk was slowly sinking, in spite of all we could do. The sleeping man woke; the Chinese stood in the bilge up to their hips, passing up cobblestones in crates and baskets to be cast overboard; but despite the loss of ballast, the junk continued to settle in the sea, until the men had to flee from the hold.

There was no time to lose. At our direction, the lowdah emptied two large bean-sauce pails and sealed them tightly, and there were lashed on each side of our deck sampan to buoy it up. A jug of water and a can of biscuits were hurriedly stowed under the forward thwart, and the boat was edged to the rail. Because of its low freeboard, the sampan could not hold the five of us in any seaway, and our only hope was that we might be picked up. A rag of sail, probably a drifting fishing boat, showed some miles to the westward. Perhaps we could reach her before dark or before the weather changed and swamped us! We emptied a kerosene tin on the sail over the ship's hatch and set it afire, hoping that the pillar of smoke would attract attention to our plight; but the flames were soon quenched as the junk's deck settled lower and lower.

Merci and I were about to run below to bring up our sole remaining possession—the box of treasure—when there was a cry from the side where the Chinese seamen were tending the sampan. The junk gave a last quiver, and started to roll. She was going over! The natives screamed as the sampan slipped with them over the deck to leeward. The little boat hit the sheer plank and fell into the sea, bottom up.

I crawled up the slippery, rising deck to the rail. Merci, who had already plunged into the water, yelled to me to get clear of the foundering *Fu Kien.* I was going to drown; I was sure of it, and sure that my people would never know where and how I had died. There was no time to pray. I jumped, and came up near the overturned sampan. I could not swim, but somehow I struggled enough to keep my head above water. Merci grabbed me by the arm and hauled me over one end of the flat-bottomed craft.

Shaking the water from my eyes, I tried to see the sail of the distant fishing boat that was now our hope of salvation. It seemed further away than before, but that was because we had lost the elevation of the deck and were now at water level.

One of the three Chinese hanging to the sampan pointed to our junk and shouted in his own tongue. We looked, to see her finishing her last roll. Gurgling in her quiet death throes, with the wind vane at the truck standing stiffly from the welter, she lumbered over and vanished. We were left alone, clinging to a tiny boat, amid a jetsam of kerosene tins, bits of grass cordage and matting, and a few drifting planks. And many fathoms beneath us, settling into the primordial mud of the Formosa channel, was a heavy wooden box containing the gold we had won only to lose.

Somehow the five of us righted the sampan and bailed her with a wooden bowl that we found floating. One of the natives swam off and came back with the sculling oar. With this we worked the boat toward the far-off fishing craft. It was getting dark when we reached her, but our hails were heard. Hauled aboard, we threw off our soaking garments and put on borrowed Chinese trousers and coats. The fishermen accepted our promise to pay them for a passage to Woosung, their home port. Late that night, when Merci and I crouched under the break of the poop of the native vessel with a warming little charcoal stove between us, he pronounced the requiem of our little argosy and her quest:

"Good-by, *Fu Kien!* You were never much of a ship at best; and even the finest ship couldn't stand up against fate. I'm sorry, boy, that with her sank your little brig with her awnings and bow chasers. You deserved better luck than to share the misfortunes of old has-beens like the *Fu Kien* and Merci Fabre."

"Let's not talk about it, Merci. I've learned something from our cruise, I think. *M.p.G.d.,* eh?"

He grinned ironically. "The old inevitable law!" He glanced at his forearm.

"And even though we're down to a set of soaked underclothes, we're still not licked, are we?"

"No, lad. You still have a chance to get that ship of yours. But I say, stick to the land. The sea is a harlot. I know. When you get back to God's country, find a job far from her tricks, and you'll win. As for me, I'm too old to change." He stood up. "Now, it looks as if we're going to spend a few weeks helping to navigate a Chinese fishing junk through the typhoon season. Let's bear a hand, and see what tricks the sea can play on us next!"

Chapter XX

LULL BEFORE THE STORM

Twenty-two days later, Merci Fabre accompanied me in a tender to Woosung, where I embarked on a Canadian Pacific steamer for the States. We had wound up our affairs at Shanghai and arranged with the American consul to send some money to the relatives of the men who had been lost overboard on our voyage to Formosa. We had little to say to each other, but I felt as if I were parting from someone very close to me. Merci said he was going back to "the islands," and I never heard from him again.

My passage home across the Pacific and through Canada consumed the larger part of three years' savings, but the welcome of family and friends was as warm, I am sure, as if I had come back with all the wealth of the Orient. With Merci's admonitions in mind, I thought of settling down to a snug shore job. The first opportunity to earn a livelihood away from the sea came in the offer of a place as special writer on the staff of the Philadelphia *Times,* which featured my stories of the navy and of China.

The old hankering for the sea did not disappear, however, and, recalling the suggestion of John R. Bell at our last meeting, I went one day to Washington to inquire of the Navy Department whether I could rejoin as a student in the gunnery school. I was told that my discharge, showing a clear record for more than five years, counted for nought. I would have to present personal references from officers who had known me.

Digging about in the list of naval officers then in the capital, I discovered that my old first luff of the *Portsmouth,* Dickie Rush, was berthed in one of the shore departments. The old disciplinarian said that he couldn't recall my face or my service under him. Perhaps if I could remind him of some serious offense that I had committed, that would sharpen his recollection. He found it impossible to believe that I had never been at "the mast" before him; but if that were so, well, it was just too bad for my prospects!

At last I remembered a day when the *Portsmouth* had been at Hampton Roads, the only time when I had appeared before him in a criminal role. I recalled to him how, on that blustering gray morning, a crew of us boys in the running boat had been carried steadily past the ship by a stiff current, and out toward the open sea. The boat was heavier than the combined weights of crew and coxswain, and although like galleys slaves we toiled at the oars, we could not make headway. Glancing up at the ship's quarter, we could see Mr. Rush with his arms on the rail, his whiskers fluttering in the driving wind, shaking his fist at us and shouting: "Pull, you lubbers, pull! You need exercise, and you'll get it when you come aboard!"

We knew that the exercise he meant consisted in having to race barefoot over the masthead. That was the last straw, and one of the boys quickly boated his oar, followed by the rest of us. It was a near mutiny, but we knew that another boat would be sent out to bring us in. On the rescue journey, the wind and tide were so stiff that we had to haul harder than ever, and the seasoned men of the cutter that towed us were all exhausted when at last we tumbled aboard the *Portsmouth.* Our fat executive had fumed and blustered about the coddling of sailors nowadays; but there was no masthead drill. As I recalled these incidents six years later, my former first luff chuckled throughout his great bulk.

"Sure, I remember now! I'll be glad to help you to get in the gunnery school. I always thought the tide was really too much for you boys that day!"

But fate again intervened, and when I once more set foot on a naval vessel, it was neither as seaman nor as gunner. I had heard that the *Monongahela,* a real sailing ship, was about to be commissioned for cruises with midshipmen from the Naval Academy. One fine day I stepped aboard her at Annapolis, re-enlisted in the navy as ship's writer, or clerk to the executive officer, with the rating of writer, first class.

The *Monongahela* was a three-masted, full-rigged ship that had served with Admiral Farragut at Port Hudson. She had a 2,100-ton displacement and had been built for steam power with propeller, but the auxiliary equipment was dismantled shortly after the ship was caught in November, 1867, by a tidal wave in the harbor of Frederickstad, St. Croix, which landed her high in that West Indian town. She was carried back by the returning sea. Five of her crew were lost, but the ship suffered no serious damage.

In this vessel I made one long cruise to European ports with a crew of three classes of "young gentlemen" from the Naval Academy. She was a comfortable and peaceful ship, and even when we ran into bad weather the orders issued were given in a manner free from the noisy urgency and apparent confusion of the older wind-ships I remembered. There did not seem to be a great respect evidenced aboard for the fine points of seamanship under sail; all the talk of officers dwelt more on strategy and high-powered guns than on evolutions under canvas. The young men went up the rigging in a leisurely way, stepping gingerly and touching the shrouds as if they were hot.

On the voyage, and especially on the lazy passage home, when we glided along under studdingsails and not a sheet or brace was started for weeks except at drill, I came to know many of the midshipmen, some of whom have since reached the top in their profession. Aboard the *Monongahela,* few of the cadets were exempt from the qualms of seasickness, and they could be just as miserable lying in the scuppers as any horny-handed apprentice boy or coal-heaver. At the morning scrubbing work, when outer clothing

The *Monongahela,* tied up at the Naval Academy wharf in 1896, the year Buenzle reenlisted.

was stripped off, the students and the youngsters of the enlisted crew could hardly be distinguished, and it was difficult to tell whether one lad might be a blooded cadet or a poor Jack with little prospect of advancement ahead. But although both might have left equal opportunities ashore, one would be destined to turn wire splices all his life and roll out to reeve a foretopgallant brace in a freezing gale, while the other, who had come into the service through the front door, had only to continue as he started and the highest command was open to his efforts.

The old ship suited me, and the smell of the sea was like wine. When we reached our home port and for the last time I went on the gun deck of the *Monongahela* and stood against the cabin partition by the oil lamp under which for many months I had performed my duties, I let my reluctant gaze wander over the wide sweep of timbers, guns, and ports toward the bows of the gallant old warship. Above were the great hatches, through which the sunlight swept down the oak ladders to silver the gleaming planks and coamings and glint on the ruled lines of deck seams. From overhead came the creak of a swinging block and the rustle of wind in the shrouds. There flashed into my head a verse written by an enlisted man who also had known the beauty of sail.

> "*Marion, Trenton, Tennessee,*
> *Nipsic, Kearsarge, Ossipee*—
> Lo! A phantom fleet appears
> Looming through the mist of years
> Breasts of ebon, wings of snow—
> Grand old ships of long ago!"

It was a valedictory to my sailing days, and to the ships of oak and pine that aroused the love of the sailor as no vessels of cold iron could ever do. I realized what a privilege it had been to challenge the sea in such stanch craft. Few men now living can remember sharing those Homeric days of our sail navy, days that are gone never to return.

My new assignment was to serve as ship's writer on the U.S.S.

Brooklyn, a great cruiser that had recently been launched. The crew was assembled at New York, and a special train took us down to her at Philadelphia on December 1, 1896. She was the finest ship of her class in the world, an improved version of the armored cruiser *New York.* It was my first experience of the new navy, and the men were of a different stamp from those I had sailed with in earlier years. Young men I had known on the *Lancaster* were serving as petty officers of deck force and gun divisions and took the lead in the work of the crew, which was made up of hundreds of green landsmen, many of whom were oilers and stokers who had never before felt the swell of a ship beneath them. The few old shellbacks still remaining in the service had been put in charge of gangways and the lower decks.

The *Brooklyn* was fortunate in her officers. Captain F.A. Cook was an exceptional leader who soon won the affectionate regard of his men; the executive officer, Commander N.E. Mason, whose writer and clerk I happened to be, was equally respected. The first mission of this new ship was a cruise to England to take part in Queen Victoria's second Jubilee. We carried aboard Rear Admiral J.N. Miller as the representative of our nation; anticipating a great deal of work that would be facilitated by a stenographer, he selected me as his personal writer. The green crew was whipped into efficient shape as we hurried over to England to take our part in the famous Jubilee.

Squeezed into a shouting throng at the entrance of London Bridge, it was my pleasure to watch the procession led by the wise old lady who had ruled the British Empire for sixty years. Before us passed a score of kings, princes, and potentates, among them the unimpressive Emperor Wilhelm II of Germany.

Ashore in England, seamen of all the foreign fleets taking part in the celebration were given the same warm welcome extended to the British man-o'-warsmen, and all were treated as guests of the people. The theaters and inns were wide open to men in uniform. Again I could not help contrasting this cheery reception with conditions in our own country. That Great Britain should ever

The *Brooklyn*.

have difficulty in enlisting a sufficient number of good seamen to man her navy, understanding as she did how to make service attractive to them, was hardly imaginable.

The naval review at Spithead, at which our ship was the sole vessel representing the United States, was, I am sure, the grandest display of floating fighting-power that the world had ever seen. There were ships from every maritime nation under the sun; but none was so impressive as the *Brooklyn* with her snowy white hull, her three extremely tall stacks, and the swift tumble-home of her sides. I think that when our executive officer, who was a man of great originality in many ways, trained the shafts of our searchlights upon our flag at the truck, it was the first time that such naval illumination had been used by any nation.[1] At any rate, our ship was the only one to light the sky with shifting beams. I felt personally that, for beauty, an armada of Queen Elizabeth's time, with decorated sails and gun-fanged bluff oaken sides, would have been an infinitely more lovely sight. But the world had changed, as it must change. I must move ahead with the times, and perhaps forget that once I had been a real sailor, a bluejacket of the days of tall spars and whipping canvas and cordage.

The new navy of which I was now a part had gone into construction in the year 1883, when the two "steam corvettes" *Atlanta* and *Boston*, the "steam frigate" *Chicago*, and the dispatch boat *Dolphin* were laid down. (The plan of naming these first ships of the White Squadron in A-B-C order was soon abandoned because the city of

1. Regarding the visit of the *Brooklyn* to Spithead, England, in June 1897, as representative of the United States at Queen Victoria's Diamond Jubilee naval review, Buenzle states that her training of searchlights on the ensign at the truck was "the first time such naval illuminations had been used by any nation." Robley D. ("Fighting Bob") Evans in *A Sailor's Log*, however, quotes his diary entry for 28 July 1895, apropos of Kaiser Wilhelm's visit to the *New York* at the celebrations on the occasion of the opening of the Kiel Canal. "The emperor took the time himself, and in one minute and a half the entire ship was ready for action with all water-tight doors closed. It was 2 A.M., the royal standard at our main and the searchlight of the *Columbia* turned on it, the ship ready for action, and the emperor complimenting the captain on the forecastle."

Newark did not care to wait until construction had reached the N's.) The *Dolphin* was considered an unlucky ship from the time her keel was laid; she broke her builders in Chester, Pennsylvania, was forever damned by her crews as an uncomfortable and cramped sea vessel, and was condemned by the political opposition as a "junketing" boat for naval bigwigs. In 1897 she was in service as the president's yacht. After our English cruise was over, as a result of the recommendations of Rear Admiral Miller I was detailed to the *Dolphin.* I believe I was the first shorthand writer in the navy to be assigned to a ship as captain's clerk.

The vessel carried an inconsequential armament, and a large space aft was devoted to the quarters of the captain and official guests, including the president, for whom there was a roomy cabin de luxe on the lower deck. The commanding officer was Captain H.W. Lyon, and his executive was Lieutenant W.H.H. Southerland, an ex-apprentice who had won his way to the wardroom through the hawsepipe. The captain's wife and son were with us most of the time. The nine-year-old boy was the pet of the ship, and when my duties permitted we would fly box kites from the quarter-deck or shoot at sharks with a subcaliber rifle, while he listened to my yarns of pirates in China and treasure on the Formosa coast. In later days young Harry Lyon was to follow in his father's footsteps through the Academy at Annapolis, and thirty years after our *Dolphin* cruises he sensationally navigated the airplane *Southern Cross* from San Francisco to Australia.

We were a contented and congenial crew, perhaps because we were never at sea for protracted periods. It was a sailor's honeymoon in the beautiful white ship. I had a chance to amuse myself in many ways that had not been open to me in my harder years of sea life. There were few drills for the men of the crew, among which many an old "plank-owner" was numbered. Most of the men were steady married fellows, and among them were tailors, weavers, and even a goldsmith.

The leisurely arts of the older type of seaman had almost vanished. The strictness of uniform regulations no longer allowed leeway for the wearing of fancy seagoing clothes, and the decorated mustering caps and blouses embroidered with stars and silk diamonds that had been the joy of our old liberty-days were no longer made. The storerooms no more contained frames for making daisy mats of fluffy wool or waste Manila. If perchance a man was found in the crew who showed an inclination to cover ropes with sennit and intricate knots of white cotton, he was turned into a coxswain of a gig or barge as quickly as navy regulations would permit. The makers of ship models had also almost disappeared from the service. The horny-fingered oldsters who would labor for weeks on a cherished model with exquisite little blocks, deadeyes, fittings of brass and bone, all done with a penknife and needle, had lost their cunning and their patience. There was no room for them on the busy decks of the steam navy. Space became more cramped as the number of officers increased, and they soon moved up into the roomy spaces forward, the forecastle, which had always been the stronghold of the enlisted men. The bearded salts of full-rigged days gave way to the schoolboys, the bang-haired landsmen, the transient workers who enlisted to get a warm berth for the winter, the oil-smudged engine-room artisans.

In the *Dolphin* we sailed up and down the Atlantic coast with hardly a thought except that of pleasure. We poked her bow into quiet bays and inlets, picked blueberries on uninhabited isles, and made the acquaintance of many seaboard Indians and their wandering families. In the luxurious cabins aft we carried famous company at times. During a review of the North Atlantic fleet off Long Island the ship held many naval attachés and diplomats, and men like Frederick Remington, the artist, and Richard Harding Davis, the writer.

One day I entered the cabin to find a stranger seated at my desk. He was a rugged-looking, pleasant man who gave me a flashing grin and asked if he might finish his writing. I recognized him by his smile. It was Theodore Roosevelt, former Governor of New York, who had recently been made Assistant Secretary of the Navy.[2] When he finished his letter, he turned to me and opened a bombardment of friendly questions. How did I like the navy?

2. Assistant Secretary of the Navy Theodore Roosevelt earlier had been a member of the state assembly of New York (1882–1884), a United States Civil

The *Dolphin*.

What about our food, our ratings, our pet aversions? How many of the seamen were married and had their own homes? Where had I served my apprenticeship? What had become of the other boys of the *Lancaster?* I informed him that, at a rough estimate, about half of them were still in service, most of them as petty officers.

"What was the matter with the other half? Why didn't they stick in the navy?"

I told him that the service was not to blame, but that the

Service commissioner (1889–1895), and president of the New York City police board (1895–1897). He was elected governor of New York in 1899 and vice president of the United States in 1900.

treatment of our men on shore left much to be desired, and perhaps that was one reason why good recruits did not always care to wear the naval uniform all their lives. Self-respecting men, I ventured to point out, should be made to feel proud of the official garb they were required to wear in their country's defense forces.

The assistant secretary showed an intense interest in this topic, and asked me for specific instances of discrimination against the uniform ashore. He took notes on what I had to tell him, and when Captain Lyon and his wife entered the cabin, the captain verified my statements and added other instances of his own.

Captain Lyon told Mr. Roosevelt that I had been an officer in the army of the Imperial Chinese government, and the friendly official continued to evince the trait of kindly interest in the affairs of the humblest citizen that made Theodore Roosevelt one of the greatest presidents the United States has ever had. He questioned me for more than half an hour regarding the treatment given us by the Chinese, and when I told him we had been replaced by German officers as soon as the war was over, he laughed and said:

"That's just what one would expect. The Germans will lose no opportunity to try and keep control over there!"

That evening, the conversation in the cabin was turned again by the Assistant Secretary of the Navy to the matter of discrimination against the uniform. Richard Harding Davis expressed his opinion that very little could be done in the absence of any law to cover the case. Mr. Roosevelt did not agree. He asked me to take a memorandum to the Secretary of the Navy, stating, "We must make a determined effort to create a public opinion so strong and aggressive that every class of people in the United States who pretend to be patriotic Americans will not dare to erect a barrier against the uniformed man of our national defenses, whether there be any law governing the cases or not."

Every day while he was on board the *Dolphin,* Mr. Roosevelt dictated his letters and orders to me. He spoke frequently of the matter of discrimination against the uniform, and had evidently confirmed through others the facts I had given him. No doubt the pressure of other grave business, and the outbreak of war with

Spain that shifted Mr. Roosevelt into the army, prevented further action by him on behalf of our enlisted men. But I never forgot his expressed support of my ideas, and his implied offer of helpfulness.

Ten years after my meeting with Mr. Roosevelt on the *Dolphin,* a decade during which the United States uniform became more and more flagrantly discriminated against, I had made up my mind that something drastic must be done to end the abuse. In order to bring the evil to the attention of the people of the United States, with the approval of my naval superiors at Newport, Rhode Island, I made a legal stand against the old prejudice represented by the sign "No Uniforms Allowed." I instituted a test case against a local amusement place where seamen in uniform were refused admittance for no other reason than that they did not wear civilian clothing—a thing that navy regulations did not permit. Painful remembrances of the many indignities heaped upon my comrades in the sea service had urged me to initiate and prosecute the case at my own expense; but for long it seemed that the law was unquestionably on the side of those who turned away the decent Jack from their doors. The case progressed from court to court with discouraging slowness, and when it reached the Supreme Court of the State of Rhode Island the expense, more than a thousand dollars, had become as much as my slender salary as chief yeoman could bear.

One day in 1906, Rear Admiral Charles M. Thomas, custodian of my legal fund, received a letter from Mr. Roosevelt, who was then President of the United States, enclosing his personal check for one hundred dollars to help me pay some of the expenses of the fight. In this letter he expressed his "indignation and contempt" for anyone who treated the uniform of the United States services save with the respect that it deserved. "I feel," wrote the president, "that it is the duty of every good citizen to endeavor in every shape and way to make it plain that he regards the uniform of the United States army and navy . . . as a badge of honor, and therefore entitling the wearer to honor so long as he behaves decently."

I am afraid that had the president not come to our aid at this time, the prosecution of the case would have abruptly ended. But his letter was discussed by newspapers all over the country as well as in many cities abroad, and a shower of contributions—not only from service organizations and officers and enlisted men of the navy, but from many relatives of navy men and disinterested citizens as well—brought more than sufficient assistance to prosecute the case through the highest courts. The strenuous opinion of our president had molded that of others who had been undecided.

After two years of court reversals, we succeeded in having laws passed that made any discrimination against the uniform of our army or navy a misdemeanor in every state and territory. I knew that the greatest struggle of my life was won, and well won. No longer would grave injustices against the lads who spent the best years of life in naval service be legally condoned. The sign "No Uniforms Allowed" was taken down and shelved with other anachronisms. I hear that, nowadays, the enlisted men are told at the outset of a liberty spent ashore in our country that they are expected to report to their officers any incident that might show prejudicial treatment by owners of public resorts. No longer may the American uniform be considered a pretext for ejecting decent seamen from restaurants and theaters and public buildings, and forcing them into the arms of shore sharks in dives and water-front hangouts. The garb of the bluejacket has, in T.R.'s phrase, truly become a badge of honor.[3]

During the pleasant summer of 1897, while the *Dolphin* was at Bar Harbor, Maine, we found ourselves in company with the

3. In 1906, Chief Yeoman Fred Buenzle brought successful suit against the Newport Amusement Company for discriminating against men in uniform, and President Theodore Roosevelt's contribution to its costs gave the problem national publicity. Rhode Island banned such discrimination in 1908, but only New York, California, Connecticut, Massachusetts, and Maine enacted similar legislation during the next decade. Elsewhere, also, discrimination against the uniform diminished with the steady rise in the Navy's popularity. Completion of the cruisers and battleships of the New Navy became prime press news and staple material for the popular illustrated periodicals, and their spectacular performance at Manila Bay and Santiago heightened national pride. After the

Atlantic fleet. Ashore one day, I happened upon my old friend John R. Bell, carrying a basket of vegetables and meat. He was serving as steward for Captain C.D. Sigsbee, of the U.S.S. *Maine.* John had aged considerably since I had last seen him at Woosung, China. His hair was white and his body was more bent than ever. But time could not dull the cheeriness of his voice or the comfort of his quiet presence.

Bell had heard, from time to time, of my progress after reenlistment, and was glad to find me back in service. He spoke prophetically of the Assistant Secretary of the Navy, Theodore Roosevelt, as a man who was sure to become a world figure. I asked John why he didn't retire from service and go to "his people." He laughed and shook his head. The steel ships were damp, he admitted, and aggravated his rheumatism; but even though the last of the wooden ships of the old navy might be abandoned, he'd stick to the flag no matter what kind of vessel it flew over. On the dock I shook hands with Bell, this humble old fellow who was respected by every naval man who had ever known him. It was the last time I was to see him. A few days later his ship, the *Maine,* sailed for Havana Harbor for a rendezvous on February 15, 1898, with a flaming catastrophe that was to arouse the American nation to arms.[4]

---

war's conclusion the Navy extended recruiting to the Midwest and South. The fourteen-month world cruise (December 1907–February 1909) familiarized the public with the peacetime Navy as never before, and the fleet's appearance at widely publicized expositions such as the Jamestown Tercentenary (1907) and Hudson-Fulton (1909) and at presidential reviews in the Atlantic seaboard cities reinforced this identification. With the entry of the United States in World War I, the surge of patriotic support for the armed services submerged traditional hostility to their uniforms, though some wearers then resented the imposition of the accompanying ban on serving them alcoholic drinks. The coming of peace in 1919 brought about some revival of the old discrimination against the uniform; it remained a very minor problem, however, until the impact of Pearl Harbor effected its complete and permanent elimination.

4. The *Maine* did not go directly to Havana after leaving Bar Harbor on 31 August 1897. The next six weeks were spent exercising with the North Atlantic

The *Dolphin* was ordered out of commission at New York on November 27, 1897, and I received a command to report to the new battleship *Iowa,* as clerk to Captain William Thomas Sampson. It was something new for an enlisted man to be detailed to this position, which had formerly been held only by commissioned officers. The captain was ashore on my arrival, and for a day or more I wondered what sort of man my new superior would prove to be, and what would be the nature of my work. On the evening of my second day aboard, a bell in my office rang, and I hurried past the marine sentry and knocked at the cabin door. A gentle voice said: "Yes? Come right in!" I found a tall, thin, gray-bearded officer, with the stoop of a scholar, sitting at a desk at the far end of a cabin that seemed crowded and stuffy. He looked up, and although he was ill, he smiled as he asked: "Are you the new clerk?"

He put me at my ease at once. He wanted to know if I was comfortable in my mess forward. Did I have a good place to sleep? What had been my former duties? Captain Sampson had recently been Chief of the Bureau of Ordnance in Washington, and Secretary of the Navy Long has suggested to him that he get a shorthand writer in his next command to aid him in preparing certain autobiographical work he planned to do. The captain had a full understanding of the need of dictating with clarity and smoothness, and proved to be the most thoughtful and considerate official whom I ever worked for. Never for a moment did he lose the cool powers of judgment and foreplanning that proved so important later when he prosecuted the West Indian campaign that ended in the extinction of the Spanish fleet.

Those stormy days were not far ahead, but there were no premonitions of war as we sailed for Key West to take part in squadron drills. Captain Sampson, upon our arrival, had some-

Squadron, followed by a month at Port Royal, an overhaul at Norfolk, and six weeks at Key West, from where, on 24 January 1898 the *Maine* was ordered to Havana. She arrived and came to her designated—and final—anchorage on the following afternoon.

The wreck of the *Maine.*

what recovered his health, and looked forward to a period of active command as well as private study. But on February 16, while we were anchored with the squadron at Dry Tortugas, the appalling news was flashed to us that on the previous evening the battleship *Maine* had been completely destroyed by an explosion in Havana Harbor. The reverberations of that flaring disaster immediately resounded throughout the civilized world with threatening force.

Captain Sampson was immediately ordered to Havana to serve as president of the American court of inquiry, and on the same evening we left the fleet on the lighthouse tender *Mangrove,* taking with us a number of naval divers and experts. At daylight on the following morning we were anchored within a cable's length of the destroyed battleship.

I was appointed stenographer of the court during its early sessions, pending the arrival of veteran reporters from Washington. As the board did not convene at once, I had a chance to visit the wrecked shell of the *Maine,* parts of which were still above

The *Maine* court of inquiry; from left to right: Captain French E. Chadwick; Captain William T. Sampson; Lieutenant Commander Adolph Marix; and Lieutenant Commander William P. Potter.

water in the shoal mud of the harbor. There I found her chaplain, a Catholic priest named Chidwick, who was being rowed about in an effort to identify bodies as they came to the surface.

The chaplain asked me how many shipmates I had lost on the *Maine.* Although I had not yet seen a complete list of the dead, I was able to mention eight or ten of my acquaintances on the *Portsmouth* and *Lancaster.* When I named John R. Bell, the priest said that he had received more cablegrams and messages regarding the fate of that one old Negro than he had concerning any other person of the *Maine* crew.

I stepped from my boat to the part of the twisted, flame-seared ship that had been the bridge. Everything was a tangle of bent iron and splintered wood. At low tide, one of the main hatch openings leading down from the spar deck was flush with the stagnant surface of the bay. The ship's ladders of this hatch, being made of wood, had floated upward as the ship settled, and had crossed under the deck opening, acting as an imprisoning barrier to prevent the poor fellows trapped below from making their way to the surface. Below this, a tangled mass of bodies could be seen, a huddle of arms and legs swaying with the motion of the tide. Through a hold that had been blown in the deck extended the frail arm of a boy, tattooed with an arrow-pierced heart above a girl's name, "Beatrice."

There was no possibility of retrieving those bodies until the divers we had brought could remove the obstructions. Every hour thenceforward the pathetic remains were salvaged, as the movement of divers, or the tension of ropes pulling up objects to be introduced as exhibits for the court of inquiry, dislodged them. After some hours had passed, no more bodies appeared, and it was thought that those still missing were locked in compartments or wedged by wreckage deep in their watery steel tomb.

Day after day I expected to hear from Chaplain Chidwick that he had found a wizened old body bent by many years of toil and self-sacrifice in the navy's service. But never a sign of Bell's mortal remains appeared. Captain Sigsbee, who had survived the disaster, mentioned in his first day's testimony before the court of inquiry that his steward had been one of the last men he had spoken to on board the *Maine* before the explosion. That was the last I knew of the fate of John R. Bell until years later, when the ship was raised and towed out to sea for her final burial. Then someone found a gold watch with Bell's name engraved on the cover, the only relic of the presence aboard of any of the men who had died without warning on that fatal night. The ruined warship was sent to rest in the blue depths of the ocean, and when I heard of these last rites there came to me a recollection of the old man's premonition that night on the *Lancaster* years before: "I shall be buried deep in the sea I love, in clean water."

Vale, John!

Chapter XXI

WAR IN THE TROPICS

The clouds of war were gathering fast, and over the anxious country sounded louder and louder the cry: "Remember the *Maine!*" The woes of the oppressed Cubans under the butchering hands of Spanish generals cried out to heaven for redress, and in the name of humanity the American government presented its demands for the withdrawal of Spain from the turbulent island off our coast. On April 21 the proclamation of the president declaring a blockade reached our fleet at Key West.

Here Captain Sampson had withdrawn after the work of his board of inquiry was completed, and shortly before the declaration of war he had been promoted to the rank of rear admiral and given command of the North Atlantic fleet with the *New York* as his flagship. Happily I remained with him in his new command, for his friendliness and consideration had bound me to him with ties stronger than those of duty.

With his characteristic promptness, Sampson gave orders to sail that night for the Cuban coast to open the blockade. On this passage of the fleet, the first shot of the war was fired when the *Nashville* captured the Spanish merchantman *Buenaventura,* and a

Admiral Sampson's flagship, the *New York,* off Cuba during the Spanish-American War.

few hours later the *New York* ran down the *Don Pedro* and sent her north as a prize. She proved a welcome prize to every one of us, from the admiral to the lowliest coal-passer aboard. My share amounted to more than three hundred dollars, and this I spent a few years later to establish a monthly service magazine, *The Bluejacket,* which was to have a lengthy and useful career as a publication devoted to the interests of the enlisted man.

The blockade had begun, and the waters of the Caribbean were no longer safe for Spanish vessels. On April 27 we of the *New York,* in company with the *Puritan* and the *Cincinnati,* had our first taste of warfare when our gunners bombarded the port of Matanzas and silenced the shore batteries that had fired on the blockaders. We then returned to our station off Havana.

Many people living today will recall the alarm that spread over the Atlantic seaboard when war broke out and the whereabouts of the Spanish fleet was completely unknown. As a retaliation for the concentration of our ships at Key West before the declaration of war, the Spanish had sent ther squadron under Admiral Cervera to the Canary Islands in the latter part of March. The strength of this force was speculative, but as it turned out it comprised two big cruisers, the *Infanta María Teresa* and the *Cristóbal Colón*, four modern torpedo-boat destroyers, and three torpedo boats. A report that the squadron had left the Canaries was received by the Navy Department on April 2, and thenceforward for several months the possibility that this squadron might harry our coasts was present in the minds of all. There was a fear that the cruisers might descend upon any point on the Atlantic seaboard, as the British had come burning in 1814; and people living in coastal cities hid their silverware and prepared for flight. Commodore Winfield Scott Schley was given command of the "Flying Squadron," consisting of the *Brooklyn,* the *Massachusetts,* and the *Texas,* to protect the Atlantic coast. Later reports showed that the Spanish had advanced to the Cape Verde Islands, to be joined by two other 7,000-ton cruisers, the *Vizcaya* and the *Almirante Oquendo,* and rumors of their arrival in American waters were rife.

In the belief that this threatening force might be intercepted,

Sampson left his blockading station and steamed to the eastward. His intention was to give battle if possible, to delay the enemy by all means, and to discover at the least whether the Spanish ships had taken refuge in any of the numerous harbors of the West Indies. Cheered by the news that on May 1 the Spanish fleet in the Orient had been destroyed by Commodore Dewey at Manila, the squadron under Sampson's command set out on the hunt in battle formation, the main body in single column, with the torpedo boats, destroyers, and other auxiliaries on the flanks or scouting far beyond the horizon.

Now it was "Clear ship for action!" with a vengeance, and the admiral issued orders to jettison everything aboard that was not absolutely essential for battle. Most of the ship's lifeboats had been left at Key West, but other woodwork had to be sacrificed to prevent the danger of flying splinters should the ships come under fire. Partitions, doors, wainscoting, and beautiful panelwork were pried off with crowbars, and, together with the handsome furniture that filled the cabins of officers in those days, all went overboard. For miles astern we left a wake of floating polished oak and mahogany, and the crowbars of our crew created more damage than, as it turned out, the Spaniards were ever able to do.

Advices received from the north indicated the possibility that the Spanish ships had headed for the port of San Juan, on the island of Puerto Rico, to take on coal. On the evening of May 11 we had arrived off the north coast of this island and steamed along slowly until sunrise, when we found ourselves nearing the port. Sand was scattered on the decks to give secure footing, and with the admiral and his staff aboard the battleship *Iowa,* the bombardment began under his direction. It soon became clear that the dreaded fleet was not hidden behind the defenses of the town, but the fire from the shore batteries was heavy. Three times the American ships ran in and shelled the forts, and during the two-hour engagement one of the Spanish shells hit our superstructure, killing one man and wounding several others. It would have been possible to put the shore batteries out of action, but had a landing been effected there were not sufficient men with us to hold the town. If the sortie had no other effect, it showed our officers and men that Admiral Sampson, though cautious as a great leader must be, dared to push ahead and carry attack into the teeth of an enemy position regardless of heavy fire.

During this engagement I was close to one of the 4-inch rifles of the *New York*'s secondary battery, and after the firing was over I felt a sharp pain in my ears, which later grew to a continual hammering and echoing inside my head. Cotton soaked in oil was stuffed in my ears, but this did not reach the seat of the trouble. Many weeks later, on service with the ships blockading Santiago, an alarm rose one night at general quarters than an enemy torpedo boat had ventured out and was trying to escape. A strange light suddenly appeared on the shore side—it was later discovered that it came from a railroad train filled with Spanish soldiers—but under the impression that it was a ship, our batteries opened fire. I happened to be looking out one of the ports when a gun near-by exploded so close that for the moment I thought we had been struck by an enemy shell. From that time on, the pain in my head could hardly be endured, and when it finally did cease I found that my hearing was badly impaired. Gradually I drifted into the peculiar isolation that comes to the deafened.

The uselessness of lingering in the vicinity of San Juan, after the bombardment, was clear. In the words of Captain Chadwick of the *New York:* "Cervera's fleet was not there; it was already two weeks out from the Cape Verdes; our squadron could move only at very slow speed on account of the monitors; we were a thousand miles from Havana, which had to be covered; the Flying Squadron, as far as we knew, was still north; we had no land force with which to hold the place, and no time to spare to await one if were were to look after Cervera—all those considerations made immediate movement westward imperative."

Sampson therefore returned to Key West, to be joined by the cruisers of the Flying Squadron. He received orders to maintain a strong blockade off Havana, while Schley of the *Brooklyn* on May 19 was sent to the south coast of Cuba with the *Massachusetts,* the *Texas,* and the *Iowa* to look for Cervera's squadron. Unknown to any of us, on that very same day Cervera had taken refuge in the bottle-shaped harbor of Santiago, where his four big cruisers and two destroyers were protected by the strong fortifications of that south-coast city.

Those were busy days for the American fleet. Cruisers arrived and departed on new missions; scout ships and dispatch boats dashed in and out to report their observations; supply ships and colliers came close alongside when weather and sea permitted, or transferred their coal and stores by lighters. They were anxious days, particularly in our cabin, where the admiral and his chief of staff, Captain French E. Chadwick of the *New York,* were in hourly consultation with the officers of the various ships under Sampson's command, directing expeditions along the coast and worrying out the ever pressing problem of obtaining an adequate coal supply and getting it into the ships. I was busy taking dictation from the admiral and his chief of staff until past midnight, and every morning before breakfast found a stack of memoranda neatly written in the admiral's hand which I must turn into letters. It was a wonder to me how the old man's enfeebled physique could stand such a strain.

Reports from our scouts and from the Navy Department indicated that Admiral Cervera had coaled at Curaçao and had probably found haven at Santiago. His ships had been seen in various places in the West Indies, and one report had it that they were sighted off Martinique, heading northward. From there the logical place for them to go would be to Santiago in Cuba or San Juan in Puerto Rico, and Sampson felt certain that Santiago would be the port chosen by the Spaniards. The admiral was cautious in reaching decisons, but once he was convinced he had a way of making everyone else share his assurance. To hold the enemy ships in their harbor, and there to destroy them, now became Sampson's chief concern.

On the south coast was Rear Admiral Schley and his squadron, with the speedy *Brooklyn* as his flagship.[1] He had orders from

1. On 6 February 1898, Captain Winfield Scott Schley was promoted to the

Sampson, and from the Navy Department as well, to keep close to Santiago and prevent the escape of the Spaniards should they be sighted in those waters. For some reason not explained then, nor even in later years during a lengthy court of inquiry, Schley's orders from above were disregarded, or were obeyed only in a tardy manner that cast doubts upon his judgment or his eagerness to do battle. On May 21 Schley was given two orders to proceed to Santiago, one of them conditional upon not finding the Spanish fleet at the port of Cienfuegos. Two days later Schley was still lingering at Cienfuegos, although almost every officer of his command was convinced that the Spaniards were not there. On the twenty-fourth, insurgents ashore gave positive news that Cervera was not at Cienfuegos, and Schley's *Brooklyn,* reinforced by a number of auxiliary ships, moved eastward. At noon on May 26 the Americans were within sight of Santiago, and conviction grew that the Spanish fleet must be there. But when at dusk the ships were expecting an order to dash toward the harbor entrance and draw the fire of the forts, the amazing message winked out from the signal lights of the *Brooklyn:* "Destination Key West as soon as collier is ready *via* south side Cuba and Yucatan Channel. Speed nine knots."

It was a bewildering and disappointing message, for the squadron was only twenty miles from Santiago and no effort had been put forth to make sure whether or not Cervera was there. The ships actually started back for Key West at nine-fifteen that night, but the necessity of towing the damaged collier *Merrimac* held up their progress, and before repairs could be completed the *Harvard* reached Schley with orders for him to remain blockading Santiago no matter what happened. The Navy Department had become alarmed at Schley's determination to retire to Key West and leave the enemy squadron completely unguarded, free to slip off northward and harry the coast and North Atlantic shipping.

---

rank of commodore and a year later, in recognition of conspicuous service during the Spanish-American War, was advanced to the rank of rear admiral.

Orders to remain at Santiago were received by Schley on the morning of May 27, but the ships remained idle all that day, and at night a futile attempt was made to transfer coal from the *Merrimac* into the *Texas*. It was not until the afternoon of the twenty-eighth that the squadron under Schley steamed within fifteen miles of Santiago, and then halted while the unarmored cruiser *Marblehead* ran across the opening of the bay and distinctly observed the Spanish flotilla at anchor. At sunrise the next morning the entire squadron, led by the *Brooklyn,* steamed across the harbor mouth and every bluejacket could see with the naked eye that Cervera's fleet was lying in Santiago Bay. Through glasses, the Spaniards could be seen strolling about the decks; not a gun was fired by them, nor did they even stand to quarters, so secure did they feel behind the harbor fortifications and the mines of the channel. Schley steamed ten miles out to sea and scattered his squadron in blockade formation.[2]

2. Schley's seemingly dilatory movements from Cienfuegos to Santiago were due, as he later stated, to the belief, shared by Sampson, that Cienfuegos, since it was the only southern port in rail communication with Havana and Cervera and was understood to be bringing ammunition to the Havana army, was the most likely objective of the Spanish squadron. They were due also, according to Schley, to the conditional nature of Sampson's orders and to the positive assurances received from the commanders of the three converted liner scouts off Santiago that the Spanish squadron was not in the harbor—assurances which were repeated until May 29, when Schley's ships actually observed the *Cristóbal Colón* at anchor in the entrance.

This phase of the Santiago campaign strikingly reveals the rudimentary character of the gathering and disseminating of intelligence by both the Navy and the Army. After the outbreak of war, the cable office at Key West was operated solely by Signal Corps personnel. Captain James Allen, in charge, negotiated a friendly agreement with Spanish cable officials in Havana to permit the interchange of personal and commercial messages, subject to censorship at each end. He then made arrangements by means of a code suitably disguised in commercial terminology to make use of the agreement for military advantage.

On May 19, Allen learned of Cervera's arrival at Santiago before the last Spanish ship had entered port, and he immediately notified Admiral Sampson, Commodore Remy, the base commander, and General Greely, the Chief Signal Officer, in Washington. The next morning, Greely personally informed Presi-

Two days passed idly, and on the thirty-first Schley decided to make a "reconnoissance," which consisted of firing on the forts at a range of four or five miles. This had little effect except to strain the carriages of the *Iowa's* guns—a strain due to the extreme elevation necessary for such long-range work—so that they were almost ruined.[3] The Spanish ships, with the exception of the *Cristóbal Colón,* which defended the channel, retired out of sight beyond the hills at the mouth of the harbor, firing at random. But Schley, as a result of his long-range bombardment, was able to report that he was "quite satisfied the Spanish fleet is here." It had taken him, from the time he had received orders to go to Santiago and discover whether the fleet was there, no less than ten days to make sure of Cervera's presence in the harbor—ten days during which the Spaniards, had they wished, could have descended at any time upon the American coast like wolves on the fold.

During these anxious days of developments along the south coast, Admiral Sampson was held by Navy Department orders at his station on the north coast, far from the scene of possible action.

dent McKinley and Secretary of the Navy Long, who immediately changed the plan of campaign from a landing of the expeditionary force then assembling at Tampa in the Havana area to a landing to capture Santiago. Despite the confirmations from different sources received daily by cable from Havana, the Naval War Board, which included Mahan, rejected them as unreliable. Such doubts within the Navy Department, coupled with suspicions of deliberate Spanish "disinformation," seemingly lay behind the conditional character of Sampson's first instructions to Schley to proceed from Cienfuegos to Santiago.

3. The bombardment of the harbor fortifications at Santiago on 31 May was ordered by Schley for the purpose of "developing" their precise locations and strength. These fortifications did, in fact, include some 6-inch and 10-inch guns, and Schley had received directions from the Navy Department to avoid damage to his ships from shore batteries while Cervera's squadron remained intact. He therefore limited his ships to a minimum range of 7,000 yards. The *Iowa*'s 12-inch gun mounts received some damage from the high angle of elevations involved, but it proved not to be serious and repair was quickly effected. Later, during the battle of Santiago, the *Oregon*, in chasing the *Cristóbal Colón*, fired from similar ranges and her forward turret guns suffered the same disability.

On May 27, the fatal day when Schley was held back from his decision to retire to the base, Sampson's ships were at the rendezvous in Nicholas Channel, and a conference of their commanding officers was called in the admiral's cabin. Every one of the men present could note how the uncertainties in the situation were troubling the mind of the commander-in-chief. Navy Department orders that he should hold his station were mandatory, but on the south coast he was not receiving the eager co-operation that he might expect from his subordinate officer. Sampson was burning to be off to the scene of action, for regardless of the vague reports received from Schley, every act of the admiral was based on the unerring presumption that the enemy's naval force had reached Santiago.

At this council, the admiral first mentioned to the commanding officers of his ships the advisability of preventing the escape of the Spanish fleet by obstructing the mouth of Santiago Harbor. He explained that in the Civil War some of the southern ports had been effectively blocked by sinking hulks across the channels. In his precise way he elaborated a plan that had formed in his analytical mind.

"I think," he said, "that it would be quite practicable to use some of the prizes we have captured, and fill them with granite blocks obtainable at Key West. Sunk in the channel at Santiago, they would hold Cervera inside for a time."

The admiral's usual signal for me to prepare for dictation was the lifting of his right forefinger, and I settled down for what I felt would be a long and detailed outline of his plans. Captain Chadwick, who had written a history of Spain and was later to write a definitive two-volume work on the war, remarked:

"This reminds me, admiral, that it's just three hundred years since Sir Francis Drake, with a strong English force, anchored his ships in the spot from which we bombarded the San Juan forts on the twelfth of this month. But at that time it was the Spaniards who sank ships at the mouth of the harbor to keep the enemy out and to protect the great treasure in gold and silver that was amassed there."

The admiral smiled. "It will be worth a greater treasure, Chadwick, if we can keep Cervera bottled up in Santiago. Until that is done, our transports cannot put out from Key West. Holding the Spanish in the harbor will give General Shafter and our army a chance to make a landing east of Santiago. Then it will be up to them to force a surrender and thus release our fleet for its campaign through the Suez Canal."

Captain Converse of the *Montgomery* deplored the delay required to fill any ships with stone and haul them to the desired place. In the meantime, he said, the enemy ships would have an opportunity to make all needed repairs, to refuel, and then to make a dash to Puerto Rico or else to our own coasts. But he agreed that the army could not stir out of its embarkation ports while the menace of the Spanish fleet existed. Another officer—as I remember, it was Captain Folger of the *New Orleans*—added that it would give the Spaniards time to transfer their ships' guns to the shore batteries. However, Sampson's idea was born, and in council it was to be expected that the plan would be elaborated upon until some fruitful conclusion was reached. Captain Chadwick's next suggestion seemed to solve the difficulty.

"We all know," he said, "that Admiral Schley has one ship, a collier, which it is claimed has retarded the movements of his whole fleet. That ship, which has serious engine trouble, could be run into the Santiago channel and sunk there. For that, only a few hours of preparation would be needed."

The admiral and some of the others were quick to see in this a practicable scheme offering success. Commodore Watson deplored the necessity of destroying so large a ship, but Admiral Sampson had a reply to that.

"If those warships of the enemy get out of Santiago, Watson, and are not engaged in a decisive battle that leaves one of our squadrons victorious, we'll stand to lose a great many of our merchant ships. To save us from that, we are sacrificing only one vessel, a broken-down collier. I think it is a good plan."

Charts of the south coast of Cuba from the Isle of Pines to the eastern tip of the island were consulted, after which the admiral dictated a letter to Captain Folger, in his presence, ordering him to proceed in the *New Orleans* at the highest possible speed to find Schley and orally inform him of the need for sinking a collier to obstruct the thirty-foot depth of the channel at Santiago. The details of the operation were left to Schley's judgment, after verbal explanations by Folger. In this letter to the commander of the southern squadron the admiral concluded with the words: "The importance of absolutely preventing the escape of the Spanish fleet is so paramount that the promptest and most efficient use of every means is demanded."

A curious incident that occurred during the drafting of this important letter remains in my mind. This was the confusion of names regarding the ship that was to be used as the stopper of the Santiago bottleneck. The admiral had the misconception that the collier *Sterling,* which had nothing whatever the matter with her, was the damaged vessel. Each time he dictated to me the name of the *Sterling,* Captain Chadwich would interrupt with "*Merrimac,*" admiral!" The pages of notes were so marked up with interpolations that when they were finally transcribed the confusion resulted in having the letter direct the destruction of the *Sterling*, and in that form it was received by Rear Admiral Schley; but Captain Folger's verbal explanations easily set the matter right. A copy of the letter was rushed around the east end of the island by another vessel.

Our suspense mounted as the days passed, and we counted hours and minutes until we might expect to hear from the south that the Spanish fleet was imprisoned in a bolted harbor. But when news did come it was the horrifying word that Schley was still lingering off Cienfuegos, many miles to the westward of the danger zone. The dispatch from him stated that he was returning to Key West with his ships for coal. The admiral fretted, as did every man of us, and he requested permission from Washington to change his own base to the southern coast. The pent-up feelings of our squadron gave vent in a mounting cheer when the bow of the *New York* was headed for Key West, where our squadron was joined by the famous *Oregon,* which had just made its record sixty-nine-day run around the Horn from San Francisco. On May 30 the *New York,* the *Oregon,* the *Mayflower,* and the *Porter* were pointed eastward to race for a final grapple with Cervera's fleet.

During the remarkably speedy passage around the east end of Cuba, Admiral Sampson, who was an ordnance expert, drew plans for the sinking of the collier with special torpedoes to be made aboard. The old man had been up all night, and marks of weariness lined his face. He sent me down to the wardroom with a message to Naval Constructor Richmond Pearson Hobson to confer with him in the cabin. Together the two officers went over the plans of a ship similar to the collier *Merrimac,* and designated the places where torpedoes would be most effective in sinking the vessel. It was to be expected that the ship used would be under a heavy and concentrated fire from the shore batteries all the while, and would have to be sent to the bottom quickly once she had reached the appointed spot. With his characteristic methodical coolness, the admiral was leaving nothing to chance. On the half deck abreast of our offices a number of large copper canisters were filled with cordite from our magazines, and then sealed up with wooden disks and a coating of pitch.[4] These were then hooked together with cables that led to a board containing a series of dry cells to explode the charge.

Early on the following morning, June 1, we arrived off Santiago. There Rear Admiral Schley acknowledged having received instructions to sink a collier in the channel, but gave no explanation why they had not been carried out. Never since the Battle of

4. Captain Chadwick has stated that the ships of the American squadron carried no cordite or other type of nitrocellulose (smokeless) explosives—except the guncotton in the squadron's torpedo warheads. Hobson's request to use this guncotton was refused by Sampson on the ground of its being too powerful for the purpose intended. Each of the "torpedoes" or scuttling charges actually exployed to sink the *Merrimac* consisted of an 8-inch gun charge of brown powder contained in its magazine storage canister and arranged to be detonated by an electrical primer. Ten torpedoes were secured outside the hull below the waterline on the port side, but only two were successfully exploded, the electrical connections of the others having been severed by Spanish gunfire.

Lake Erie during the War of 1812 had a naval officer so flagrantly disobeyed the orders of his superior.[5]

The *New York* was driven close into the mouth of the harbor, where we could see the Spanish cruiser *Cristóbal Colón* and another cruiser of the *Vizcaya* class moored near the grim fort of the Morro, but they soon got up anchor and withdrew inside the channel.

Our next move was to go alongside the collier *Merrimac,* the ship whose poor condition had caused so many delays, and soon she was stripped of everything that could be removed from her except sufficient coal to carry her on her last short voyage. That night she became, in fact, nothing more than a derelict, except that her engines were put in good running order. The torpedoes we had made were secured to her sides beneath the water, and their wires were led to a control board under the ship's bridge. The collier was a good-sized vessel, and it was believed that if she could be swung

5. The alleged "disobedience" regarding the Navy Department's and Sampson's orders to obstruct the Santiago channel inside the harbor entrance later became the subject of considerable controversy. Sampson's directive to sink the *Stirling* as a blockship was delivered on 30 May by Captain Folger who joined Schley from Sampson's squadron with the cruiser *New Orleans* and the collier *Stirling*, loaded with 3,000 tons of coal. The order was confusing; it mistakenly designated the *Stirling* instead of Schley's own ill-equipped collier *Merrimac* as the blockship, as originally intended by Sampson.

The adverse weather that had hampered the at-sea coaling of Schley's ships moderated sufficiently on the 31st to enable the *Texas, Brooklyn*, and *Marblehead* to replenish bunkers from both colliers. Next day, June 1, Sampson arrived off Santiago with the *New York* and *Oregon* and two additional colliers, each fully loaded. With the blockaders' fuel problem thus resolved, Sampson, on June 2, ordered the *Merrimac* to be prepared for sinking in the harbor channel.

Schley, in conferring with Sampson at this time, opposed the operation, pointing out its difficulties and arguing that Cervera should rather be enticed out to be intercepted by the American squadron than bottled up in the harbor where his ships provided strong support for the city's defense against the American army. In retrospect, the generally unsuccessful experience with blockships in the Russo-Japanese and First World Wars would appear to support Schley's doubts about the feasibility of blocking enemy harbors with hulks.

by the tide and sunk crossways at the proper spot in the shallow channel, which just inside the entrance narrowed to a width of about a hundred yards, her hull would effectively block the Spaniards in their self-chosen trap. It was now a question as to what men should be picked to guide the doomed ship to her last resting place.

A call went out for volunteers for one of the most dangerous exploits ever planned in modern naval warfare. Only six men were needed. A thousand men of equal daring and courage could easily have been selected from the lists of volunteers that poured into our office from all the ships of the fleet, and the six who were finally chosen were the envy of all those who could not go with them into almost certain death. Among the officers there was a spirited contest for the command of a ship that no doubt would be ripped to pieces by enemy shellfire even if her own torpedoes failed to do the trick. Captain J. M. Miller, who had commanded the *Merrimac* when she was a collier, with tears in his eyes begged for the privilege of remaining in command. He claimed that his familiarity with the ship and her steering qualities entitled him to the honor, and I believe he should have had it. Finally the admiral decided to grant the command to Naval Constructor Hobson because he was already familiar with the means adopted for sinking the ship.

Although the *Merrimac* was ready and the men were at their stations, the expedition was not sent out early that morning as planned. The tide and the setting of the moon were right for the venture, but there was an unavoidable hitch somewhere.

Now that we were at last off Santiago and in sight of the enemy, there was great change in the admiral. The worries of the previous week seemed to drop from his shoulders. He entered into the *Merrimac* scheme with the enthusiasm of a boy, and perfected the plans and details which had been hurriedly outlined the day before. That afternoon he sent a message to Secretary of the Navy Long, reporting that the Spanish fleet was in Santiago Harbor and that its ultimate capture and destruction were a certainty. The army transports were now free to sail unmolested to Cuba and there bring the war to a close.

Shortly after three o'clock on the morning of June 3, after the admiral had personally taken leave of her crew, the *Merrimac* silently crept off on her mission to plug the neck of the Santiago bottle. Admiral Sampson refused to allow any more men to go in her than merely enough to work the ship, but in addition to Hobson and the six enlisted men chosen, Rudolph Clausen, a coxswain of the *New York,* joined the intrepid band by stowing away under cover of darkness. Each man knew his particular task, and each could have had little hope of escaping after it was done, although a life raft was laid on the deck and a steam launch from the *New York* trailed the gutted collier in the hope of picking up any survivors.

Although the night was cloudy, it was almost certain that, because of the narrowness of the mined channel, the vessel would be seen by the gunners of the batteries above and by the pickets that lined the two-hundred-foot cliffs on either side. A few moments after she left us, a hell of flame spouted from the guns of the Morro and from the broadsides of the *Vizcaya,* on guard just around the bend. The Spaniards evidently believed that the whole American fleet was trying to run the channel, but their marksmanship was fortunately so poor that no vital damage was done until the ship reached Estrella Point. Here was the place to sink her, and Hobson pressed the button that tore open the sides of the ship under him.

To the crew of the *Merrimac* it seemed for a moment that the daring scheme would succeed, but the vessel filled so slowly that she drifted lengthwise of the channel and well to one side before she struck bottom, leaving room for heavy ships to pass in and out. The intrepid plan had failed; but as for its execution, let those criticize who have undertaken exploits equally dangerous and important, and have carried them through to success. Had the *Merrimac* managed to bar the channel that night, the navy's absolute and glorious victory of a month later could not have been.

Chapter XXII

DAY OF DEATH

We had watched our shipmates vanish on the *Merrimac* into darkness and a sudden storm of gunfire. When morning came, the masts of the sunken vessel could be seen above water; but the anxiety of the fleet for news of our friends was unrelieved until the Spanish tug *Colón* came out of Santiago in the afternoon under a flag of truce, bringing a letter from Admiral Cervera commending the bravery of the American volunteers. The message was brought on board the *New York* by Cervera's chief of staff, Captain Joaquín Bustamente. He reported that all our men had been picked up at dawn by Admiral Cervera himself, and would be held as honorable prisoners of war.

Captain Bustamente was a fine-looking officer, courtly and gracious, and he spoke some English. The other officers who accompanied him were also polished gentlemen. Bustamente accepted twenty-five dollars in gold which our admiral wanted him to give Hobson to purchase comforts for his men. As the Spaniards sat around the cabin table, taking refreshment and chatting sociably, with Captain Chadwick acting as interpreter, their senior officer wrote out a receipt for the money. I could not help wondering why we were waging a bitter war of destruction against these men and their nation. Why were we firing our huge guns to demolish them, giving the greatest praise to those of us who could kill the greatest number? . . . Bustamente himself was killed that same night in the trenches outside Santiago.[1]

Hobson was honored with advanced rank, and his men were given appointments as warrant officers. Some of them received swords from their states. Handsome Hobson was sent north on a special mission in connection with raising the *Infanta María Teresa*, which he did, but lost her somewhere off the Bahamas. He was received in the States, dined and kissed and lauded as the popular hero of the war. Like Perry in 1813, Dewey and Sampson, and many others, he soon learned that popular acclaim may last a shorter time than the short war which had brought it to him.

The attempt to block the channel was not repeated, but on June 6, a few days after Hobson's feat, the navy made an attack on the shore batteries, and in the month that followed, not a shot was fired from these batteries at the blockading fleet. During that time our curious dynamite-thrower, the *Vesuvius*, also helped to terrorize the Spaniards ashore. This vessel, through 15-inch tubes built into the hull, by means of compressed air fired huge 250-pound charges of guncotton, which on landing exploded with a horrifying roar and plowed up holes in the earth the size of a celler excavation. The drawback to this newly invented type of battery was that it could be aimed only by steering the ship into position, and the gunners could never ascertain whether the charges had inflicted any damage on important works ashore; so the idea embodied in its design was never carried out on any other ship. However, the fear of *Vesuvius* shells undoubtedly did much to cow the Spanish gunners during the blockade.

The days and weeks that followed were marked by other bombardments, in which the *New York* took part on June 16 and on

1. Captain Joaquin Bustamente was mortally wounded while leading the naval detachment in support of the troops defending San Juan Hill on 1 July, twenty-eight days after the sinking of the *Merrimac*.

July 1 and 2—a welcome diversion from monotonous blockade duty. Our ships were disposed in a semicircle of six miles during the day, and at night, after June 8, two battleships would put in at dusk within a mile of the harbor entrance and flood the dark gut of the channel with searchlights. Days were spent in intensive drilling by our crews for the clinch that was sure to come when the Spanish fleet decided to emerge from their trap. Things were growing desperate in Santiago, for on June 10 the harbor of Guantánamo down the coast was captured by our marines to be used as a coaling base, and on June 21 three thousand men of the army were landed with no opposition at Daiquirí, a little port seventeen miles east of Santiago. The men of General Shafter's force were approaching the city on the landward side, and the weary blockade maneuvers of the fleet were effective in closing off any help to the besieged from the sea.

The many dispatches and letters, ciphers and cables, kept our little office force busy; but soon after our arrival off Santiago I asked permission to print a daily log of events for the benefit of the enlisted men, using the office duplicating machine. The men of the fleet were not privileged to hear wardroom talk that filtered through from dispatches and letters, and when they did get news of the progress of the war it was merely rumor that might or might not be true. The admiral doubted that I would have time for such extra work, but approved the idea provided everything published was first submitted to Captain Chadwick. The chief of staff thought so well of the plan that he made himself editor of the newssheet, as well as its censor. There was such an immediate demand for these "Squadron Bulletins," as they were called, that the printer had to come to the rescue after the first few days of publication. The issue ran into the thousands daily, and helped not a little to keep the morale of the men at a high pitch.

The men of the old navy—men whom I had lived with for most of the nine years since I had joined as a raw apprentice—were ready for their hour of trial, each bluejacket eager to do his duty and knowing precisely what must be done. Men of a score of nationalities were united to fight under the old gridiron flag of America against a common enemy. Yet as I remember, our chief feeling, in that time when we were daily in sight of the foe and momentarily awaiting the cry that the Spanish ships were coming out to do battle, was not one of do-or-die bravado or flag-brandishing. Rather it was one of dull waiting until the hour might strike when our bloody task—the task that we had been trained over the years to perform—could be victoriously accomplished and the war ended.

The strain told upon us all. So long as the Spanish fleet, supposedly well equipped and manned by seasoned crews, remained afloat, eternal vigilance had to be our watchword for every hour of day and night. Boys and men forgot what it was like to swing in their hammocks, and they bedded themselves as near their guns and stations as they could. Our food was neither plentiful nor good. Many days intervened between the serving of rations of fresh meat, and when supply ships reached us after days of steaming through tropical heat, the food they carried was sometimes spoiled. There were the usual man-o'-war grumbles, but all of us knew that the admiral's declaration that the Spaniards would not escape meant just that.

The burden of suspense and care fell heavily on Sampson. His health had not improved. Night and day he had to give his attention to the thousand and one details of the campaign. Problems had to be solved without reference to higher authority; future movements had to be planned, and the pressing matter of co-operation with the land forces was growing more acute. Captain Chadwick had the operation of the ship under his direction, and coaling problems and other tasks kept him busy. Another efficient officer, whose indefatigable energy helped much to keep the fleet records straight, and who untangled many an involved cipher message, was Lieutenant C. C. Marsh, our flag secretary. In the broiling heat we toiled many hours a day, unaware that the crisis was drawing close and with it our opportunity to bring the war to its desired end.

On the night of July 2 the admiral had me in the cabin until after midnight. He was drawing up a new set of battle orders with

Captain Chadwick. At about five bells in the morning, half past two, there was a knock on the door of the little office in which I had my bunk, and when I pulled aside the drapes I saw the admiral standing behind his orderly, in striped pajamas, his wide staring eyes dry and hot for want of sleep. He read to me from his own writing a cablegram he wished to rush off on a waiting torpedo boat. He explained some changes he wished to have made. It was about the trip he was to make ashore the following morning to meet General Shafter to the eastward. There was some friction between the army and navy authorities at that time—a clash of orders and different views of what assistance each should give the other. The admiral looked tired and worn, and I wondered as I typed if the old man ever slept. Yes, he did, for when I took the finished message into the cabin for his approval he was sitting at his table, his head down on his arms, an untouched cup of tea alongside him. What a pity I had to awaken him!

The next day was Sunday, and while our crews were making ready for general muster the *New York* separated from the blockading fleet off Santiago and headed to the westward. It was the first time that our flagship had left her station except to procure coal at Guantánamo. We had proceeded about seven miles when the sound of gunfire and the breaking out of the long awaited signals from mastheads proclaimed that Admiral Cervera's ships had chosen this moment to make their desperate effort to escape from the harbor.

Admiral Sampson and Captain Chadwick were on the flying bridge. The admiral was dressed in fatigue uniform, with leggings, since he was to make a landing at Siboney to carry out the important consultation with General Shafter, in command of the besieging army force. The admiral was dictating to me a memorandum to guide his conversation with Shafter when Chief Quartermaster Charley Squires from the platform below reported coolly: "They're coming out, sir!"

We all turned and without glasses could see the brown shape of an enemy ship emerging beyond the brow of the Morro, her guns blazing away at our ring of cruisers, which had already shrouded themselves with the smoke of their own gunfire, immediately hiding their signals from our sight. The gallant *New York* trembled like a greyhound eager for the chase, and heeled far to starboard as the helm was put hard over and the engines were urged to their utmost power. We were always cleared for action down there in those days of watchful waiting, but now an order was given to take in the awnings that had been spread. Otherwise, there was little that we might do until the scene of battle could be reached.

The admiral stood pressed against the railing of the bridge, his upper body bent forward, his eyes fixed ahead. No doubt his mind was certain as to the inevitable result of the sea battle, for he had provided in his orders for every possible contingency. It was simply a question of how long the Americans would take to destroy the last vestige of Spanish dominion in the Western hemisphere. Without turning his head, the admiral motioned to me that he would postpone further dictation. Taking a paper-covered parcel from the pocket of his linen coat he handed it to me with the words: "Please give this to George. I won't need them today."

George Strollum was the admiral's steward, and the package contained three sandwiches that had been made up for the officer's lunch ashore. The action was significant of Sampson's precise manner of handling detail in everything; in the most dramatic moment of the whole war he could give his cool attention to a trivial matter as well as to keeping track of ship movements in the crisis of a long campaign.

It was nine-thirty by the charthouse clock when the *New York* turned on her heel and started plowing back to the westward. Her engines were soon tuned to maintain, in the ensuing race, a speed that she had not made since her acceptance trial years before. In the stokehold the men gasped as they heaped fuel high on the fires, and black smoke flattened from our hot stacks as forced draft roared into the furnaces. It was to be a stern chase and a long chase.

Cervera had chosen a lucky moment for his attempt. Another ship besides the *New York* was also off its station—the *Massachusetts*, which had been sent to Guantánamo for coal. Captain

Francis J. Higginson, the "Poppy" who had commanded the tiny brig in our apprentice battle off Newport, would forever regret missing this more deadly battle.

"The remaining vessels," runs Sampson's official report, "were in or near their usual blockading positions, distributed in a semi-circle about the harbor entrance, counting from the eastward to the westward in the following order: The *Indiana,* about a mile and a half from the shore; the *Oregon*—the *New York's* place was between these two—the *Iowa, Texas,* and *Brooklyn,* the latter two miles from the shore west of Santiago. The distance of the vessels from the harbor entrance was from two and a half to four miles, the latter being the limit of day-blockading distance. The length of the arc formed by the ships was about eight miles. . . . The auxiliaries *Gloucester* and *Vixen* lay close to the land, and nearer the harbor entrance than the large vessels."

Our ships in their wide arc centering about the Morro had been swaying to the gentle swell, with only a wisp of smoke coming now and again from their funnels, for steam was low and only enough coal was used to keep pressure for an emergency. It was a sparkling morning, and the men were standing at their posts for the regular Sabbath inspection when the lookouts raised the cry and a boom from the *Oregon's* 6-pounder signaled the alarm. At once the men broke ranks and ran joyfully to their guns. In two minutes the order to cast off had been obeyed, and the fleet charged in like bulldogs toward the enemy steaming against them.

In the van of the Spanish cruisers was their flagship, the *Infanta María Teresa,* which cleared the main channel and ran half a mile toward our ships before she could clear the shoals and head about on her determined flight to the westward, firing a full broadside at the nearest of our ships, the *Indiana.* Another enemy, the *Vizcaya,* followed a few minutes later, pouring hot metal from every gun she could bring to bear. Then, following the *Cristóbal Colón,* came the *Almirante Oquendo,* which had to take the brunt of the rear-guard fire and was hammered hard. The *Colón* was less stricken, for she ran inshore of her companions and was partly shielded by them from the vicious gunnery of the American batteries. Each ship

The *Almirante Oquendo* after the Battle of Santiago.

headed to the westward as soon as she rounded the shoals, but at every minute the fire from our converging ships became more concentrated and deadly. Guns spouted their roaring burdens of fire and bursting metal through shrouding curtains of black smoke, and it was not easy to pick out our own vessels from those of the enemy. But a groan arose from our men as we saw that the Spaniards had chosen to flee to the westward, drawing away from us instead of in our direction.

In hot chase, we were approaching the fortifications of the harbor entrance when the enemy torpedo destroyers *Furor* and *Plutón* made their dash from the channel, to be checked by the guns of our plucky little *Gloucester,* a converted yacht manned by naval reserves from Michigan and commanded by Captain Richard Wainwright, a survivor of the *Maine.* The shore batteries on both sides of the entrance were getting the range of the *New York,* and their shells fell thick and close about us. As we passed beyond the *Gloucester* we fired a volley of four-inch shells at the *Plutón.* The *Furor* was already beached, and the *Plutón* sank soon after, stern first. From our decks, as we drove close along the shore, we could see wounded survivors from the two smaller Spanish ships being carried into the brush by their comrades.

One fatal defect in the construction of the Spanish vessels was to put them out of action almost at the start. Their decks were of wood, and the first hits of the American shells set them on fire. The wind of their motion fanned the blazes and quickly converted the ships into floating holocausts, with the gunners finding that the deck planking was burning away under their feet and their light ammunition stored on deck exploding in all directions. A few minutes after the *María Teresa* started westward, a shell cut the steam line and another wrecked her water mains so that it was impossible to fight the blaze. At ten-fifteen the flagship ran ashore, hauling down her flag as she became hidden by clouds of smoke from her blazing body. Fifteen minutes later the *Oquendo,* terribly cut up by American gunfire, found her last berth a few cables' lengths to the westward of the flaming *María Teresa.* Half the strength of the Spaniards was now reduced to burning wreckage.

The fine cruisers *Vizcaya* and *Colón* were being battered and mercilessly shelled by the Yankee guns, bot duggedly raced westward with the harriers in close pursuit.

As we came abreast of the *Almirante Oquendo,* listed on her bilge where she was stranded in shoal water, an explosion that overtopped all the minor explosions aboard her sent up a dense cloud of oily smoke, mushrooming at the top like a giant umbrella and streaked with lurid flashes of fire. The main magazine had caught. On the rim of this hellish upheaval appeared solid fragments of iron and wood, and the blasted shapes of poor seamen who would never see an armistice. For them the war was over.

"How dramatic! How sad it all is!" remarked Captain Chadwick, shaking his gray head. He could well appreciate the tragedy of it, he, the chief of staff of a fleet heavy with death-dealing instruments, he who at the call to action could become savage in the desire to kill and destroy the enemy. And an hour later that same captain could receive prisoners with a gracious manner that made him one of the most kindhearted officers of the navy.

Perhaps most of us were like that, I pondered—one moment thirsting for enemy blood and the next moment suffering in spirit with them in their pains. As I stood on the bridge of the *New York* and saw human beings burning alive, all my love of peace surged in me. When I had enlisted, I now realized, it was because I was fascinated by the sea and the romance of sailing from one strange port to another. I did not at that time associate the quiet, uneventful life of the sailing ships of the navy with war and the slaughter of seamen like myself, men who chanced to sail under another flag. And yet every moment of my nine years in training had as its ultimate object just such a day as this off the coast of Cuba, and all our labors aboard the warships had been to sharpen us to deal a destructive blow to other ships.

It was a disastrous day for Spain, nor was it a joyous day for most of my comrades. Few naval engagements of history have been so one-sided as the encounter off Santiago. The terrible loss of life and complete destruction of the Spanish ships, and the insignificant damage inflicted on our fleet, made it a cheap victory. It might be a glorious victory to the newspaper-readers back home, but there was little glory in watching the smoke rise from flaming Spanish warships on the Cuban beach that fine Sunday morning. I was sick at the thought of the enemy's suffering, and I wondered how many of my companions must be feeling as I did. I was a man of peace always, and I think that our commander-in-chief and many of his officers were no less so than I; never had I heard the admiral utter an inimical or warlike word. As for the men of the American service—men who never missed attendance at divine worship, many of them soft-spoken fellows, some of them fathers of families—it was impossible that they could feel lighthearted in the face of so much human suffering. I never wanted to hear the word "war" again; and I determined, on that day, while the air was yet filled with the sour tang of smokeless powder and the crash of exploding shells, that I would be glad to exchange my naval billet for the humblest calling on shore if there was any more murdering to be done on the sea.

We were speeding on at an increasingly fast pace, making signals to our ships as we passed them. It was at this time that the *Vizcaya* turned ashore well ahead of us, while the shells of the *Iowa* and *Texas* were perforating her superstructure and stacks and causing terrific explosions in her innards as she lost way and rolled drunkenly, out of control. Fires had broken out on all her decks, black smoke shot up from her hatches, bursts of flame came through her ports and licked up her starboard side. Naked men hung over her rails to escape the blistering heat; some of them were clinging to her anchor cables near the waterline, and others with hair afire jumped into the sea. Her flag was still flying at her main truck, but she was wrapped in ruinous flame as her crew dropped off into the water when their hands blistered and burned, or when a splinter of metal from a shell put them out of their miserable dilemma.

One of the poor wretches floundering in the water shrieked out, as our ship thundered past him: *"Madre de Dios, ayúdame!"* He had good reason for his appeal to the Mother of God, for the sharks were feasting that day and many a day after; moreover, he feared that he was about to be picked off by the rifles of the North American barbarians in the great ship. I happened to be in the after cabin with some of the crew of the 4-inch guns stationed there, and we grabbed the chaplain's pulpit—which for some reason had escaped jettisoning—rested it on the gallery rail, and dropped it overboard, altar cloth and all.

Billy Plummer, a little coxswain of long service who stammered when he was excited, and who was blasphemous at all times, cried out: "Cling to the c-cross, you s-s-spiggoty, c-cling to the c-cross!" We had no time to observe whether the drowning Spaniard had time to accept this sacred means of rescue, for already we were far beyond the burning *Vizcaya*. How many poor fellows we passed who no longer needed any help from us! . . . The next day, when many of us visited the captured ships, the hulls were still burning, and coins, swords, and bayonets were found to be fused to the metal of the ship by the action of the heat from which the seamen had been driven overside during the unequal battle.

It was past one o'clock when the last of the Spanish cruisers, the *Cristóbal Colón,* caught up by her pursuers some fifty miles from Santiago, ran ashore and surrendered. It was soon learned that her crew had opened some of her sea valves, and had also thrown the breechblocks of their secondary battery overboard. The ship was filling with water and lay dangerously near the edge of a beach that shelved so precipitously that we were able to approach closely and push her farther inshore, the *New York*'s ram lunging steadily against her armor plate. But the fine Spanish ship filled completely during the night, rolled over, and sank on her side with the bilge keel and the guns of her port battery pointing vacantly upward. It was impossible to salvage her, and she, like all the rest of the proud ships of Admiral Cervera's fleet, was lost to us.

During the afternoon, at a time when it was known that the last of the enemy ships was about to surrender, Captain Chadwick and Flag Lieutenant Staunton discussed the wording of a cablegram report of the victory to the Secretary of the Navy. At the end of the discussion Chadwick went off to attend to other details, and Lieutenant Staunton dictated to me the brief message, which opened with the words: "The fleet under my command offers the nation as a Fourth of July present the whole of Cervera's fleet." In these few words was expressed the sentiment of officers and men of the two squadrons, at last relieved from the tension and anxiety of constant watchfulness for an enemy whose strength was not known to us. If there was undue boastfulness implied in those words, it might have been overlooked as an expression of the ebullient spirits of our officers and men. The telegram, of course, was signed "Sampson," as all official communications from the flagship were signed. But the admiral had nothing to do with the precise wording of the telegram; this trivial detail was left to his subordinates, and no doubt he never gave it a thought, for his mind at the moment was filled with the problem of taking more than a thousand Spanish prisoners on board our ships and transporting them north. Yet what a howl those few words raised in the mouths of the political friends of Schley, the junior flag officer, when the notorious controversy that dimmed the luster of the victory was set under way some time later!

Rear Admiral Sampson was a man who rose to his position and high rank by virtue of merit alone. Unassuming, unpretentious, he was prepared to take whatever blame might accrue from his conduct of a campaign that he had carefully planned and which under his direction had reached a decisive ending. It is not with any intention of adding to the unfortunate controversy, now all but forgotten, that I give here the facts regarding the origin of the telegram that his enemies considered to be a blemish on his conduct after the sea battle off Santiago.

In this battle, which forever ended the power of Spain in the Western hemisphere, the American fleet lost but one man. He was George H. Ellis, who two years before had served with me on the *Dolphin*, who had been my companion on many liberties in New England ports, and who later took my former billet as ship's writer on the *Brooklyn*. Ellis was decapitated by a Spanish shell as he was reporting the range of the *Vizcaya* from an exposed position alongside the forward turret of the *Brooklyn*. This single fatality was an anomaly of fate, for Ellis was a yeoman, a noncombatant, and known to be one of the most peaceable men in our entire force. He was in his twenty-fifth year, and a proud and devoted father of a family; I remember that on the *Dolphin* he had spent part of every day writing a long letter to his wife. His body was buried with full honors.

On the other side, the Spaniards lost 323 killed; 151 were severely wounded, and 1,782 were made prisoners. Most of those who escaped death reached our ships without clothing, and Admiral Cervera himself was taken nearly naked on board one of the *Iowa*'s boats. It was surprising that in a modern battle such terrible punishment could be given to one contestant while the other remained almost unscathed. The answer is in the excellence of American gunnery, but almost as much in the morale of the two forces. The Spaniards, who knew that their expedition was being sent forth as a piece of bravado and that they were condemned to be burnt offerings on the altar of national pride, were whipped before they started fighting. Their flight from Santiago was a forlorn hope against a superior force, and they could do little except to die bravely.

In pity we rendered every assistance in our power to the struggling men in the water and on the beaches after their surrender, and at one time our commander ordered the *New York* to slow down so that we could give aid to swimmers. Many a Spaniard was saved by Americans from the Cuban insurgent snipers who lined the beaches to pick off survivors. The feelings of all were expressed by the famous admonishment of gallant Captain John Philip of the *Texas* as he came abreast of the burning *María Teresa*: "Don't cheer, boys; the poor fellows are dying!"

Rear Admiral Cervera was sent to the United States as a prisoner of war. When he made his report of the battle to the Spanish government he devoted a paragraph of eulogy to the chivalry of the Americans: "They clothed the naked, giving them everything they needed: they suppressed the shouts of joy in order not to increase the suffering of the defeated, and all vied in making our captivity as easy as possible."

Admiral Cervera died in 1909, loaded with honors by the nation that he had represented so honorably and courageously. His conqueror was not to have such a gracious end. Rear Admiral William T. Sampson died in May, 1902, broken in health, in spirit, and in heart. There is little doubt that his end was hastened by the bickerings of small-minded men, who can always find time to wrangle after history has been made and great achievements won. Those who knew Sampson best admired him most, and many loved him. He was a gentle man, a great man; those who were unfair and unkind to him did not know him. Few men have deserved so well of their country, and few have received less honor where honor was due. That many petty minds have been wilfully blind to his worth cannot detract from his inherent greatness as a cool, clearheaded leader of men, nor from the certainty that posterity, when partisan bias and the rankling of personal envy have passed, will do justice to the character and deeds of this man. His name will shine among the resplendent names of American naval heroes forever.

Not by any words of Sampson was his personality embroiled in the controversy regarding the conduct of his subordinates during the Cuban campaign. Lieutenant-Commander Hodgson—the bearded "Billy Buttons" of my *Portsmouth* days—was the navigating officer of the *Brooklyn* during the battle. He it was who charged, a year after the fight, that as the Spanish ships came abreast of the *Brooklyn* and the *María Teresa* charged to ram her, Commodore Schley, instead of putting the helm hard astarboard and turning his vessel toward engagement with the enemy, gave the opposite order and turned her away from the fight in a swerving circle. This maneuver resulted in a near collision with the battleship *Texas,* and caused the *Texas* to stop, then go astern, and thus halted that ship's valorous attack upon the enemy. Hodgson also charged that he called Schley's attention to the danger of giving such an order, thinking that possibly there was an error or that he had not heard aright, but that Schley replied: "Damn the *Texas!* She must look out for herself!"

Three years later Edgar S. Maclay, a civil service employee at the New York Navy Yard, published a three-volume history of the navy, in which the author referred to the incident as an attempt at flight, and described the maneuver in words which Schley considered intemperate abuse and defamatory language. He therefore demanded a court of inquiry upon his action. The court was in session for nearly six months, and its proceedings cover more than two thousand pages. The opinion of the court resolved itself into a vote of censure to Schley for repeated delays in his movements to cover Santiago as ordered, and stated that his action in turning the *Brooklyn* away from the enemy during the battle of July 3 was characterized by vacillation, dilatoriness, and lack of enterprise. President Theodore Roosevelt, in reviewing the case, declared that had Schley "turned the *Brooklyn* toward the enemy instead of away from them she would undoubtedly have been in more 'dangerous proximity' to them. But it would have been more dangerous for them than for her! This kind of danger must not be too much weighed by those whose trade it is to dare greatly for the honor of the flag."

The death of Spanish power on our side of the Atlantic was also, in one way, the deathblow to the old navy that I had known. My comrades of fo'c'sle and gun deck had helped to win that struggle, but their day, like the day of the towering sailing ships that had bred them, was over. The navy became a service calling for a new type of man. The apprentice system was abolished, and age requirements for enlistment were sent up a notch. Naval strength grew so rapidly that less and less time could be allowed for shore training of seamen, and the old wind-ships that had schooled thousands of young sailors were dismantled forever. Pay was increased, and during the presidency of Theodore Roosevelt many benefits were showered upon the enlisted men, benefits of which the old navy's people might have vaguely dreamed, but which the new service took for granted. The steel decks of the dreadnoughts were no place for the Jack Robinsons, the Basil Bonos, the Tom Dunns, and the John R. Bells, the gallant rascals and the lovable seagoing men whom I had been proud to call shipmates.

I remained in the navy, it is true, for many a year after the flames of Cervera's burning squadron had turned to ashes; but it was as a mere pen-pusher, and the romantic days of "Rise tacks and sheets!" and "Man the captstan bars!" were over for all of us. All hands now looked toward a navy of speedy cruisers of steel, floating fortresses bristling with mighty guns of hairbreadth precision. When the officers took up their quarters forward and drove the seamen back to the part of the ship that had for centuries been the stronghold of gold braid and bright buttons, the few old man-o'-warsmen still living threw down their marlinspikes in disgust and made application for berths in the sailors' home. It was just as well, for like spare pump handles their place was on the shelf. Quietly they might sit and dream, as I dream now in retrospect, that the past years have been hard ones, but not without their sunshine. There was too much drill in the old days, too many hours at the oars, and too few precious days on shore. My hammock slings enticingly on its hooks, and I can hear the soft tread of the officer of the deck overhead, mingled with the flat-footed tramp of quartermaster Stevens. There is the music of restless wheel ropes, and the thrumming of cordage. The bugler rasps my hammock as he passes softly up the ladder for his last chore of taps. Strangely my thoughts revert to my officers—the many whom I feared in the old days; but my bitterness evaporated long ago, absorbed by the kindness of the hundreds who won my respect. Their many faces resolve into the patriarchal visage of bearded Sampson, the florid cheeks of Chadwick, the aesthetic features of Hobson, and so on, and on. Burn me! After all, those who chose to be harsh did their duty as they felt it should be done, and all our intentions flowed in the direction of a superior navy.

Now I have heard the sweet refrain of taps; the old boatswain comes up from the berth deck, fingering his silver whistle. As the trilling notes reach the lower decks I coil up my last piece of gear, and hoist the signal of

"END HO!"

INDEX

ABOUT THE EDITOR

Neville T. Kirk is Professor Emeritus of the U.S. Naval Academy, where he taught history and political science for 34 years, and Captain, U.S. Naval Reserve (Retired). Raised in Brooklyn, he attended the New York State Nautical School—now the New York State Maritime College—and was trained under sail in the schoolship USS *Newport.* With undergraduate and graduate degrees from Columbia University, he joined the Naval Academy faculty in 1942. From 1945 to 1948, he was the academy's first exchange professor at the U.S. Military Academy at West Point. He is co-author of *American Sea Power since 1775* and *Sea Power: A Naval History,* and the author of articles on naval subjects.